A Little Love
and Good Company

A Little Love
and Good Company

Cathleen Nesbitt

FABER & FABER
3 Queen Square
London

First published in 1975
by Faber and Faber Limited
*3 Queen Square London WC*1
Printed in Great Britain by
Western Printing Services Ltd, Bristol
All rights reserved

ISBN 0 571 10280 8

How a little love and good company improves a woman!
from 'The Beaux' Stratagem' by George Farquhar

Contents

Prologue   *page* 11

Chapter 1   1888–1904: The Schoolgirl   15

       2   1904–1906: The Au Pair Girl   31

       3   1907–1909: The Drama Student   43

       4   1910–1911: The Irish Player   51

       5   1911–1912: Perdita   57

       6   1912: Rupert Brooke,
            The First Four Months   71

       7   1913: Rupert Brooke, The American Year   82

       8   1914: Rupert Brooke,
            The Last Three Months   89

       9   1915–1917: The War Years   101

      10   1919: The Halcyon Summer, Sunninghill
            Park   125

      11   1920: Antony and Cleopatra   139

      12   1922: The Married Woman   151

      13   1933: Two Houses   166

      14   1938–1939: Around Europe with the
            Old Vic   182

      15   1939: The War Begins   188

      16   1940–1945: The War Continues   197

      17   1949: Life Begins at Sixty   206

Contents

18   1962–1965: Three Years in Lotus-Land   224

19   All My Friends   234

20   All My Sons   248

Epilogue   257

Index   259

Illustrations

~~~~~~

(*between pages* 80 *and* 81)

1. Myself aged one, 1889
2. Myself with my mother, 1891
3. The Nesbitt family, *circa* 1898
4. Myself at Victoria College Belfast with Helen Waddell and school friends
5. As Perdita in *The Winter's Tale* with Dennis Nielson-Terry as Florizel, 1912
6. Henry Ainley as Romeo
7. As Mary Ellen in *General John Regan*, 1913
8. Rupert Brooke's favourite portrait of me as Phoebe in *Quality Street*
9. My favourite portrait of Rupert
10. As Jessica in *The Merchant of Venice*
11. My wedding; with bridesmaids: Tanis Guinness, Claudia Johnson, whose father lent us a white Rolls-Royce, and Zara Mainwaring
12. My son's christening in the House of Commons Chapel, with godparents

(*between pages* 176 *and* 177)

13. With my children Mark and Jennifer on the beach at Studland

14. As Mona the Streetwalker in Fred Lonsdale's *Spring Cleaning*
15. E. Kapp's cartoon of a love scene in *The Grain of Mustard Seed*
16. Myself in *The Grain of Mustard Seed*
17. As Yasmin in *Hassan*
18. As the Grand Duchess in Terence Rattigan's *The Sleeping Prince*, with Barbara Belgeddes
19. Sir Cecil Beaton in his winter garden
20. Lynn Fontanne and Alfred Lunt when I first knew them
21. Cecil Beaton's costume design for Mrs. Higgins
22. Robert Coote and me as Mrs. Higgins in *My Fair Lady*
23. In Cecil Beaton's garden in Wiltshire, aged 84

Prologue

~~~~~~

When, some fifteen years ago, my friend Anita Loos suggested
that I ought to write my memoirs, I scoffed at the idea. I assured
her that I was not a writer, and having all my life admired, this
side of idolatry, the writers of good books, and scorned the
scribblings of indifferent ones, I was *not* about to join the great
army of the scribblers.

But Anita is a very persistent persuader. She took me to lunch
with the editors of a well-known American publishing firm and
I ended up with a contract!

It arrived on a morning of a day I was going to Hollywood to
do a television programme, so I took it on the plane with me.
I felt I needed a few days' thought.

I was fascinated by the five closely printed pages of the contract. It provided for every possible contingency, from insisting
on my guarantee that 'there would be no scandalous, injurious
or unlawful matter' and their guarantee 'to print publish and
market it . . . in the United States of America . . . the Philippine
Islands (why the Philippines? I wondered) . . . and the Dominion
of Canada.'

So impressed was I by seeing myself designated as The
Author, as I turned over the pages, that I almost found myself
designing the book-jacket.

Then came a phrase that arrested me: 'the MS of the Work
(how important that capital W looked) shall contain not less than
85,000 and not more than 95,000 words.' Eighty-five thousand
words! I have never learned to type and my handwriting

11

is so illegible I can't even read it myself. I began to ask myself whether I could even write *one* thousand words that would interest anyone but me. I returned the contract, explaining that as I had no memory at all, I couldn't write a memoir, and as I had never kept a diary I had no framework to give a shape to an autobiography and I remained, 'theirs regretfully'.

But Anita remained a very persistent persuader; when I got back to New York she scolded me with 'sheer laziness – you haven't even tried. How do you know you can't do it?'

'But it's all so difficult, I don't even know how to begin.'

'Nonsense, you begin at the beginning, and you'll soon find you can remember more than you think you do.'

When I got back to London Cecil Beaton was equally importunate. His first greeting was, 'Have you started on your book yet? You really ought to get down to it.'

'Qui s'excuse s'accuse!' I can't truly pretend that it was 'because people wanted me to' that I finally succumbed to the temptation. One only does what one, perhaps even subconsciously, wants to do oneself.

'I want to be remembered,' says Mrs. St. Maugham in Enid Bagnold's play *The Chalk Garden*. To be remembered, perhaps that is the spur. And one longs for one's friends to be remembered, the people who have been kind to one, the people one has admired.

> *Memory fades, must the remembered*
> *Perishing be?*

Gwen Raverat in her enchanting *Period Piece* warns her readers: 'This is a circular book. It does not begin at the beginning and go on to the end; it is like the spokes of a wheel sticking out from the hub which is me.'

I must warn readers that this book is really a 'wandering' book, my 'spokes' are just lying about in disorder because I can't find a hub. I can't really find a me.

Like anyone who has been on the stage for over sixty years, I have been written about by those whose business it is to write about actors, from dramatic critics to gossip-columnists, and I have formed a picture of how other people see me. But it conflicts so bewilderingly with the picture of myself that *I* see, that I have given up even trying to find a real self as a 'hub' for my book. It just 'wanders', so I humbly preface my first 'essai' with a line from that greatest and wisest essayist of all time.

Loe reader, here is a well-meaning booke.

ONE

The Schoolgirl
1888–1904

My birth certificate tells me that I was born in Liskeard, Cheshire. Why Liskeard? I suppose it must have been a quiet village near a port – Liverpool, perhaps, or Birkenhead? Where my mother awaited the return of her sailor husband and the arrival of her first child. I never heard of it again. Indeed I have no recollections of living anywhere, till I went to sea with Father in the tramp steamer, the *County Antrim*.

I have a dim memory of having fallen in love with a ravishingly beautiful principal boy in the local pantomime. She was superb, dressed in naval uniform, glittering with gold braid and buttons, singing a sad ballad about 'The loss of the *Birkenhead*'. 'I'll go down with the ship, lads, you have children and wives.'

Another memory was of creeping out of bed and crouching at the top of the stairs to hear the 'sailor home from the sea', singing in a sweet tenor voice, and Mamma accompanying him at the piano.

Mamma was a very good pianist and had a beautiful contralto voice. She and Papa loved to sing duets; or sometimes there was an evening of Gilbert and Sullivan, 'Willow, tit willow, tit willow', or 'I am the Ruler of the Queen's Navee', or best of all, a sentimental ballad about 'The garden of sleep where the puppy dogs grow'. It must have been 'where the poppy doth grow', but I always heard it as 'puppy dogs' and thought what a lovely garden it must have been. I can remember nothing of those early years, nor have I any recollection of where we lived, or where and when my brothers Tom and Hugo and my sister

Anna were born. I must have been a singularly stupid child! I was probably about seven or eight when an old friend of Father's who owned the County Shipping Line offered him the command of the merchant ship the S.S. *County Antrim* and Father decided to take his family with him. Oddly enough I have a vivid memory of the night we boarded her. From *where* we came I have no idea, but I remember the dock at Greenock where the ship was berthed. My brothers Tom and Hugo and myself, Mamma and baby Anna in her arms, and Nelly the nursemaid, shepherded by Dick, the Second Mate, slipped and slithered on the wet cobbles of the wharf. It was a dark wet windy night and the little cabin with oil lamps burning, seemed wonderfully cosy. It was exciting to be shown a sort of shelf sticking out from the wall called a 'bunk' with a little round hole above it called a 'porthole'. 'Here's where you sleep, and in the morning when you look out of the little window you will see nothing but the sea,' said Father.

Years later when I read Masefield's

> *Dirty British coaster with a salt-caked smoke stack,*
> *Butting through the Channel in the mad March days,*
> *With a cargo of Tyne coal,*
> *Road-rail, pig-lead,*
> *Firewood, iron-ware, and cheap tin trays.*

I tried to remember what cargoes the *County Antrim* carried, not that she was a *dirty* British coaster; no ship under Father's command was ever dirty, even if it carried cheap Tyne coal.

What cargoes *did* we carry? All I could recall was the blissful time when her cargo was raisins, juicy big plump raisins – very different from the little wrinkled things mixed with almonds that we used to be given for a Christmas treat – and we must have eaten pounds and pounds of them.

I do remember that we ran into a terrible storm in the Bay of Biscay. Father sent Dick down to warn Mamma to get us all wrapped up warmly in case we should have to take to the boats. Oddly enough, we were all quite calm, including little Nelly, who nevertheless put on her macintosh and galoshes and had her umbrella at the ready. 'If it's drowned the ship is going to be, *I'll* go to Heaven dry,' she announced.

How I wish I could remember the daily life on board. We had

a goat for milk, and there were chickens and a pig for slaughter. My bloodthirsty little brothers loved to see the killings. Was there any kind of refrigeration? What did we eat? How many sailors were there to make friends with? It has all faded into the mists of time.

I made friends with Dick, and had the run of his cabin which contained a wonderful library of books left there by one of his predecessors, obviously an American. That was my undoing. I imagine that the reason I don't remember all the interesting things that happened aboard, or on shore, was because my real life was in my reading. There were *Little Women* and the 'Elsie Dinsmore' books. The 'Elsie Dinsmore' books were to Americans what the 'Bibliothèque Rose' was to the French. How I rejoiced and suffered with Elsie Dinsmore and her fascinating and inconsiderate Papa. They were far more real to me than anyone on board. And *Little Women*, where I first read of 'hot gingerbread and apple sauce'; it was a pudding I vowed I would one day go to America to taste. When I did eventually go to America, 'Elsie Dinsmore' procured me a delightful friendship with Alexander Woollcott who was enraptured to find that an Englishwoman was a 'Dinsmore' fan.

There were great piles of *Harper's* magazines too. Most of their essays and articles must have been above my head, but I met Mark Twain in their pages and learned much about the rift between the Yankees and the Deep South, and hero-worshipped Robert E. Lee. My only enduring memory of those months was of sitting in a cosy nook, my back against the warm funnel, my nose in a book, seeing nothing but a great width of sky and a grey waste of water and the tall mast, carving a wide parabola from port to starboard on a day when the ship rolled.

Certain places I can still see vividly. Buenos Aires for instance. We went ashore there for several days, and so clearly were its wide streets, its white buildings, the tree-lined avenues – all dancing in the brilliant sunshine – etched in my memory, that years later when I first saw Paris on a summer day I thought instinctively, 'Why it's just like Buenos Aires.'

My parents did their best to make me take advantage of my opportunities to see the world. They showed me the catacombs in Alexandria, let me sit up all night for the miracle of Kronstadt, the port of St. Petersburg, on the longest day, where there was nothing but sunlight for twenty-four hours from dawn till dawn, save for an hour or two of faint dusk about midnight. Papa picked me up from my bunk and carried me on deck to show me Constantinople by moonlight.

How it was wasted on me. Unobservant and unresponsive to anything that I hadn't *read* about, I only remember that I have been to these cities. All that remains clear in my mind's eye is 'the lonely sea and the sky – the flung spray, and the blown spume, and the seagull's cry' and perhaps even those are simply Masefield's memories imprinted on my faint recollection.

Father made two round-the-world trips on the *County Antrim*, but during the second my brother Tom and I were left behind to get some education and to give Mamma a rest. The baby Anna was coming up to the dangerous age of two, so much to climb over and under and up that she couldn't be left out of sight for one moment. In fact, I believe she did once fall overboard in a harbour and for several years she regaled her friends with the dramatic statement of 'how I fell right down to the bottom of the sea and Father dived after me with all his clothes on and catched me when I came up the third time, bodies always come up to the top three times.' I've always meant to inquire whether there is any truth in that sailor's legend.

How shocked Papa and Mamma would have been if they had known the acute misery in which my brother and I lived during that six months. Some relation of my father's had recommended the Misses Hoey's 'School for the children of parents serving abroad'. Many generations of children must have suffered there, judging by the age of the Misses Hoey but by now we were the only boarders. Miss Katherine was quite mad and was removed to a home soon after we arrived, having chased her sisters round the house with a large carving knife. Miss Elizabeth taught apathetically, 'History', 1066 and all that; 'arithmetic' and 'geography' (the names of the principal industries of the principal towns of Great Britain and we never even saw a map); and 'religion', a number of dreary hymns to learn by heart. Miss Jane, the youngest sister, was a sadist. She was excessively religious and really enjoyed chastising the unruly in the name of the Lord. She liked to say 'Hold out your hands' and give us strokes across the palm with a ruler. It was extremely painful, but I think children are usually stoic about pain. We were in a continual state of terror because she liked to give us 'bad marks' and add them up to ascertain the number of strokes we deserved on those horrible Saturdays. They must have been for sins of omission rather than commission for I'm sure we would never have dared to be naughty. Those six miserable months seemed to go on for ever and ever, then suddenly we were free!

We were to live now in Belfast in a house in the Antrim Road, a house with a splendid wild garden, and I was sent to a day school run by beloved Quaker Sisters, the Misses Hanna, who were like enchanting Fairy Godmothers, making up to me for having been kept prisoner by the Wicked Witch.

Belfast was a very quiet, stagnant town in those days on the surface. There was the usual fighting on the 'Glorious 12th' when the Orangemen took to the road with their banners and bands, and the Catholics awaited their return in a stretch of common land behind our garden. We children used to creep out of bed after dark and climb an old apple tree to see the fun. There was usually a grand battle, but no guns or bombs, just fists and hurley sticks, and most of the participants staggered home bloody but unbowed.

Looking back, I realise now that there was a smouldering resentment among the Catholics at the arrogant 'superiority' of the Protestants. The Protestants, bigoted Methodists and Presbyterians, mostly of Scottish descent, looked down on the Catholics as 'lazy savages'. We had a wonderful 'general', as a maid-of-all-work was known in those days, a sandy-haired raw-boned woman of incredible energy, but an obstinate bigot.

'Ye can't buy sweeties *there*,' she would say, 'that's a Papist shop, like as not they have dirty sweets that would poison ye.' 'Papists', we gathered, were an 'ignorant class of people who worshipped the Pope and some mysterious creature called a "scarlet woman"'.

When Mamma engaged a pleasant young girl, Delia, to take us for walks in the afternoon, Eliza was furious. 'She's a Papist, ma'am,' she muttered, 'she'll be up to no good.'

Delia took us out to her home once for tea. How Eliza found out we never knew. We wouldn't have told for worlds, we enjoyed it too much. But that was Eliza's chance. She played her trump card.

'That girrell takes the children to her own home, ma'am, and

19

it's just one big room and a scullery and a dozen of a family in it, all of them *blaspheming* as like as not and the children picking up bad words and *diseases*.' That did it, Delia was sent away and we mourned. It was so mysterious and thrilling, the dark cavern smelling of strange smells and full of friendly people laughing hilariously at each other's jokes and ours.

'Oh! isn't she the witty one', they cried when I made a joke.

Mamma explained about the fear of disease – 'so many people in one room', but no one could ever quite explain blasphemy. Why should it be all right to say 'O God! please make me a good girl', and terribly wrong to say 'O God! what have I done now?' as Delia did? 'Devil, and hell and damn' were very bad words, so why should Eliza be allowed to tell an 'elevating' story of a Christian child's deathbed? 'And this little fella only three years old he was, and him knowin' he was on his deathbed, sat straight up in his little cot: "To hell with the Pope", he says, "and let the damn devils get him", and with that he lay down and died.' Not that she would have told it in front of us, but we heard her regaling her friends with it.

I don't remember how long we believed the myth about the Catholics, any more than I remember when we stopped believing that other myth about Santa Claus coming down the chimney.

There were some happy years while I was at the Misses Hanna's school; my reports were good except very often for a mild reproof: 'does well but could do better, lacks perseverance and concentration' – faults which have dogged me all my life.

As Noël Coward was to answer me many years later when I asked him why I was not a better actress: 'You don't *concentrate* enough darling,' he answered honestly. Perhaps it's because I don't concentrate that I often don't *see* what I'm looking at, that I forget places and people I have seen often enough to know them by heart!

It's very strange to me now not to be able to remember the faces of any of my family except that of Terence the youngest brother, who was 'my baby' from the first, as Mamma was ill for a long time after his birth. There are only two faces clear in my mind from those years. One was that of Terence, the other was that of Mrs. Clancy. Colonel Clancy was stationed at the Curragh Camp for a time, and Mrs. Clancy, bored with Belfast, amused herself with a little flirtation with my father.

How did I know? I had never even seen them alone together in a room. How did I know that Papa was 'in love' with her, and that Mamma was jealous and tried desperately not to show it? Perhaps I guessed at all that, because I was in love with her myself. My heart always beat faster when I heard her high clear voice: 'Where is Sinbad? Where's my Sinbad the sailor?' and saw her sweep into the room like a ship in full sail. She was a tall woman, well rounded in the Edwardian fashion with a delicate straight nose, a short upper lip and wonderful teeth, 'like pearls', I thought. But it was her eyes that fascinated me – very large and gleaming, with a myriad tiny lights in them. Whenever I heard afterwards the lines 'Stars; stars and all eyes else dead coals', I thought of Mrs. Clancy.

But the regiment went away and Mrs. Clancy with it. I missed her sadly, and longed for just one more hug from her, one more of those wonderful moments when she would take me in her arms ruffling my hair, and calling 'Sinbad, where are you?' Father was always 'Sinbad the sailor' and I was 'the sailor's child'. And she smelt so delicious, like the garden in the evening when the tobacco plants were out.

The next excitement in my life was something that was to have more influence than I realised at the time: my first visit to a real play. Belfast was not a theatre town, and no good company ever tried to play a full week there. But sometimes, when a big star was playing in Dublin, the company would take a train after the Wednesday performance, arrive in Belfast about 2 a.m., have a short rest, play an early matinée performance, and immediately take the train back to Dublin for the evening performance there. It was known as a 'flying matinée'. Father found out that Sarah Bernhardt was to play in a flying matinée in Belfast. He had a friendly acquaintance with her, having been in command of a ship on which she had sailed from South America before I was born. She had come aboard with a collection of baby animals: a puma, a leopard and, I think, a lion cub. The terrified passengers protested vigorously, but Papa soothed them by taking all the cubs up on the bridge – he loved small animals, and more than once we had baby monkeys and bears at home. Sarah was ecstatic at having triumphed over the other passengers and at being the only one to be allowed on the sacred 'Captain's bridge'.

21

Papa told me I might come to the station with him to meet the night train and present her with a bouquet of flowers. I was almost ill with excitement. We waited patiently for the train as the Dublin train was always late. In the green light of the waiting-room I looked at myself in the glass and was enraptured to see that my face looked quite white. I always longed to have a pale, interesting face, and writhed inwardly when people said, 'What a lovely complexion you have, such nice rosy cheeks.'

We finally walked on to the platform to meet an elderly lady swathed in white scarves and woollies and a long flowing cape, supported on each side by a bearded gentleman. One of them had been her interpreter and manager on many tours and recognised Papa at once. Poor lady, the last thing in the world she could have wanted at that hour was to be presented with a bunch of flowers, but she smiled an enchanting smile at Papa, patted me on the head and said a few words to her manager, who told Papa that Madame would arrange for 'two very good places' at the matinée for 'Le Bon Capitain' and his little girl.

It was the first play I had ever seen. It was *La Dame aux Camélias*. (I have often wondered why it is always called *Camille*. Camille is not French for 'Camelia' and there is no one called Camille in the play.)

I did not understand a word of it, but instinctively I knew what it was about. The French language sounded infinitely beautiful to me, and Sarah's emotion was my own. I had dissolved in tears by the end, and they were still rolling down my cheeks when we went round to her dressing-room. I think she was touched by my involuntary tribute, and gave me a picture postcard of herself gazing soulfully into the heart of a red rose, surrounded by all that lovely *diamanté* that French picture postcards used to be strewn with. She wrote 'Adorable jeune fille' on it and signed it.

I can remember the exact moment when the play came alive for me. I had been a little disappointed at the beginning, unable to follow the dialogue or gather who was who, then I suddenly felt that Sarah was looking at *me*, saying, 'I suffer, comfort me, or suffer with me.' The great actress's magic was working – we all felt it, everyone in the audience, and we all began to suffer with her, to reach out to her in the same way as she was reaching out to us.

It was then I think that the seeds were sown of an ambition – hardly an 'ambition' even, just a vague fantastic longing, for a future in which I could speak French, and be an actress, in that order of importance.

I had taken part in the annual school 'plays', scenes from *Uncle Tom's Cabin* playing Topsy with a black face, and *The Little Mermaid* playing a wicked witch. But it had not interested me. Indeed I grudged the time spent in learning lines and re-hearsing, when I could have been *reading*.

Time! Time! There was never enough time for reading, for escaping into what was always for me the real world, inside the pages of a book.

Reading in bed was forbidden and the one gas light was too far away for me to get to it in time when I heard a footstep on the stairs. But I found a way I could see to read beautifully by the light of a street lamp on the road just under my bedroom window. I spent many happy hours curled up on the window seat – I don't really deserve my still very serviceable eyesight!

Now the time approached when I would have to leave the Misses Hanna, who only took '*little*' girls'. We couldn't really afford school fees, but Mamma was determined I should have the best teaching available in Belfast. She discovered that Victoria College had very generous scholarships for 'promising' girls.

I wasn't an 'intellectual' but I had a very useful 'examination' memory. I could cram my brain with assorted knowledge at fantastic speed and forget it all within a week! Mamma found some specimens of typical papers. We swotted over them to-gether for six weeks and I won a scholarship.

Oh, what bliss it was to be alive! Victoria was the best school in Ulster. Mrs. Byers, the Head, was a wonderful old lady, who made a grand tour of the classrooms every day; all the girls rose to their feet at her entrance and remained respectfully standing until her exit. The teachers seemed to me splendid women with a real vocation, and the acquiring of knowledge became really exciting. I, who had always loathed arithmetic, fell in love with the mathematics teacher who had rabbit teeth sticking out oddly but even those seemed beautiful to me, and to gain merit in her eyes I applied myself eagerly to the magical world of mathematics.

I was thrilled with algebra and Euclid and came to derive

great pleasure in solving difficult problems. I even found them a game more fun than chess, and one could play it alone. I picked up a book called *Algebra for Beginners* in a bookshop the other day to see if I could recall any of those triumphant victories over a complicated formula, but I could not understand a word of it!

But the most exciting class was that of Miss MacWhirter, who taught history and literature, and like 'Miss Jean Brodie' she had her little group of 'special' girls of whom Helen Waddell was the bright star, and to which I was admitted. Even at that age I was a snob, not that I was interested in money or 'class', but like the great Lord Clarendon, I loved 'the company of my betters'. He wrote of himself: 'He owed the little he knew, and the little good that was in him, to the conversation he had still been used to of the most excellent men in their several kinds that lived in that age. He never took more pleasure in anything than in frequently mentioning and naming those persons who were then his friends, and used often to say that he was never so proud or thought himself so good a man as when he was the least man in the company, all his friends being in their qualities, in their fortunes, and in their faculties and endowments of mind very much his superiors.'

And indeed throughout my life, I have always felt most at home when I 'was the least person in the company'. I fear that I shall appear in this book as a most inveterate name-dropper, for I too take 'most pleasure in mentioning and naming my friends'.

To return to Victoria. I found 'my betters' in Meta Fleming, because she was the best-loved girl in whatever class she was in; Helen Forbes, because she was the most beautiful girl in the school; Helen Waddell because she was the most intelligent. And I loved the little extra study classes that Miss MacWhirter held for us.

Helen Waddell and I used to walk home from school together, sharing our growing delight in poetry and our first religious doubts. These doubts, combined with our intensive reading of Darwin and Huxley, led us to discard *all* religions, though we admitted 'from our heights of mental superiority' as Miss MacWhirter used to say scornfully, 'that there was great poetry in the Bible and the Koran'. What little prigs we were; we could not wait to announce to our respective families that we were 'no longer Christians'. Helen's God-fearing Methodist parents were scandalised. My mother was shocked, more on social than religious grounds I suspect, when I remained silent and motionless when the congregation turned to the east to recite the Creed. Ours was a very High Anglican church but I think the vicar must have been a man of good sense. When my mother begged him to come and talk to me because I refused to be confirmed, he humiliated me deeply by depriving me of the theological arguments I'd so looked forward to by patting me kindly on the head and saying, 'Dear child, when you are a little older you will be able to examine your beliefs with more understanding.'

One day Helen and I, passing the Roman Catholic cathedral on our way home from school, decided to go in. We had never been inside a Catholic chapel. We were deeply moved and impressed by the magnificent ritual of the High Mass. Helen even made the sign of the Cross as we left! 'It's strange how difficult it is to throw off old superstitions,' she said when we were outside. 'I almost expect the Lord God to hurl a thunderbolt on our Protestant heads for consorting with the "scarlet woman".' We had neither of us, I think, heard of Edmond de Goncourt, but how we would have applauded his summing up: 'A gentle scepticism is the height of human happiness and wisdom. You should not believe in anything, not even your own disbelief.'

Helen usually won the monthly essay prize donated by Miss MacWhirter, but every now and then it came to me. Once the subject was 'If you were allowed to choose a gift at birth from a Fairy Godmother, which would you choose? Character, Intellect or Beauty? And why?' I think I won the prize that time for saying that I would rather have beauty than *anything*, with intellect and character far behind. Miss MacWhirter always said, 'Try to say what you really think about everything – not what you are expected to think.' Every 'good' girl was expected to put Character first!

Mrs. Byers herself gave a £20 prize for the best historical essay written by one of the school leavers, at the end of term. Helen and I tied for the prize, and it was divided between us. The money was supposed to be spent on books, but I had a wonderful idea: couldn't it be spent on further education? A trip to Paris? I confided in Miss MacWhirter that I had once met Sarah Bernhardt and that ever since my dream had been to learn to speak and write French perfectly. For £10 I could go by bus and train and boat and train again and spend a week at the Girls' Friendly Society's headquarters in Paris while I looked for a post as au pair English teacher in a school or family.

Miss MacWhirter was wonderful. She co-operated in every way and gave me a going-away present of a splendid Larousse's French dictionary. Mamma stitched away at a couple of new dresses. How I took for granted those hours she spent at the sewing machine, so that I and my sister should be decently dressed. I feel ashamed when I look back on it.

Poor Mamma, it was not till long afterwards that I realised what a gruelling life she had led. Her marriage was not a very happy one but I think it might have been better if she had not hated so much the years in Belfast. She hated all my father's relations. 'Middle class people with lower middle class minds like every one in Ulster,' she would say when she looked back.

How fiercely she battled with the Belfast accent. We must have picked it up from the children we played with or went to school with or even from Eliza. However poor you were, at your wits' end to pay the butcher's bill, you had to have a 'servant girl' – who would slave for fifteen hours a day for a pittance of a wage. In fact I think during lean periods in the South, Ulster people who didn't mind having a Catholic in the house could have had several for no wage at all but their meals, and a bed.

Our Eliza was a stubborn, narrow-minded Ulster Protestant who thought all Catholics were 'scum'. Father had to fight the superstitions and prejudices we learned from her, as firmly as Mamma had to fight the Belfast accent. If we had lived in the South I don't think she would have minded a touch of the brogue – but the Belfast accent *is* the ugliest in the Kingdom, except perhaps the Glaswegian.

Mamma had even had a miserable girlhood; she was a pretty girl and her sister was a beauty, but they never had any money. They had one pleasure, they rode well and some friends would always mount them for an occasional hunt. But they couldn't go to parties because they never had any clothes.

Her wicked old father had not been rich but had had what was known as a comfortable sufficiency, which he spent entirely on himself, giving nothing to his wife and children. He treated his two daughters as slaves till they escaped into matrimony and upon his wife's death married the drunken cook who had been his mistress. They drank themselves to death, but not before they had broken or sold all Grandmother's beautiful china which had been promised to her daughters.

I learned all this much later, I only saw him once when I went to 'visit' as a small child and found the kitchen a magical place. I was allowed to turn the handle of the knife cleaner; in the slot one inserted a stained steel knife (no stainless steel in those days); two turns of the handle and out it came shining and spotless. And the coffee grinder, another handle to turn and watch the freshly roasted coffee-beans turn into fine powder.

And at 11 o'clock Grandfather would give me a slice of sponge cake with caraway seeds in it, and a tiny glass of Madeira while he scolded Mamma for not having taught me a single word of Welsh.

It was when at last she left Belfast for ever and settled in London, that life really began for her – so many 'believers' like herself, crusading for so many 'causes'.

The most appealing was the 'Women's Rights' movement. So fervently did she believe in 'Votes for Women' that she even went to prison for the cause. She and her friend Mrs. Bennett went forth early one morning with their little hammers and broke all the windows of the Baker Street Post Office. She listened scornfully while the magistrate rebuked them for their unladylike conduct, but was really stung by his remark as he sentenced them: 'Bennett, six weeks, Nesbitt, in consideration of your age, four weeks.' She had always thought Ethel Bennett older than herself!

When I went to visit her in Holloway Gaol I found the ladies all having their daily exercise in the prison courtyard. Two by two round and round they marched bravely chanting the Women's Freedom Song, conducted from the window of her prison cell by Ethel Smythe using her toothbrush as a baton. Mamma's fine contralto voice rang out gallantly among some of the quaverers.

I found it so moving that when years after they finally *did* get the vote, I volunteered to Mamma, who by that time was rather crippled with arthritis, to march in her place from Trafalgar Square to the Albert Hall at the suffragettes' final triumphant celebration. The only time in my life that I ever 'demonstrated' for anything. I'm ashamed to say I don't think I ever used that vote won so hardly by so many brave women.

By the time Mamma became altogether crippled and had to live in a wheelchair, she had, thank goodness, found a riveting interest that lasted for the rest of her life. She became an astrologer. It had everything for her, an honourable ancient history, a touch of necromancy and, to Mamma's eyes, was so *scientific*! It used to make me dizzy to watch her plotting the heavens with her little compass, searching for the exact position of all the planets, even including the newly discovered Uranus. And it amazed me to see the people who would come to her to have their fortune predicted. Sir Sefton Brancker, Air Chief Marshal, was one of her devout adherents, always coming to her for advice when the 'women in his life' became too demanding.

'Mamma darling', I said on the day after the 101 Disaster when practically all the top brass of the Royal Air Force were killed, 'Mamma darling, Sefton was here only a few days ago – didn't you foresee his sudden death?'

'It was remiss of me, of course it *was there* quite plainly, but I was too intent on his House of Venus which was what he was so interested in at the moment.'

'And then of course,' she would say, 'one can so seldom get the exact *moment* of birth which is so important. To think that no one thought to notice the time of your birth. All that *I* know is that it was around midnight on a Friday. The nurse used to joke about: "Friday's child is loving and giving, Saturday's child works hard for its living." '

'Well now you know. I'm certainly a Saturday's child.'

'But if I'd only known what I know now I'd have predicted it before you were weaned!'

Oddly enough it made her more tolerant. When I displeased her in some way instead of assuming what I used to call her 'tight face' she would shake her head and say, 'Of course you can't help it, it's the Gemini in you.'

'I thought I was Sagittarius?'

'Ah yes! but Neptune was on the cusp and he rules Gemini.'

28

I can't quite remember the correct terms but I gathered that Neptune was responsible for my wavering and fluctuating nature!

She even was able to indulge her great weakness, a love of gambling. She took to casting the horoscopes of the horses. And by some chance had a very lucky run of winning outsiders. One day when she was backing a favourite the gentleman at the telephone at Ladbroke's said, 'Backing the favourite for a change Mrs. Nesbitt?'

'Yes, I have done his horoscope and it really *is* his winning day.'

'You did his *what*, madam?'

'Cast his horoscope. Oh dear! how I wish I could be actually at the meeting – then I could put a 2s. 6d. bet on at least half a dozen horses; I could cast the jockeys' horoscopes as well and solve some interesting problems, but you see I live in a wheel chair and can't get about.'

'Madam,' said the gentleman at the telephone, 'you may put 2s. a time on *any* horse, and as *many* horses as you please from now on.'

I think she must have been the only person from whom Ladbroke's have ever accepted so many and such minute sums! More and more as I look back on my mother's life I realise how much she had to contend with and how gallantly she faced it. But while she lived I fear I did not *love* her, in the way I loved my father.

'Ah, that's typical, a question of sex, son loves mother, daughter loves father,' the Freudians will say. Not so in our family. My mother and her eldest son Tom did not even *like* each other nor was she very interested in Terence. Hugo and Anna adored her and she loved them both passionately.

Her enthusiasms, her eager credulity, her willingness to embrace any new faith from theosophy to astrology I had found embarrassing. I always froze inwardly. My father's mind appealed to me, cynical, tolerant, sceptical. And he was always fun to be with, and entered into the lives and games of us children much more than Mamma ever had the time or the energy or even the wish to do. She never *enjoyed* children as some mothers do.

Father too had had a 'star-crossed' life but he had a happy

temperament and did not suffer as Mamma did. As a boy he had escaped from his family shipbuilding firm and been a midshipman in the Navy, where he was supremely happy.

But after a serious illness and a long convalescence at the Haslar Naval Hospital, he was invalided out at an early age. I forget what impediment prevented him being up to Navy standards, but it did not keep him from the sea. He was Captain of a vessel which must have been a forerunner of the modern passenger-freighter, for that was when he had Sarah Bernhardt as a passenger.

Poor Father, how ready he was to try anything and everything to make money but he never succeeded in making very much – perhaps his heart was not in anything but sea-faring. I was so happy for him when he got back into the Navy, or rather 'Royal Naval Reserve' at the beginning of the First World War. He was given the rank of Commander, and a shore job in Calais dealing with supplies arriving for our allies.

'Allies?' said Father ruefully, 'I have never seen such senseless hostility between two groups of human beings, as between our naval ratings and the French *matelots*, except perhaps that between the Catholics and the Protestants in Ulster.' And how he fretted against the bureaucracy in London which had assigned him to a depot receiving horses, about which he knew nothing, rather than to one receiving engineering supplies and spare parts about which he knew a very great deal!

How I run ahead of myself! Several pages ago I was a schoolgirl in Belfast on the brink of a great adventure till I found myself reminiscing about my parents.

'Revenons à nos moutons,' which is one of the few French phrases I knew at the time!

TWO

The Au Pair Girl
1904–1906

〜〜〜〜〜〜〜〜〜〜〜〜〜〜〜〜〜〜〜〜〜〜〜〜〜

The night before I left for France, Mamma came and sat on my bed and talked a little of this and that, wondered if the lock of my trunk would hold (I had filled it too full as usual).

I have had since then well over sixty years of continually packing and unpacking and have never yet mastered the art, invariably the trunk, suitcase, even overnight case is too full to close properly, and invariably something essential gets left behind.

I could see that there was something that Mamma wanted to say, some parting word of advice, then suddenly she got up, blushed scarlet and stammered 'Take care of your modesty darling,' and hastened from the room. 'Modesty?' I thought vaguely. 'Why shouldn't I be "modest"? God knows I have nothing to be vain about.' I hadn't the slightest idea that poor Mamma probably felt guilty about never having breathed a word to me about the facts of life, and felt too shy to broach the subject now. I had learned from my small brothers, back from a holiday on a farm, that they had seen baby calves and baby lambs come out of their mothers, and that real babies came from inside their mothers too. But how they ever got inside to begin with, and how my belly button could ever stretch enough to let them out, was a mystery. Such a little hole, but perhaps it blew up like a balloon? I naturally assumed that the navel was the exit. Oddly enough, I can't remember ever having had much curiosity about it. Even if I had, I was brought up in an atmosphere where discussion of any of one's bodily functions was 'rude'. Even the explanation of menstruation was hastily confined to how to cope with it with a napkin and safety pins and a belt, and when I asked glumly whether it would really happen every month forever and forever, I was told that it was some kind of primeval curse that God had laid on women. I vaguely connected that with Eve and the apple and forgot all about it.

I set off on the long journey by train and boat and train and arrived safely at the Girls' Friendly Lodge or Hostel, or whatever it was called, in the rue Danton, and was well looked after till a suitable post was found. An English 'Miss' was wanted in the 'École Secondaire pour Jeunes Filles' in Lisieux, a little town in Normandy. I gathered that it was one of the new Government secular schools, but run on strictly Convent lines by les Demoiselles Duputel; the English 'Miss' would be expected to help with the little ones and to chaperon the older girls if a male teacher was taking a class. (I found that even dear old Herr what's-his-name who taught German and was well into his sixties, might not enter the classroom unless I was installed in a corner of the room!) In return for which I was to receive French lessons and a small weekly sum of pocket money. 'You really won't find anything to spend it on in Lisieux,' said the secretary of the Girls' Friendly as she put me on the train. It was due to arrive at 7.30, but owing to a derailment at some junction I didn't reach Lisieux till 10.30 p.m. The solitary porter must have been astounded to see a young girl descend from the train and shyly hand him a piece of paper with the name Duputel and the address of the school written large upon it. He managed to rout out an ancient fiacre, and we rattled along the dark cobbled streets and stopped before a grey edifice, dark within and without. The driver tugged at a bell which resounded alarmingly, and after a time there was a grinding of bolts and a clicking of keys. The door opened on a dark hall and an old woman with a square white face looking like the Duchess in *Alice in Wonderland* peered at me, her lamp held high in her hand. My schoolgirl French deserted me completely. I stammered something about 'Mademoiselle Doo-pootell m'attend'. 'Ah! la *Miss*,' she barked. I caught the word 'heure' and gathered she wanted to know what on earth brought me at this hour. Then the driver addressed her as 'Mademoiselle Maria' and they held what sounded to me like a furious argument. Finally

he humped my trunk on his shoulder and we climbed endless
dark stairs with the lamp flickering before us. I handed my purse
to the driver and said 'Prenez' helplessly. Under Mlle Maria's
stern eyes he extracted what I guess was the correct amount
and she ushered him down. I heard from afar the locking and
bolting of doors, and after a long pause Mlle Maria returned
bearing in her hands a briquette, a kind of brass bottle or flask
filled with boiling water which she placed in my bed. I nearly
burst into tears at the kindness of the thought; for a moment I
had felt as if I were abandoned in an ogre's castle! It's odd how
I slept in that little room for over nine months and haven't the
remotest recollection of what it looked like or how it was
furnished. I only remember that it had a window overlooking a
great garden and that on summer nights the most heavenly
smells were wafted up from the shrubs and trees below – lilac?
syringa? I never discovered the names. But when the nights
began to smell sweet I would lean out of my window and murmur the whole of the Balcony Scene to the perfumed air, savour-
ing the delicate mischief of 'I forget why I did call thee back';
and always stopping at Juliet's reply to Romeo's 'I would I were
thy bird' – 'Sweet, so would I – Yet I should kill thee with much
cherishing'. All the rest seemed anti-climax. How Shakespeare
understood the need a passionate woman has for a sudden
frivolous line, something inconsequential, to 'toy' with love that
is too overwhelming.

I gradually discovered that the gruff Mlle Maria, whose
bark was worse than her bite, was the housekeeper, matron and
general manager of the school; and Mlle Duputel, her elder
sister, was the headmistress, who, with the help of two resident
mistresses and various visiting professors, was responsible for
the morals and education of some fifteen boarders, ranging from
eight to sixteen in age, and countless day-girls. Mlle Duputel
was a cheerful, rotund old lady who prided herself on her
English, which was almost as elementary as my French. She
always called me to her office when she had to interview a
parent so that she might hold a little conversation in English. I
always made a point of asking her a number of unnecessary
questions about my work and that of my 'pupils', and was careful
not to strain her vocabulary too far. She did so love to bask in
the awed admiration of the *bonnes bourgeoises* of Lisieux I think

it must have been about that time that the Government had decreed secular schools and that the boys' lycées (grammar schools), and the girls' 'cours secondaires' (high schools) should be taught by lay professors rather than priests and nuns. The Duputel ladies were strict Catholics and for the boarders it was very like a convent. They all wore black overalls with coloured sashes, white, red, black, orange, blue, yellow, to denote which class they were in. It astonished me to see how healthy and happy and *slim* they were – I was extremely 'fat conscious' – under the regime. For breakfast, a great bowl of soup with hunks of the unleavened Normandy bread in it. For lunch, always the same menu for the same day of the week – 'Lapin et lentils,' Monday; 'Boeuf et nouilles,' Tuesday; 'Gigot et Haricots', Wednesday. Hardly ever a green vegetable or salad. For supper a vegetable soup, potatoes and carrots and aubergines and onions and many other légumes unknown to me – after which one went up to the long table where Mlle Maria stood behind big earthenware bowls of 'compôte de fruits' in season – apples, pears, apricots, prunes. The eldest girls went first, then on down to the youngest ones who found decision difficult – 'abricots? non! prunes? oui! non! j'aime mieux des pommes' – Mlle Maria would grow impatient – 'Choose, choose at once, I can't wait all day'.

Nanette, the seven-year-old niece of les Demoiselles Duputel, adored and spoiled by everyone, had her own way of solving the problem. 'De *tout* ma tante,' she would say, pointing to all the bowls and Mlle Maria would smile indulgently: 'Que tu es gourmande,' she would scold, while putting a little of everything on the plate held out. Ever since when I have been confronted in a restaurant with a trolley full of goodies, I have had an urge to say greedily 'De *tout*, ma tante' to the waiter.

There were no walks, except to Mass on Sunday; the girls just ran around the great garden during the morning and afternoon breaks. A bath once a week. Two large baths with cold running water only, which was slightly warmed from a great can standing on a little gas stove. In a row on a long table were the bath-gowns, long cotton smocks under which they modestly undressed and in which they plunged into the baths two at a time. I can't remember whether the water was ever changed! Emerging they would drop the bath-gown on the floor, clutch a towel around their damp little bodies and after a perfunctory 'drying' get into a clean nightdress and so to bed. I can't ever remember having seen a naked body during any of the bath sessions.

I, as an *Anglaise*, belonging to that strange race which wanted daily baths and daily exercise, was permitted to use the bath whenever I wanted. (I confess that in winter once a week was quite enough for me.) And as my status was more that of mistress than pupil I was allowed to walk about the town completely unchaperoned on my days off and during the holidays. As I look back I think it was fortunate that I was short and fat and completely without feminine allure, for the town was always full of soldiers from the neighbouring barracks. Sadly, I was never once accosted or even winked at. A combination of lack of curiosity, lack of observation, and a childhood of rigid taboos had somehow preserved me from the elementary knowledge of the facts of life that at my age I should certainly have known. I even survived the persevering attempts of Jean-Paul to educate me. Jean-Paul was the fourteen-year-old son of Madame Maugis, the town's music mistress. I had a great longing to go back to Belfast and astonish my mother with my ability to 'play a piece on the piano'. Poor Mamma, she had struggled valiantly to teach me. She herself could play anything at sight and had a beautiful contralto voice. Sir Hubert Parry had offered to train her free. He thought she should be a concert singer, but her father had been shocked at the idea and turned it down promptly. The complete lack of music in my soul had bitterly disappointed her. How lovely to go back and play a Chopin nocturne from beginning to end without the book!

Madame Maugis quickly discovered that I had no talent, but found that Jean-Paul liked my company so much that she gave me two lessons a week for a ridiculously small sum, on condition that I stayed to keep Jean-Paul company for at least an hour, and, incidentally, drink delicious hot chocolate. She did succeed in enabling me to play a Chopin nocturne (with, I'm quite sure, 'un excès de sensiblerie marrant' as she had once said of another pupil). I looked up 'sensiblerie' in my dictionary and thought what a good word it was for 'maudlin sentimentality'.

But Jean-Paul never succeeded in his ambition to make me more 'wordly-wise'. He had lain on his back for many years and was always having treatments for some spinal injury; but he was always cheerful and would welcome me with 'A new book for you Missy, Miss'. He was a voracious reader and had never had anyone with whom to discuss his reflections and reactions. By this time I had enough French to be able to follow and respond. Mademoiselle Duputel's method of teaching was very successful. For an hour or so every day I sat in with the 'Dictée' sessions of the infants' class, gradually proceeding upwards. I would make exactly the same mistakes as the little ones in spelling and grammar, writing 'ritme' for 'rhythm' and 'foi' for 'foie', though I didn't go so far as to write 'omm' for 'homme'! The dictation went so quickly, to my ears, that it took great concentration to even spell words I knew perfectly well. But the grammar! I thought that would never come right; one learned to say 'J'amais', 'J'aime', 'J'aimerai', and 'Je pensais', 'Je pens', 'Je penserais' – only to be confronted with 'J'allais', 'Je vais', 'J'irai'. I felt like an English child just learning to talk must feel when told, 'You don't say "I runned" or "I felled down".' As for the subjunctive, the rules for that were and will ever remain a complete mystery to me. But every evening Mlle Duputel, who rather enjoyed reading aloud, would read a column of the daily paper and a page or two of some French classic and tell me to translate them the next day into English. I would return the French pages to her after I'd done it and a few days later she would make me translate my English version into French again and let me correct myself with the original French in front of me. It became a fascinating game and I ended by sensing the 'feel' of a phrase and I would write 'ce n'est pas certain qu'il *ait* recontré' or 'il aurait fallu que je *fisse*' quite automatically.

It was there that Jean-Paul helped so much. He lent me books that I really enjoyed reading, and discussed them with me. I must have read through the whole *œuvres* of Balzac, Zola, de Maupassant – to say nothing of all the 'Willy' books, *Claudine à l'école*, *Claudine en vacances*, *Claudine en Ville*, etc.

The thing that teased him more than anything was the desire to know whether I was really so innocent as I appeared. It was after a great 'scandale' at the school that he lent me the 'Willy' books. I had never heard of such a thing as lesbianism. I had no idea that the resident mistress Mlle Coudray, a slender, auburn-haired woman with green eyes, who would have been a beauty

but for her too long nose and too tight mouth, was a lesbian who
had been having love affairs with some of the older girls under
the unsuspecting eyes of Mlle Duputel (who was probably as
ignorant as I was about many things). But she made the mistake
once of transferring her affections from the Dark Twin to the
Fair Twin, as we called the beautiful fifteen-year-old twin
daughters of the local doctor. His wife had left him so the girls
were weekly boarders. The Dark Twin was a smouldering
passionate creature who raged with jealousy for a week, and
suddenly confessed to her father that Mlle Coudray had 'seduced' them both. Most of the girls like myself did not know
what all the drama was about, why the doctor descended
Jupiter-like and thundered, and took his daughters away with
him; why Mlle Coudray departed in tears; why Mlle Duputel
and Mlle M. scowled for days; why a strict order was given
that no girls must ever walk about the garden 'à deux' – it must
always be 'à trois'; that no girls must ever hold each other's
hands or embrace each other, except on the first or the last day
of term.

I found myself suddenly in great demand. 'Miss, marchez
avec nous voulez vous?' 'Miss on veut s'asseoir dans le grotto,
soyez la troisième voulez vous?' I even had more chaperoning
to do. The older girls had never been allowed to be without a
chaperon during the classes of Herr A the German teacher – or
Monsieur B the mathematics teacher – or even Monsieur C the
old gentleman who taught a curious subject: choral singing!
Now Mlle Gérard, who lived in the town and came to replace
Mlle Coudray for history and literature, had to have *her* classes
chaperoned. I always enjoyed the chaperonage. If the subject
interested me, *I* could learn too. If it didn't no one minded my
reading a book.

Jean-Paul was delighted with the whole affair: questioned me
increasingly about it 'Eh! eh! Mlle Coudray, Je m'endoutais
bien vous savez! Elle les aimait beaucoup les petites filles de
M. le Docteur? La petite blonde? est ce qu'elle allait dans la
chambre de Mlle Coudray la nuit? Hein?'

How boring it must have been for poor Jean-Paul to find that
all the implications of the whole affair had gone over my head like
water off a duck's back. It was then that he gave me the 'Willy'
books. I didn't know till long after that I had been reading the

first stories by Colette. Jean-Paul's is the only face I can see clearly of all the faces I saw during that year (except perhaps the square frog face of Mlle Maria) – a little dark monkey face with eyes brimming with *malice* – that French word for which there is no English translation – our 'mischief' is too light, our 'malice' too dark – as he bent over a very 'explicit' chapter – even by modern standards – of Zola, asking 'Est ce que ça vous fait quelque-chose?' looking in vain for a blush of comprehension. But what I am most grateful for was his introduction to the poets. Balzac and Zola and Romain Rolland I would surely have found for myself. But Laforgue and Baudelaire and Mallarmé and Rimbaud – they 'hit' me then just as Dowson and Swinburne and Christina Rossetti did years later. Now as I leaned out of my window at night I could indulge in delicious orgies of world-weary sadness. 'La chair est triste, hélas, et j'ai lu les livres.' 'Il pleut dans la ville, comme il pleut dans mon coeur.' Not that there were 'Tears in my heart' any more. I had become cosily integrated into the world of the school; I had learned to change my winter hat for my summer hat, and to sew roses round my summer hat for Easter Sunday. (The girls wore black velours with cherries for winter and white straw with roses for summer.) To know all the words of the Litany 'Sainte-Marie mère de Dieu priez pour nous' and to kneel and stand at the right moment at Mass. Even to have a conspiratory smile at 'Les toutes petites' when they sang under their breath with surreptitious giggles 'nous sommes crétins' for 'nous sommes chrétiens'. I had to look up 'cretins' in a dictionary before I quite saw the joke – but no dictionary could help with the 'silly' dialogues – 'Toi t'es bis bisbique' 'Et toi saucisse!' 'Et toi boudin!' I discovered that 'bisbique' meant 'silly old goat' and 'saucisse' was a very witty substitute for 'aussi', and 'toi boudin' meant 'you are a big sausage'. Hardly hilarious when translated. But try to translate 'You're bonkers! You're bonkers! You're bonkers donkey!' which convulses my small grandchildren, into French!

A child's humour doesn't change much from country to country or from decade to decade. I was really happier with the smaller children – the older girls were too near me in age for confidences as I was after all one of the 'maîtresses'. I once overheard a conversation between two of them: 'Have you seen the

dress "Miss" made for herself? I have – it's so provincial, and
what a colour.' 'She is so fat, she should wear dark materials.'
'Ah well, she has no taste.' For months afterwards I imagined
every time I saw one of them looking at me, that they were
despising me as a 'provinciale', a creature without taste. I even
tore up the hideous green muslin dress on which I had spent so
many hours. But on the whole I enjoyed the ten months I spent
there and rejoiced that I could speak and write French fairly
well. But not well enough. I went home for a short holiday and
persuaded Father and Mamma that I needed another year for I
wanted to try for my 'Brêvet supérieur' and afterwards – an
ambitious dream that I kept to myself – to get a Baccalauréat,
the coveted 'Bachot', something that even very few French girls
achieved. So back to Paris and a job in Paris this time, so that I
could study at the Sorbonne.

The Girls' Friendly Society found me a post as governess to
Mimi and Pierre Gary, aged six and eight respectively, who
lived with their grandmother. 'Papa', a widower, spent the
weekends at the apartment in the Boulevard Emile Angier – but
during the week he lived in his bachelor's apartment. It's
strange, I haven't the least recollection of what the children
looked like – or even Monsieur Henri – but old Madame Gary
I can still see plainly. Hers was the face of the old woman in Van
Gogh's *La Mouleuse de Café*. A 'concentrated' face with hooded
eyes and a tight mouth. What a matriarch she was. She had two
other sons and three daughters and the whole family with their
wives and husbands had to lunch with her every Sunday. No
nonsense then about the 'generation gap'. They were all grown
men and women with children of their own, but they deferred to
'Ma mère' and listened to her laying down the law every weekend; only the eldest son's wife, Madame Laure, ever talked
back and she was the old lady's favourite. She had enormous,
shining, very blue eyes – 'Les yeux de myope,' said old Madame
Gary – and ever since when I see exceptionally large, brilliant,
blue eyes, I think instinctively 'short-sighted'.

I was allowed five hours to myself every morning, while the
children were at their schools where they lunched. I took them
to school, hastened to the Sorbonne, and returned to pick them
up at 3.30. I received a small salary which just covered tram
fares, candles and cream buns! Candles, because Madame Gary

didn't allow reading at night; 'Waste of gas', she would say abruptly as she turned off the supply from the meter in the hall. The 'servants' quarters' for each apartment were on the top floor of the building and their gas supply was connected with the hall and landing lights which were left on all night – only those living in the no-man's-land of nannies and governesses were subject to the whims of the employers day and night. So I bought candles and studied into the small hours.

Cream buns! On Saturday afternoons when the children went out with 'Papa' I used to go to the Bois de Boulogne with a bag of two or even three great éclairs or 'Napoléons' oozing thick whipped cream – no wonder I grew fatter than ever; I began to wish I could wear a uniform to disguise it, as worn by the 'nounous', the children's nurses with their great billowing skirts over starched petticoats, their splendid flowing capes, crisp white bonnets with multi-coloured ribbons hanging down behind or fluttering in the breeze. You could be as big as a house underneath all that panoply as you proceeded down the avenue du Bois behind a magnificent white lace-decked 'voiture d'enfants'.

On weekday afternoons Madame Gary kept me busy with a thousand small jobs, teaching the children games, making inventories of linen or china – she believed firmly that the devil always finds work for idle hands to do – and if there should be a book in those idle hands, that was even more 'suspect'. I've always hated sewing and the thing I most disliked was darning the children's stockings. I'd done too much of it with three brothers wearing those ridiculous woollen stockings that always went into holes at knees and toes. But one day I had an inspiration. I asked Madame to teach me to darn a sheet. Higher education for women was still slightly frowned on in those days, and as a sop to prejudice no female could get a 'Brêvet supérieur' unless she got good marks in a special subject, darning fine linen! Thanks to Madame Gary I passed with top honours in that, and oddly enough it was the beginning of something like friendship between me and the formidable old lady. She liked the way I really concentrated on the darning, pulling fine threads out of the material itself, special pieces of worn pillow cases were kept for the purpose, and weaving them in and out with almost invisible needles. After a time I confessed

my reason for wanting to do it particularly well and she began to
take an interest in my 'studies' and gave me the key to the splendid
glass-fronted bookcases that lined one wall of the salon, so that
I could browse among the classics. I sometimes wonder if I
should ever had discovered Saint-Simon or Voltaire if it had not
been for those precious bookshelves. As time went on Madame
gave me more and more responsibility. I was given the key of
the wine cellar and the names of the wines to be brought up for
the Sunday luncheons, taught the correct hour to uncork the
Burgundy so that it should have time to 'breathe' at room temperature, how long to keep the Montrachet in the ice-box but
not to let it get *too* cold – quite a lot of wine lore that I have
completely forgotten. I even bought the children's clothes.
Mimi wanted a red coat 'Je veux que ça soit rouge, bien rouge,
un rouge vif, n'est ce pas Grandmaman?' 'All right – darling,
"Miss" will take you to the Galeries Lafayette and you shall
have a red, *red* coat.'

But suddenly the old lady was taken ill. Bronchitis followed by
double pneumonia. One day when death seemed very near and
all the family was gathered in her bedroom, Madame Laure
came into the study where I was sitting with the children. 'Ma
mère vous demande,' she said sounding a little incredulous.
'Moi?' I replied equally incredulous and went in, wondering.
Madame Gary raised her head from the pillow, 'Come closer,'
she whispered and when she had pulled me right down close to
her ear she said 'That red coat for Mimi, have you bought it?'
'Not yet Madame.' 'Good, good! it would be such a waste, get
her a black one, she will need it for the funeral. Promise her a red
one for the autumn.' Madame Laure took me back to the
children. 'What did she say to you that she didn't want to say
to her daughters?' When I told her she shook her head half
laughing, half crying, 'C'est épatant, de tout de même,' she
murmured 'on her deathbed! How we used to tease her about
counting her pennies. The coal, the gas, the soap even – but it
isn't really that she's so miserly – she just thinks it wicked to
waste money which should remain in the family.'

I can't remember the following days at all or whether I saw
her on her deathbed. I just remember vividly the five figures of
daughters and daughters-in-law draped from head to foot in
heavy black crêpe with flowing veils, like mourning figures on a

tomb, while the entire congregation passed before them murmuring pious condolences.

They were all very good to me afterwards and took me to Boulogne with them for the holidays. They had two or three villas there, into which all the five households decamped, and we spent long lazy hours on the sunlit sands watching the children splash and build, and as children do when they are tired, squabble fiercely as evening drew on. Madame Laure especially loved to make me talk. I talked more in those two weeks than I had in the previous ten months. 'Elle est épatante,' (her favourite word) Madame Laure would exclaim. 'What she has *read*! Maupassant and 'Willy!' 'Willy? oh Norty! Norty' one of the gentlemen would interrupt waggishly. Fortunately I refrained from quoting any verses from my favourite poets as I might have shocked them unutterably with verses of a sexual implication of which I was completely unaware. I think I must have been slow-witted to the point of idiocy; once in Paris, a large man seated beside me on top of an omnibus started fiddling with his flies and drew forth an object which made me rise indignantly. My only thought as I hastened down the steps was 'What a dirty man – he was just going to pee on the bus, degoûtant!'

After two delightful weeks of being 'made much of', something that had never happened to me before, I was really sad to leave them all. There had been vague discussions as to whether there was any way I could have stayed on, but of course it would have been totally 'indecorous' and 'inconvenable' for a jeune fille to have remained in the household of a widower; they would have had to engage a chaperon as well.

THREE

The Drama Student
1907–1909

When I arrived home from Paris I found the Nesbitt family fortunes at an all time low. Father and Uncle Courtney were struggling to shore up the ruins of Nesbitt Brothers, working from dawn till dusk and extracting at the end of a month less than any of their unskilled labourers. There were no Government subsidies for failing shipyards in those days, and anyway Father's firm was no Cunard Line. It had never prospered since the day when Grandfather Nesbitt had 'axed' his business partner Mr. Wolff for pulling off a deal that Grandfather considered dishonest, even though Mr. Wolff could prove that it was 'strictly legal'. Mr. Wolff had very quickly found a job with another small firm, Mr. Harland's. 'Harland & Wolff' was on its way to becoming world-famous, and 'Nesbitt Brothers' was soon to sink without a trace.

In the meantime Mamma was struggling. 'Taking in washing,' said Father bitterly; but she had hit on an idea that might have proved extremely successful had she had any capital or business training: a 'baby laundry', which guaranteed fine woollies to come back as soft as new, and baby robes as white as snow. Eliza washed all day and Mamma ironed and threaded baby ribbons all night, and I was pressed into service to pack them all into pretty boxes tied up with ribbon, and often deliver them surreptitiously to back doors if the delivery boy was too rushed.

I gave French lessons to as many pupils as I could find, and among them was an elocution teacher, with whom I exchanged skills: I taught her French and she taught me elocution. How or what she taught I can't remember, but she did teach me to make 'wind noises' in a terrible poem that started: 'Did you ever hear the wind go who-o-o-o?' and was intended to be recited at children's parties.

My silent moan for weeks was: 'Dieu que les jours sont quotidiens!' There seemed no hope of any end to the monotony. I had a vague desire to go on the stage, but where? when? how? And I had only to look at myself in the glass to add a mental mocking reservation: why?

But suddenly everything began to happen. The elocution lady belonged to an amateur dramatic company, the Belfast Footlights. I was, at her insistence, given a part in their next production. I was going to be *on the stage* – on the stage of the Theatre Royal, Belfast. Then from mother's rich cousin Sophia in Chile came a *cri de coeur*: her husband had died of a heart attack. 'Could dear cousin Thomas and dear cousin Cassy come out with the whole family and help her? She so needed a man with business acumen to run the ranch as she did not trust Chileans or Spaniards.' Mother was swift to move. Dear Papa's business acumen was hardly his strong point, but he was a *man*, and honest as could be, and *did* know a good deal about handling men. Mother wrote at once: Father would go and was practically on his way. For the moment Mother was tied up with the children's education, etc., but very soon she would come out with the younger ones, and soon we would all be with her. In the meantime Papa would have to give up his own business (Mamma never hinted that the business had practically given up anyway), he would have to keep a family this side of the ocean – she trusted Sophia to think of these things when naming a salary. Sophia had indeed generous ideas and poor Papa was shipped off. He would have been more than willing to take a job as a housepainter and send his children to the 'national schools', rather than be parted from his family. But Mamma wanted the Great World and a Great Place therein for her offspring.

The week after Father left, the performance at the Theatre Royal took place. For years I treasured the review in the Belfast *Northern Whig*: 'One of the bright spots of the evening was Miss Cathleen Nesbitt as a merry and buxom widow. If she intends to make the stage her career she should do well.' I suspect that the reviewer was a boyfriend of my elocution teacher and she had inspired the last lines! But I didn't think of that at the time. Nor did Mamma. Here was an excuse for us all to get away from the town she had always hated so much.

Within a few weeks we were in London, and living in Lynette Avenue, Clapham Common. And I was to be interviewed by Rosina Filippi as a prospective pupil.

What an utterly self-centred little brat I must have been. I remember nothing of that momentous move, getting rid of the Belfast house, finding a house in Clapham, getting Anna into a Convent school on Clapham Common and Terence into the American Choir School in Paris (I must have at least managed that I suppose), finding out that Rosina Filippi was supposed to be the best teacher in London, how? I haven't the faintest recollection of how it all came about, so I guess Mamma must have accomplished it on her own.

I remember surveying my wardrobe with dismay and finally dyeing a very dim grey coat and skirt in the bath. It came out an improbable shade of true vermilion, 'un vrai rouge bien vif' as Mimi would have said. It looked a little too much even to me, so I tried to tone it down with a large black hat (it must have been Mamma's) and black gloves which certainly were Mamma's. I must have looked just like a freshly painted pillar-box. I was just about that shape too. I took the tram to Victoria Station, then walked through a lovely park and up Park Lane, ravished by all the fairytale houses of the rich, up Baker Street, past where Sherlock Holmes lived, and so to Bickenhall Mansions.

My first emotion on seeing Rosina was of a mild elation. 'She is fat too and she is a big success. She is playing in a musical comedy at this minute. Perhaps fat doesn't matter if you're a good actress.'

'Rosina Mother', as we all called her, was a very good actress but she was also an inspired teacher. She was a half-sister of Duse: one of them was illegitimate, I was told, but I never dared to ask which: illegitimate was a truly sinister word in those days.

I think my mother had told her that we had very little money and that if I had no talent, the sooner I faced it the better. After a talk she decided I should try for one term, and promised that if I was no good she would tell me so honestly. I didn't really have any over-weening ambition. I had often told myself that there were two kinds of people in the world, the 'actor' people and the 'audience' people, the 'speakers' and the 'listeners', the 'doers' and the 'watchers', the 'leaders' and the 'led'. I had always, indeed I do still, placed myself in the second category, but I felt I would be content to earn my living on the stage playing cooks and charladies and perhaps one day graduating to the nurse in *Romeo and Juliet*.

We had mostly speech lessons. 'No one can teach you to act,' said Rosina, 'but you can learn to speak.' We also had movement and dancing lessons. I remember struggling with the *pas de basque*: 'Don't just *plonk* your foot on the ground, turn your leg in a graceful curve, a parabola, sway a bit'; and learning how to sink gracefully into a chair, seeing to it the while that one's feet ended up in a position from which one could rise suddenly and yet elegantly.

At the end of the term Rosina was a little nonplussed: 'I think you have *something* there, child, but it's all knotted up inside you – you think too much – you have no spontaneous instinct.'

However, she made a delightful proposition; that I should continue to come to the morning classes, and in the afternoon take on her twin daughters, Fanny and Rosemary, chaperon them to their art classes, their music lessons, their visits to museums and art galleries. Au pair again! But what a difference this time. To begin with the twins were so beautiful that it was sheer pleasure just to look at them. They had those lovely Botticelli faces one sees in the *Primavera*.

Sometimes old pupils came to visit and see the little monthly shows she would give, showing pupils in scenes from plays. How awed and self-conscious I became when I saw Owen Nares. He was the current matinée idol of the town, blond and slim with melting blue eyes. If anyone had told me that one day I would play his blackmailing ex-mistress clad in filmy pink pyjamas in an Edgar Wallace melodrama, I would have choked with disbelief.

Rosina had her own way of teaching diction. 'Consonants!' she would say. 'I want to hear *full* vowels, *sharp* consonants.' We had to recite stirring ballads, singly, then in unison:

> *King Charles and who'll do him* right *now*
> *King Charles and who's ripe for* fight *now*

or

> *The Assyrian came down like a wolf on the fold.*

As we chanted with what we thought was savage 'attack', there would come a groan. 'Stop! Stop! There are two F's there – a wol*f* on the *f*old.'

The first time I met Rachel McCarthy (Lady David Cecil) I found that Rosina had taught at her school, and though a good generation younger than me she too had rolled out 'King Charles and who's ripe for *fight* now' on Rosina's weekly visits.

I had a lovely few months, struggling to learn my craft in the mornings, and in the afternoons watching the twins draw from the life in their art studio, play duets at their music studio, and best of all visiting the British Museum and the National Gallery, insisting to my receptive pupils that Greek art was infinitely superior to Egyptian, and Chinese far above Japanese, and Leonardo's *Virgin of the Rocks* an infinitely greater picture than the *Mona Lisa*, with the dogmatic fervour of one who knows nothing but 'knows what she likes'.

At the end of term Rosina would give a performance at the Court Theatre for the parents and friends of the pupils, and for her friends among the London managers. I was cast to do a tiny part of a French wet-nurse. I think all I had to do was enter, cross the stage with a beaming hearty 'Bonjour Messieurs, Dames', and return a few minutes later, this time looking grim and with an icy 'Bonsoir Messieurs, Dames'. I loved my part. I knew just how a *nounou* walked and dressed: not for nothing had I watched the splendid creatures parading in the Bois de Boulogne. I could hide my too large bosom and too plump behind under the rustling petticoat and flowing cape, I held my head high over the starched collar and under the elegant bonnet with its fluttering scarlet ribbons floating behind. I felt secure in my disguise and certain of my impeccable French. I forgot about the audience and – I suddenly discovered I had authority.

I was astounded, and so I think was Rosina, when I got a round of applause on my exit and was awarded the 'Grand Prix' of the afternoon, a contract with the famous manager of the Court Theatre, Mr. Vedrenne. I was to start in his new production a month later as understudy and to play a small part as an earnest young suffragette. I think the play was all about 'Women's Lib', but in those days it was called 'Women's Rights'. In the meantime I got a heady glimpse of the great world – the great world to which Mamma had always felt she belonged.

There was a famous group of amateur players – the Edward-
ians were very addicted to acting – called the Canterbury
Players, who gave an annual performance at the Windsor
Theatre Royal in aid of some fashionable charity. Lady Alington, the star performer, came to Rosina in despair – Lady Susan
Yorke who was playing a French maid in their new production
had suddenly come down with measles. Could Rosina possibly
find among the pupils a girl who could speak fluent French, and,
most important, was a quick study? Rosina could indeed, and
two days later I was in Windsor rehearsing. Lady Susan had
been invited to stay in the Castle with the Dean of Windsor in
his own quarters, and I occupied the room which had been
allotted to her. There was a delightful member of the company
called Colonel Foley who stayed there too. I remember being
very surprised when Lady Alington said to him, as he offered to
escort me home every day, 'Now, Frank, I am in charge of this
child. None of your flirting.'

'Flirting?' I thought. 'Why, he's an old gentleman.' He must
have been all of fifty!

Lady Alington fulfilled her duties as chaperon admirably, in
fact to my mind she overdid it. If I danced too often with the
same young man at the two balls we were invited to, she would
loom up to pry us apart! Perhaps she was more intent on saving
the young man from a possible misalliance than on preserving
my virtue.

Lady Alington was a wonderful character. I got to know her
well after the war. She looked like a barmaid with a splendid
bosom and brightly rouged cheeks and was given to bewailing
the behaviour of her two children, Napier Alington who had just
succeeded his father, and Lois Sturt, whose portrait by McEvoy
as a Bacchante was drawing crowds at the Royal Academy.

'Naps is impossible,' she would say. 'No sense of his position.
Fools about with the most terrible young men, gate-crashes at
parties he wouldn't have dreamed of going to if he had been
invited, and Lois, everyone is talking about her, on Marconi's
yacht, all alone with him! She should leave that sort of behaviour
until *after* she is married . . . a girl "blown upon" like that will
never marry'. She must have been delighted when Lois finally
did marry a young peer of ancient lineage and enormous wealth.
His mother was reputed to have died insane, and he himself was

a very odd young man indeed, but it was a good match. Lady
Alington herself had been most circumspect in her behaviour
until her marriage to Lord Alington after which there was a
great deal of gossip. There were those who hinted that none of
her children was Lord Alington's, which I was not inclined to
believe. Lady Alington had her own standards and I'm sure she
would never have allowed herself to stray until she had had a
legitimate heir to the title. But I was quite ready to believe that
the lovely and exciting Lois was the daughter of the Brazilian
Ambassador, or was it the Portuguese?

Lady Alington would sometimes reminisce nostalgically about
the country weekends of younger days:

'I can't think how they manage nowadays, they tell me there
is no such thing as a Mixing Bell any more.'

'A Mixing Bell?'

'Well,' with a ribald chuckle, 'perhaps they should have called
it an unmixing bell. Every morning a page or a little maid
would go along all the landings and ring a little bell outside every
bedroom door, just long enough before the housemaids came
with morning tea for the gentlemen to scuttle back to their own
rooms.'

These reminiscences came much later in our acquaintanceship,
but while at Windsor I thought her a very awe-inspiring lady,
and incidentally a very good actress. I remember when I was
shown my costume, a saucy black dress and a very alluring cap
and apron of frilled muslin, I ventured to say, 'I've never seen
a French maid dressed like that'. She laughed and said 'Neither
has anyone else, who has ever seen a French maid. But it's what
most of the audience expects. Always give an audience what it
expects.' She invited me to visit her at Crichel but I had to go
back to London to rehearsals at the Royalty, and the thrill of
being on the stage professionally at last. The one thing I did not
enjoy was to see myself in the long mirror placed in a downstairs passage for the small fry like me who had only little table
mirrors in their dressing-rooms. I really looked a monster in
my badly cut grey coat, just the shade to add to my already
outsize waist, my round face with spectacles (to make me look
a bit more 'mature') underneath an exceedingly unbecoming
hat. I played one of a trio of 'suffragettes'.

The play was a success: three months was a success in those

days. Real smash hits like a Hawtrey farce or a Du Maurier comedy might run for six or even seven months. Years later *Chu Chin Chow* became a legend: 'Five years!' people would say, and start telling anecdotes about that prehistoric period when there was no *Chu Chin Chow* at His Majesty's Theatre, just as people now reminisce happily, 'You know I saw *The Mousetrap* before I was married and now I have five children.'

Luckily after the play closed and before I had time to feel the misery of unemployment, a new excitement came into my life: the Abbey Players came to town.

FOUR

The Irish Player
1910–1911

ल॰

The Abbey Players were the great success of the 1911 season, and I saw almost the whole repertory. I climbed to the gallery at least four times a week; we aficionados started standing outside the gallery door early in the afternoon. Orderly queues were unknown in those days and as soon as the doors opened at 7.30, there was a wild rush, a real free for all, and we fought our way up the stairs, past the dress circle, past the upper circle and down more stairs to the front row of the gallery. There we nursed our bruises and gradually we relaxed. We watched the stalls fill up with glamorous white-tied gentlemen and ladies, 'bedizened and bejewelled like Pharaoh's Ma'. We listened to and applauded the orchestra. Then we held our breath as the curtain rose slowly on an Irish cottage interior, or a lonely Irish road. We wept with Maire O'Neill as she lamented, 'Oh! my grief I've lost him surely, I've lost the only Playboy of the Western World'; and laughed when Sara Algood rounded on the village maidens who were crowding into the shop eager for a glimpse of the boy who had 'murdered his Da' and pretending they had come for a penn'orth of starch:

'Starch is it?' she replied in a wonderful deep contralto. 'Starch is it? And you without a white shirt or a shift in your family since the dryin' of the flood.'

The actors and playwrights all seemed to me to be geniuses. I longed to stand at the stage door to watch the actors come out, but felt it would be unbecoming for one who, however humble, was after all a member of the same profession. Then came the miracle: I was invited, I can't remember why, I didn't really move in such circles, to lunch with Sir Hugh Lane, Lady Gregory's nephew, and one of the guests was Lady Gregory. During lunch I heard her speak of the projected American tour:

'The Schubert brothers who owned many theatres in New York and most of the American provincial theatres have invited us to go for six months, but it's a great deal of worry we are having with their business gentleman. . . . "Now, how many understudies have you?" he said, and I replied, "Understudies?", not quite understanding. "What do you do when someone is sick? Who plays the parts?" "Oh, that's all right, they all know all the parts, and if Sally or Molly is ill, Una or Eileen takes on their part, and one of the girls takes on their parts. But of course if it's a play with a great row of characters and we haven't one actor to spare, we just close the theatre for the night." "You can't do that in New York," he said, "you have to have a couple of 'spares' as you call them, and you have to rehearse them properly too." It's a great worry, there's not much time. We have Sydney Morgan who's over in Dublin – he knows most of the men's parts – but it's a young girl we need to satisfy them.'

After lunch I summoned up courage to attack: 'I am an actress; I am a very quick study, I practically know all the parts now.'

'Are you Irish?' she asked doubtfully.

'Oh yes,' and I proceeded to recite a part of *The Playboy* in my best Kerry brogue.

'Do you come from Dublin then?' she asked, brightening a little.

'No, I'm really from Belfast, in fact I have a better Belfast accent than Miss O'Connor.'

'You would do well then for Norah in *Mixed Marriage*, and Una never liked the part,' she replied cosily. *Mixed Marriage* was not a racial problem play as you might think, but a Protestant-Catholic marriage which was frowned on in Belfast. In the end she told me to go to the Court Theatre next morning at 10 o'clock to meet Mr. Yeats.

Dare I tell him how many of his poems I knew by heart? Dare I speak Irish to him? He was not terrifying but gave an impression of great weariness and remoteness. He asked for a specimen of my brogue, and murmured, 'It will do, near enough. Do you think you could speak verse?'

I gasped, I would recite 'The Lake Isle of Innisfree'. Poor
man, how often he must have heard people mouth that. It was
rather like his own signature tunc. I sometimes think it was
to spare himself a recitation of the whole poem that at the end
of the first verse, he raised a weary hand, 'Enough, enough, I'll
take you to Mr. Shubert's man'.

I can remember nothing clearly after that. I imagine I was
living in a dream, always afraid to wake up. There must have
been a thousand things to do: people to meet, clothes to buy,
copies of parts I was to understudy. I remember only being
summoned to Lady Gregory's cabin on board the *Zeelandia* to
be told that at the last moment Maire O'Neill had discovered
she was pregnant, and refused to go, so all her parts were to be
divided between four of us Una, Eileen, Maeve and myself.
The other girls knew the plays by heart, but Lady Gregory
would help me learn my words during the twelve days it took
to cross the Atlantic. On the fourth day a dreadful storm shook
the old boat. Everyone was seasick, except Jimmy Kerrigan and
myself, who ran from cabin to cabin, trying to reassure the
troops that death was not imminent.

KERRIGAN: How's Sally now?
ME: Terribly seasick. She keeps screaming for the captain to
  come and see her. She wants him to stop the ship now and go
  right home or she'll be dead by morning and put a curse upon
  him with her dying breath. How's Sinclair?
KERRIGAN: He's on his knees in his cabin and he's reading an
  old press-cuttings book he keeps with all his best notices in
  it, and he's praying to Almighty God, 'Ah, ye wouldn't
  drown a great actor like meself and me in me prime. . . .'
ME: How's Mr. Yeats?
KERRIGAN: A bit under the weather, I'm thinking, but Lady
  Gregory is typing away, writing a new play to keep her mind
  off the weather.

That was always my memory of Lady Gregory. When we
toured one-night stands we youngsters would crawl from the
train we had boarded at dawn, and lean against the hotel desk.
'A bed, a bed, me kingdom for a bed!' But Lady Gregory would
be asking in her gentle, faintly Irish voice, 'Have you a nice
steady table I can put my typewriter on?' She was then I think

over seventy. She seemed immensely old to me, and I remember wondering how anyone of that age could be so vigorous. For me the voyage out was spent in 'study'. I inherited a number of parts, from 'the beautiful Molly Byrne' in *The Well of the Saints*, to the oldest woman in the village, aged about eighty. Kerrigan tells a story of the opening night:

'There was Miss Nesbitt sitting in the dressing-room with a Rembrandt reproduction in front of her, putting lines on her face God Almighty couldn't see with a microscope, and gettin' so absorbed she never heard her call, and the stage manager bellowed up the stairs, "You're off, woman, you're off," and the next thing we heard was a noise like a herd of elephants lumbering down the stairs and Miss Nesbitt leapt on to the stage like a young gazelle, and suddenly remembered she was all of eighty, and crumpled up like an old besom.'

Kerrigan was my friend and supporter during the early days on the ship, and in New York, during which the company, who didn't believe in the need for understudies, did believe that I was a 'spy', and English at that, 'put in by the management', as they called Lady Gregory and Yeats. But they gradually discovered that I was humble and biddable and anxious to learn from my betters, and we became friends. Arthur Sinclair alone continued to regard me with suspicion and malice, and I really believe once tried to push me into the 'Well' of the 'Saints'. That was my favourite play. I wore a golden wig and a dazzling white blouse and red petticoat, and the *Chicago Tribune* said, 'Cathleen Nesbitt is a beauty.' How I treasured that piece of paper for years. No one had ever hinted that I had any claim to good looks. Even my mother was wont to say, 'Don't worry about not being pretty, you are intelligent and that is far better.' When I read the sonnet in which Shakespeare boasts that his love is 'as fair as any mother's child', I thought ruefully, 'Not *my* mother's child'.

Our opening night in New York was a battle between the actors and the Sinn Feiners in the pit, who had been alerted by their Dublin brethren that *The Playboy* was a wicked play and a slur on the fair name of Ireland – 'makin' a hero out of a man who killed his Da.' A large section of the Irish population of New York was in front having arrived with a variety of raw vegetables. I have no recollection of it myself but Richard

Maney, a famous theatrical columnist, swore that I threw all the tomatoes right back at the audience. I may have wanted to but I had the sense to realise my aim was bad (I could never even throw a ball), and that my tomatoes would only stain the white shirts of the gentlemen in the front stalls, if they didn't fall short into the instruments of the orchestra. The Schuberts made the most of it and sent us all home guarded by police cars with screaming sirens. For the rest of the run the box office was besieged by a number of people hoping, I suspect, for another battle.

The Sinn Feiners had a more subtle approach in Philadelphia; they suborned an old Irish-born magistrate to issue a warrant for our arrest on the charge of producing and performing 'an obscene and blasphemous play'. The resulting trial was a splendid Gilbert and Sullivan affair that drew crowds to the play itself. Urged to explain where the obscenity could be found, the old magistrate averred that 'the Playboy had *spent the night* with the girl!' Counsel for the defence shouted, 'Didn't you hear her point to the next room and say, "There's your bed now. Good night to you. Sleep till the morning" – and shut the door on him?' 'Ah!' cried counsel for the prosecution, 'but what happened when the curtain went down and a ten-minute interval before it came up again?'

'It's you that's obscene, ye dirty ould sod,' bellowed Kerrigan from the dock.

'Remove that man from the court', shouted the magistrate.

'Glad to go,' retorted Kerrigan and made for the door. Hurried whisperings from counsel for the prosecution.

'Holy God, bring him back, *he's a prisoner!*' cried the magistrate.

'Who's blaspheming now, takin' the name of the Lord in vain!' shouted Kerrigan triumphantly.

Oh, how I *wish* I'd done what I've always intended to do when in Philadelphia: look up the newspaper files for 1911 and reread the full reports of the whole happening.

We never lacked for excitement. When the actors hadn't an audience to fight they fought among themselves. There were nights when an agonised stage manager rang the curtain up and down on an empty stage because Sally and Arthur or Fred or Sydney or some couple had had a row and were muttering in the

wings, 'I won't stand on the stage with *that* one by my side,' and
we 'also-rans' didn't dare go on without the stars. But we had a
good time everywhere and were fêted by the rich and fashionable. Kerrigan whispered to me once at a party, 'Would ye
look at Sally there, preenin' herself in a red silk gown and
Yeats and her Ladyship pretendin' in the corner that they
caught us all wild off the trees like monkeys.'

Some of the company were well educated and extremely intelligent people, and most of them had more wit and manners
than the average silent film star but 'the management' liked to
preserve the illusion that we were all simple peasants lured
from the land to warble our native wood notes wild behind the
footlights. We did not live in luxury. $25 a week didn't provide
luxuries when it had to cover hotel food, make-up, and odd
pocket money. So mostly we were parked in boarding-houses,
'American-plan', where a great show was made without a great
deal of food by putting every item on a different plate, a bit of
meat with a lot of gravy on the centre plate, and half a dozen
little white saucers containing corn, potatoes, cabbage, beans,
cole-slaw or whatever grouped all round it; to which Sally's
reaction in every town was an anguished cry to the waitress:
'For God's sake will ye take away them little bird-baths and
give me a good helping of something on me plate!'

The voyage home was serene. The sun shone, we had sing-
songs on deck, and by now we were all good friends. Sally
taught me some wonderful old Irish ballads: 'I know my love by
his way of walkin' and I know my love by his way of talkin' ',
and 'If my love left me what should I do?' and the marvellous
lament 'Agadoe' which always sent shivers down my back.

I think the ship was called *America*, and Sally was hoping for
the sake of the infant that a young woman in the cabin next door
to her would not give birth until the ship docked: 'Ye remember
the poor little baby I was godmother to on the way out? – and
the way they insisted on callin' it *Zeelandia*.' 'I'll tell ye some-
thin',' said Kerrigan, 'that young woman is on her way to
Dublin and if she doesn't hold out till then ye'll have a godchild
called S.S. *America* runnin' round Ireland's fair city.'

We said tearful farewells on the quay vowing to meet again
soon, but except for Sally I never set eyes on any of them again.

FIVE

Perdita

1911–1912

~~~~~~

And so back to London and a move to Hyde Park Mansions in Marylebone Road. What bliss to be actually 'in town', no longer living out in the wilds of Clapham.

My eldest brother, Tom, had now become an actor. He had stunned poor Mamma the Christmas before by announcing that he couldn't stand the thought of being an engineer. Just before the examinations for his engineering degree began, he had come home with a beaming smile and said, 'I've got a job in the Streatham Pantomime.'

'What?' cried Mamma.

'I'm one of the four Singing Footmen. We do old English part-songs and catches.'

'How on earth . . . ?' Mamma stuttered.

'Well, I saw an ad in the local paper saying "Singer Wanted", so I went to the stage door and they asked was I a tenor or baritone? And I said, "Which are you short of?" and when they replied, "Baritone", I sang them a baritone song and that was it.'

'I thought we would have one member of the family in a steady profession,' wailed Mamma. But Tom, who made her laugh by singing the Cornish Dance in basso profundo, baritone and tenor, justified himself from the start by being always in work; and ended up, within ten years, in America starring opposite favourite stars like Ruth Chatterton and Margaret Lawrence.

In fact with Hugo happy in the Headmaster's House at Bedford School (the Head was an old friend of Mamma's) and becoming a cricket star, and Anna training for ballet (too old to begin, but none of us knew that) and Terence in his last term

at the American School in Paris, I was the only one of the family
at a loose end.

After my exciting experiences with the Abbey Players I fell
into the trough of despondency; never, I felt, would I get such
parts again. It is the actor's occupational disease, that dark
cloud of depression when a play closes: 'Shall I ever get a part
again?' Even for the stars it comes: 'Shall I ever find a play
again?'

At last I found a job through Lady Gregory, to play the part
of an old Irishwoman in her play *The Workhouse Ward*. It was
to be the curtain-raiser for Marie Tempest's new play. There
was always a curtain-raiser in those days – a one-act trifle to
keep the pit and gallery entertained while the stalls and dress
circle drifted in after their 'early short dinner' (only five
courses!). I was thrilled to be in a theatre with Marie Tempest,
but alas, I never got to be presented to her. She was the queen
in the theatre and didn't talk to the proletariat, or the proletariat was kept out of her way.

When that finished came a Protean Act at the Shepherd's
Bush Empire. The actor would recite 'One man in his time
plays many parts' and proceed to enact five or six characters
within half an hour, sometimes transforming his whole appearance in less than a minute.

There was a woman called Gwen Lally whose very successful
Protean Act allowed her to impersonate at least four or five male
characters. Looking back I think she must have had a lesbian
yen for me, or she would never have engaged anyone so inexperienced as her stooge for a week at the Shepherd's Bush
Empire – and 'tour to follow'. There always had to be a female
stooge who could come on as a Lady Love appropriate to the
period while Gwen 'made her change'. We would start with
Lancelot and Guinevere – and while Gwen rushed behind a
screen to transform herself into Charles II, I would stay on stage
reciting a few lines of Tennyson – Gwen was very 'literary',
always a nice bit of poetry. Then when Charles II made his
Dashing Entrance I hastened off to become Nell Gwynne. As
soon as ready, but never quite on time, came pretty Nell to
release Charles for another transformation. I longed to come
on crying: 'Desist good folk, I am the *Protestant* whore' but
Gwen was shocked; 'You can't use that word on the Halls dear,

we'd get the sack pronto.' I got the sack anyway before the end of the week.

'You're a nice girl dear, and I'd like to keep you for the tour, but you aren't nippy enough, you barely make it with two dressers waiting for you, what would you do on the road with only one?'

But I did get some reward, I was able to see the great clown, Grock; oh! more than clown – genius, Chaplin and Marcel Marceau combined. I saw him close to and for free, every night as I stood in the wings. Sometimes the audience simply wouldn't let him go as they stood and cheered; he was worth missing the last bus for.

I was out of work again, but this time I was incredibly lucky. I had an actress friend called Jane (I can't remember her surname), a very lovely girl with red hair and green eyes, and an impudent mouth. She took me down to the Savoy Theatre where they were casting the small parts for *The Winter's Tale*.

'We are to go to the stage door and see the stage manager, and tell him what experience we've had and he'll decide whether we shall see Mr. Granville-Barker; and I wouldn't mention that Shepherd's Bush Empire bit,' she warned me.

I was afterwards told by Henry Ainley that when Barker was told I had had six months with the Irish Players he said: 'Good! She won't have learned any damn tricks.'

Jane and I were engaged to play the two shepherdesses, Mopsa and Dorcas. (I can't remember which I was, but I think it must have been Dorcas, as in the catch-song 'whither oh whither?' Dorcas has always one line to Mopsa's three, and singing was never my strong point.)

The rehearsal plan was for one week sitting round a table, then one week 'blocking' on the stage, then a month off for Ainley to fulfil a previous contract. During the readings the Perdita disappeared after the first few days. I suppose Barker thought she wouldn't do – she had a ravishingly pretty face but a 'tinny, tiny' voice. Jane and I read Perdita on alternate days, but when we got on the stage and there was still no Perdita, Barker said to me 'You'd better read it till our Perdita arrives and mark the moves in your book for her.' I had to seek counsel from kind Enid Rowe, the Paulina. With the Irish Players one never 'marked' anything, we just kept out of each other's way. If there wasn't an empty space you sat down on the nearest chair.

At the end of the week he told me to stay behind when the rehearsal was over and told me I was to play Perdita. I wish I could go back in memory to that moment: it must have been one of such rapture. But strangely enough all I can remember was him saying: 'You must spend the whole of the coming month going daily to Margaret Morris. You realise you must dance "like a wave of the sea"?' Then he asked what salary I had had with the Irish Players. I said £5 a week and wished at once that I had said £6. I added quickly: 'Everyone said we were ridiculously underpaid. We were getting less than the stage-hands and *much* less than the electricians.' 'So you should,' said Barker. 'They were double your age, and probably twice as good at their jobs. Very well, you shall have £5 a week.'

There was no such thing as rehearsal money in those pre-Equity days, nor, as I found later on, were there any arrangements made for us to get home after rehearsing – often till 3 o'clock in the morning. Thank God I now lived in Marylebone, and could quite happily walk home if necessary. But I really did feel that I earned any salary I was about to get for playing Perdita, if only for those Margaret Morris lessons. I spent hours balancing like a figure on a Greek frieze: left foot on the ground, right foot poised by left knee, arms stretched out at right angles to the body, and then from the elbow up, parallel to the body; remain motionless for sixty seconds; then reverse feet and repeat. By that time every muscle ached. I don't know whether I ever danced 'like a wave', but at least I was more graceful, and what with all the skipping and jumping and running as well, I lost quite a bit of weight.

On 1 August we started rehearsals. I don't think I was ever again actively to *enjoy* every moment of rehearsals to such a degree. I never left the stage during the long periods when Perdita was not in a scene. I tucked myself away in some corner and watched breathlessly. Barker had the gift of galvanising the whole cast. Everyone trusted him, everyone turned themselves inside out for him. I have worked since for many famous directors – Basil Dean, David Belasco, countless others – but Barker was the only genius. And to be put under contract to him for a year was the greatest good fortune any young actress could wish for.

I had already met the company during the first reading round the table when Mr. Barker courteously presented us all to each other. I wanted to curtsy to all the famous actors I had read about, or seen from the gallery, Lillah McCarthy, statuesque and beautiful, Arthur Whitby, Nigel Playfair, Leo Quartermaine, but secretly I was eagerly awaiting Henry Ainley. There were no gossip columns in those days, but I had heard about him, even at Rosina's. How he had taken the town by storm as the most beautiful Romeo of his generation; how countless young women had been in love with him and how he had 'loved them and left them'; how he had married an American actress, Suzanne, fifteen years older than himself, red-haired and beautiful; how he had left her for another red-haired American beauty, this time a novelist ten years older than himself and had a son by her. It all sounded so romantic to me. When a tall, slender, extremely beautiful young man came in, I thought for one fleeting second 'This *must* be Ainley'. But I realised 'It can't be – too young' before Barker's introduction: 'Florizel – Mr. Dennis Neilson-Terry'. How formal we were those days. Barker called me Miss Nesbitt during the whole two years of my contract with him. At last! Henry Ainley! A stockily built solid-looking man with a ruddy face and unruly black hair. My heart sank. Was *this* the Romeo, the Lothario of every woman's dream? Before the 'reading' was over, I knew that I was fortunate to be in a company with a really great actor. He might have been tall or short, thin or stout, I could no longer tell. His eyes and his voice were so magnetic, one was 'held' fascinated. I didn't appear till the middle of the play and he was 'on' practically all the time till then. I was fascinated by the work he and Barker did together. I had not dreamed that 'acting' could be so interesting, so fraught, with problems, so tenuous an interweaving between author and actor and director, each of the latter two adding his own fraction of illumination to the glow of the original.

How we rehearsed, for at least six weeks and sometimes until 3 or 4 a.m. Then there would come the moment when Lillah would walk on in the middle of a scene, with a cup of broth or milk or cocoa, and say 'That's enough now, Harley', though the young ones in the company would want to go on till dawn. He was so exciting to work with. There was practically no scenery.

61

He said: 'There's never going to be much to sit on except an odd bench or gilded stool. You must decorate the stage your-selves.' Having had no experience and having only seen one Shakespearian production in my life, *A Midsummer Night's Dream* at His Majesty's, chock-a-block with real trees and rivulets of real water and real rabbits scuttling around, I didn't realise that the whole production was going to electrify the audiences of that day, much as Peter Brook's production of *A Midsummer Night's Dream* has electrified the audiences of today. There was little scenery but the costumes were very beautiful. He had the sets and costumes designed by the best artists of the day, Norman Wilkinson and Albert Rutherston. People like Nigel Playfair and Arthur Whitby and Henry Ainley, who had always played in splendid walled rooms, with ceilings and a proscenium, must have found the vast open stage on three levels, the lower one built out over the orchestra pit, rather a shock, but I had only played with the Irish Players where we had one 'cottage set' to find our way around in as best we could. I revelled in the feeling of *space*.

Barker had cast the play magnificently. For instance, there's a short scene towards the end of the play between the Three Gentlemen, which had usually been regarded as a bore and often cut entirely, but Barker respected his Shakespeare. I don't think he ever cut a word.

He must have thought, 'I won't cut that scene, it's there for some reason.' So he called upon Nigel Playfair, a very highly paid actor, who happened to be playing in a play in which he was killed off in the second act.

'Play a Third Gentleman?', said Nigel. 'For God's sake, I stopped playing "extras" years ago, and anyway the part can't be worth my salary.'

'I'll pay your full salary, and you will find the part worth it.'

And Nigel was so funny in it and played it with such *brio* that the other two somehow came up to his level, and the audience laughed so much at him and at the scene which followed between the Shepherd and the Clown, that it was all a marvellous burst of fun and nonsense. And then the quiet end of the play came as a lovely *andante*.

I think one of the reasons Barker was so wonderful to work for was that in many ways he gave his actors such freedom. He was not one of those directors who does a lot of homework with a set of puppets, and then says to the actors 'I have you standing stage left on that line and moving stage centre on this.' He worked *with* his actors and the only thing he ever bullied one about was *speech*, he wanted tremendous speed and clarity, a difficult combination.

I remember him standing in the auditorium of the Savoy. One could just see his face above the line of the footlights, his green eyes blazing, clutching at his reddish hair saying; 'Faster, faster, it must go at a clip. Pausing for a laugh? Nonsense! There are plenty of laughs, just ride over them till you get to a real smacker.' Sometimes Lillah would say: 'For Heaven's sake, stop *interrupting*, you never let us get to the end of a scene. You're inhibiting us.' And he would laugh and say, 'All right. I'll shut up. I promise I'll go up to the dress circle and not utter a *word* till the end of the act.' For a while there was peace. Then there was a curious drumming noise and searching for its origin we would suddenly realise that he was sitting in the dress circle with his back to the stage kicking the second row seats furiously to express what he thought of what was going on. He knew exactly what he wanted from each actor. I was astounded, and I think the rest of the cast was, too, at my being chosen for Perdita. I had thought of her as a little Botticelli nymph (some vague association with the *Primavera* I suppose), the daughter of a king. But Barker saw her as a country girl, brought up by a shepherd, and my puppy fat was if anything an asset. He had enormous kindness too, none of the sarcasm and bullying which sometimes seems built in with perfectionists. I remember once, when I had been, as I thought, doing very nicely, in the scene where I 'flirted with flowers' with the elderly gentlemen of the Court, listening to myself being very musical about the

> daffodils,
> *That come before the swallow dares, and take*
> *The winds of March with beauty; violets dim,*
> *But sweeter than the lids of Juno's eyes*

He came up to me quietly and said, 'You're being too poetical.' 'Shouldn't I be?' 'Don't you remember Touchstone's dialogue with Audrey? Touchstone says: "I would the gods had made thee poetical." And Audrey says: "I do not know what poetical

is. Is it honest? Is it a true thing?" And Touchstone says, "No.
No!" '

'Remember – be not poetical. Be *honest*, always. Don't ever
listen to yourself sing.' And at the first dress rehearsal, when
I was so shocked, the prim little prude I was, at the dress Albert
Rutherston had designed for me that I refused to put it on. 'It's
split right up one side, away up above the knee,' I cried to the
wardrobe mistress. 'It will go right up to my waist when I
dance. *Please* stitch down to just *below* the knee.' 'Oh! Miss,'
said the horrified wardrobe mistress, 'you can't go muckin'
about with a dress Mr. Rutherston designed special, I won't
put a stitch in it.' I waited till she was out of the room and
cobbled it up, or should I say down, myself. I expect Rutherston
howled in protest, but as he told me long afterwards when we
had become friends, Barker, who used to be furious when people
'cheapened' a design by wearing a wrong hair style or whatever,
just laughed: 'Don't worry, we'll snip it up again gently – she's
got an odd quality of innocence which is quite different from
ignorance. I don't want that spoilt.' It's true, real innocence *is*
different from ignorance. Perdita was a country girl. She knew
all about breeding and impregnation, but she only knew it
because she had seen it with animals. She didn't connect it with
human beings or as having anything to do with love, and I
didn't either. Barker was very careful to keep that sense of
innocence and forthrightness about Perdita. She had been brought
up from birth as a shepherd's daughter and was without any
coyness or courtly graces. Playing Perdita, I ceased to hanker so
much after a Botticelli figure with long slender legs and resigned
myself more to my puppy fat. How Barker loved his actors to
speak well. 'In the beginning was the *Word*,' he would say, and
insisted on every word being given its absolute value, except in
scenes of great passion – anguish, fear, anger, jealousy – which
need a torrent of deep emotion. At one time, when Ainley was
rehearsing the very difficult (and, *pace* Shakespeare, extremely
improbable) jealousy scene at the beginning, he stopped and
cried: 'I can't say anything as quickly as that and give any
meaning to the words. For God's sake, there are lumps of it
I don't understand myself, how's the audience going to understand them?'

'They don't have to understand with their ears', said Barker, 'just with their guts. You are really just babbling in a rage and anguish of jealousy, it's a *primitive* emotion. You can accelerate and accelerate, just sounding the vowels, till you come to the still menace of: "Is whispering nothing? Is leaning cheek to cheek nothing? Is meeting noses nothing? Kissing with inside lips?" . . . which must rise to a roar, a howl, when you come to: "The covering sky is nothing, Bohemia is nothing, my *wife* is nothing." ' And Harry could do it. I shall never forget him at the dress rehearsal, pacing up and down like a tiger, his eyes blazing, his magnificent kingly robe of crimson and gold flaring around him, his voice resounding through the theatre. He had a superb voice. It could sound like a trumpet or a 'cello or a violin. And in addition to its enormous range and power, it had that – there *is* only a Welsh word for it – that *hwyl* that kindles the blood. The only voice I ever heard again quite like it was Richard Burton's. I heard Burton recite once a war poem by David Jones, called *In Parenthesis*. I can barely remember a word from it, but I can remember the emotion it roused in the audience and in me.

I can't remember much of the opening night – except little notes from Barker we each found on our dressing-table. Mine was: 'Be swift, be swift, be not poetical.'

Were there flowers and telegrams, did I then know enough people who would be likely to send me flowers or telegrams? I can't remember. I do remember that Barker, with his usual tremendous intuition, knew that Dennis and I would be likely to be paralysed with nerves it being our début on the London stage, and having to wait till the middle of the play till we appeared. He came and gave us a pat on the back as we stood waiting for our entrance, Dennis trembling, I rigid as a leaden pipe and as empty. He waited for our cue to enter and then literally *pushed* us on to the stage. Dennis almost fell on his knees and I on top of him; by the time we had straightened up we were almost giggling and went into the slightly pompous lines of the opening scene rather breathlessly with an under-current of laughter. Someone remarked afterwards: 'What a clever idea to have the two young lovers tumble on to the stage like a couple of frisky lambs, it set the mood for the sheep-shearing Festival exactly.'

How horrified some of the critics were by the set for the

sheep-shearing Festival – no trees, no artificial roses, no sheep
even, just a little cottage 'looking as if it had been a throw out
from the Ideal Home Exhibition,' said one. 'The Elizabethan
music was not exhilarating,' said another. I agreed – it is not easy
to dance a merry measure to a Recorder and a couple of pipes!

In fact I agreed heartily with the *Daily Telegraph*, I think it
was, who respected Mr. Barker for his refusal to cut the play,
'but he might at least have cut the music to the sheep-shearing
scene, which seemed to go on for ever, as did the galumphing
village dances'. The *Telegraph* was a little disturbed by the
'pretty little Perdita' who was 'too rollicking a miss for one who
should have been rare and aloof as a king's daughter'. However,
he did think the sheer *whiteness* of the set was wonderful and the
way the palace was suggested by pillars and an arrangement of
light and colour rather than anything real. And Barker must
have been happy that so many of his own pet theories had been
justified, from 'Nigel Playfair, who aired his scholarship about
Giulio Romano and his own eloquence with such a delightful
sense of Shakespearian fun as to win the laughing homage of the
audience', to his direction of Ainley in the 'jealousy' scene:
'Mr. Ainley, speaking with a fierce speed, seemed to have no
difficulty of utterance . . . and was amazing in conveying the
mad meaning of the strange lines in which the frenzy of passion
has contorted truth and meanings.' The critic finally concluded
he agreed with the lady in front of him who had exclaimed
'I had no *idea* it was such an *interesting* play!' *The Times*,
on the other hand, declared that even though 'the old shepherd
inhabited a model bungalow from the Ideal Home Exhibition
with Voysey windows', 'the "country scenes" of the play were
the high spot of the evening', and that Perdita was 'a delicious
little romp', but that nothing could ever make Leantes and
Hermione anything but bores, that Ainley was 'magnificently
violent' but 'even violence can be dull'. There were so many
critics in those days, I can't remember what they all said.
Some of them objected to the speed of the speaking, 'as though
every one had a 100 horse-power engine inside him,' others
thought it magnificent. I can remember feeling what I have so
often thought since when reading reviews of a new play: 'Can
they all have seen the same production? Or are they all review-
ing different plays?'

When I worked with Barker years later in his own play *The Madras House* and in *King Lear*, I learned so much by watching and listening to his direction of other actors. But, during *The Winter's Tale* rehearsals, my concentration, which is the root of memory, was very much elsewhere. I was falling in love. I had been 'in love' with someone, real or imaginary, ever since I could remember, but the objects of my affection had never even noticed me. Now my Florizel was falling in love with me. The first love letter I ever received was from him. He was the first man who had ever kissed me. In the beginning it was Florizel who kissed Perdita and then it was Dennis who kissed Cathleen. It must have been thrilling to me – but I don't remember. I don't even remember how long it lasted. I think I had forgotten about it, till I came on a letter from him in a box of old papers.

> 91, Bedford Mansions,
> Bedford Square, W.C.

'Dearest, just a line to say will 1 o'clock be too early for you to meet at the Pall Mall Restaurant in the Haymarket tomorrow as I've got a matinée. Just drop me a line, or if you haven't time send me a verbal message by someone, though I should much prefer the former. You do know, don't you, how much I adore you really. Oh! don't be so horribly casual with me. I am deadly serious and love you with all my heart, so don't altogether hate me for writing this. Bless you. Dennis.'

Poor Dennis, it was with Henry Ainley that *I* had fallen in love. I loved him from afar. I didn't even think he knew it, and thought I couldn't possibly mean anything to him, even when one day he took me in his arms in the dark passage to the stage door and said: 'Beautiful eyes you have, child. "Stars, stars and all eyes else dead coals",' and then left me abruptly. I stood shaken and giddy, thinking: 'It can't be, he can't mean anything' and when he smiled at me gently at rehearsal next morning, the world seemed to spin round me again. I was so many fathoms deep in love! I did not plunge in to the well. It all happened so gradually, at first I was his 'beloved daughter', his long-lost little 'Princess', his 'Perdita'. 'May your father take you to lunch tomorrow? Where would you like, little Princess? The Carlton Grill?' And then, a little note on the table in my dressing-room: 'Will Perdita sup with her father after the play tonight? We will go across the street to Rules and sit in the corner where they say the Prince of Wales, before he was good King Edward, supped with his lady love.' Then little by little there was no more pretence that I was his 'daughter' or a 'child'. How my heart beat when I had the first letter that began 'My Caitilin, my woman'. He always called me 'Caitilin' because I had told him that spelling Cathleen with a C was copying the Gaelic version of the name, Caitilin. How I listened for the post in the morning, and ran back to bed clutching the Garrick Club envelope with the well-known handwriting on it; or perhaps it would be a knock on the door and there would be a little messenger boy with a great armful of red roses and a card: 'Oh my rose of the world, my dark rose, my Irish rose, good day to you my Caitilin.'

I had the flat in Hyde Park Mansions all to myself – my Father and Mother in Chile – my younger brothers at school – my brother Tom had his own house. Sometimes Harry would take me home and let me scramble eggs for him while he wandered about and looked at my books and went into my room and blew a kiss on my pillow and leave me in a haze. I was living in a fairyland. I would read myself to sleep with his letters and wake to re-read them. 'My most beautiful and best beloved. There has been a song in my heart all this day, a song of beautiful worship for my Woman and so I send you a few flowers and bid you dine with me tomorrow afternoon. Will you fetch me? Or shall I fetch you? Anyhow, we love each other, so we may as well fetch each other. My dear, I am your man.' Sometimes, after the play had opened, he would take me back to his house in Regent's Park where he appeared to be camping out. It's amazing to me, looking back, that I should have had so little ordinary human curiosity about his background. Where were they? His wife? His mistress? His child? I never asked. It was enough that we sat by a fire and he read Shakespeare's sonnets to me – not the sonnets that everybody knew – most of which even I knew by heart – but the rarely quoted ones.

His caresses were so gentle, and little by little became so insistent, that I was half afraid, half longing for something more – *what?* I did not know. I think it gave him a curious pride that he could in a sense 'possess' me without 'o'er stepping the bounds of modesty'.

And then there came a time when it all began to be unhappy. I felt a sense of guilt. I began to wonder about his other 'woman', the real woman, the mother of his child. When Jane said to me one day 'You won't be seeing so much of Harry now?' I thought at first she meant because *The Winter's Tale* was coming off and I was rehearsing for another play, Galsworthy's *The Eldest Son*. 'Oh, that? No, didn't you know that Bettina is coming home? She leaves the nursing home next week.' '*Bettina?*' 'For God's sake don't look like a half-wit! Bettina, the Baroness, the mother of the boy, she's had a baby girl, she has been on the danger list for weeks.' I was stunned and bewildered. I was angry and jealous, somewhere deep down was a vague relief. I had known there was an unreality about it all, that it would have to stop soon. There were several 'Farewells' in that dark corner at Rules – I didn't realise it then but he was already beginning to take refuge in drink. It was many years before it dimmed his talent, but in the end it destroyed him and robbed the theatre of a great actor. I didn't know then that his tears were the easy tears of the alcoholic when he would sit trying to explain about Bettina – 'she had no right at her age to *have* another child. She's only done it to keep us together. I'd have married her after the boy if that bitch Susanne would have divorced me.' I'd ask: 'Will you marry her now if Susanne divorces you?' 'If? If? I don't want to marry anyone – *but you*', and I would have a little pang of disbelief; the '*but you*' didn't quite ring true. I think I was by this time in Barker's next production, *The Eldest Son*. One night a strange woman burst into my dressing-room at the Kingsway Theatre and said fiercely 'Is it true that you are going to have a child by Henry Ainley?' I thought at first she must be some crazy woman who had been unhinged by the play (I was playing an unhappy parlourmaid in a stately home who was *enceinte* by the eldest son). 'I am *Mrs*. Ainley,' she said sharply, and without giving me time to speak, added: 'He's been badgering me about a divorce again. If he is going to marry *you*, I'd give him one.' I assured her that I was *not* with child, that Harry had never seduced me (she obviously didn't believe that) and that there was no question of our ever marrying. I think she believed that. Her parting words were: 'You can tell him I'll never give him a divorce to marry that *bitch*, never *never*!' I crept into bed that night and lay awake all night.

What monsters we all are, I thought. I was a culprit myself for making love with a married man; Harry was guilty for making love to another woman while the mother of his new-born child was seriously ill; Bettina was guilty for enticing him to have another child he did not want.

I felt stricken and bewildered. I had so many moments of what I thought was longing for Harry and was really only a longing for what had been. But gradually the turmoil subsided to a lingering nostalgic affection: 'The heart must pause to breathe, and love itself have rest.'

I did not know that I was soon to find another and a truer love.

SIX

Rupert Brooke, The First Four Months
1912

∽∼∽∼∽∼∽∼∽∼∽∼∽∼∽∼∽∼∽∼∽∼∽∼∽∼∽∼∽∼∽∼

I first met Rupert Brooke at a party at Eddie Marsh's flat in Gray's Inn.

Christopher Hassall, in his splendid biography of Rupert,* says that it was on 20 December 1912. He also adds that Rupert had seen me play Perdita twice, and that Eddie had given the party so that he could meet me. In Eddie's own diaries he noted on 20 December:

'Supper at Raymond Buildings. Cathleen Nesbitt asked to meet Gilbert Cannan. Rupert, Henry Ainley, Gilbert there.'

I don't remember Rupert ever telling me that he had seen *The Winter's Tale*. Perhaps it would have explained what often puzzled me at first, a kind of 'image' he had of me, as incredibly young and innocent and unworldly. I don't remember Rupert even mentioning *The Winter's Tale* at all. When we met at Eddie's I was playing in *The Eldest Son*.

I just remember a tall very good-looking, rather shy young man with extraordinarily blue eyes asking me: 'Do you know everyone here?' And my truthful reply: 'Only two people besides Eddie.'

We sat down together and talked. I said I was enjoying Eddie's new anthology *Georgian Poetry* and that my two favourite poems in the book were 'The Listeners' by Walter de la Mare, and 'Heaven' by someone called Rupert Brooke. He blushed scarlet, and I had an odd feeling that I knew him very well, and knew that it annoyed him very much that his

* Christopher Hassall, *Rupert Brooke: a Biography*, Faber, 1964.

clear delicate skin showed a blush so vividly. (I found out afterwards that this was true, he hated it.)

He laughed and said, 'You have very good taste. I wrote "Heaven", I rather like it myself!'

I think I told him then that I had come to the party wishing to meet Gilbert Cannan, whose novels I much admired, but I found it much more thrilling to meet the author of 'Heaven'; and quoted some lines from it. I don't remember that there was any feeling of 'love at first sight', any *coup de foudre*. We just felt as if we had known each other for a long time and, as always with old friends, had a great deal to say to each other. We arranged to meet at the Moulin d'Or for lunch, before we parted. But he went down with 'flu, and sent me a note from Eddie's flat asking if I would like to pay him a visit, if I wasn't afraid of infection. With it came two books: 'I was so shocked at your ignorance of Thomas Hardy's poems that I send you some to read between the acts. Will you look at it? I enclose also, to gratify myself rather than you, an even newer and drearier work. Don't bother to read it, I just found I'd like to give it to you. The scratches in it are corrections of the imbecility of compositors and the prudery of publishers.'

When I opened *Poems 1911* I found he had carefully obliterated the title of one poem 'Libido' and substituted his own original title, 'Lust'. I didn't know which to think funnier, the publisher's euphemism or Rupert's caring enough to scratch it out in every copy he owned! We wondered together whether Shakespeare could have got away with Sonnet 129 with these publishers? I sent him two books, one American, one French, and he wrote:

'I was rather shocked by the American, but I very much liked the *Dialogues d'Eleuthère*. . . . La Présidente – oh, it's very maliciously nice. But that queer second chapter, so unexpectedly outspoken and subtle. How did you ever discover Benda? I'd like to know more about him.'

Dialogues d'Eleuthère I seem to remember was mostly about 'l'amour'. Julien Benda was maliciously cynical about 'l'amour'. At that time we were both a little wary of the very word, love.

I was still somewhat shattered by my experiences with Harry Ainley, and Rupert, though I did not know about it till long afterwards, was still rather neurotic and depressed after an

72

unhappy love affair. He had been desperately in love with a woman who was in love with someone else, but who, out of kindness and pity, had consented to live with him for a time. During that time she fell in love with him, but he had grown out of love with her. He thought she was with child by him, and she had a miscarriage for which he bitterly blamed himself. He was still suffering from a guilt-complex, and I was too, in a lesser degree. Of course, neither of us knew about each other's traumas then. There was never any constraint between us, we just felt infinitely happy in each other's presence – we had so much to say to each other.

So often in the letters of that first month he'd write:

'I've so much to say, like you. What shall we do when we meet? Shall we both talk at once for an hour? Or shall we have to lay down rules like a Shaw-Belloc debate? First you half an hour, then me half an hour, then you twenty minutes, then me twenty minutes. And then I'll propose a vote of thanks to you, and you to me. And we will carry them with acclamation.'

Sometimes he would make me laugh by exaggerating his surprise that I seemed, in my letters, to be 'quite intelligent for an actress'.

'. . . astonishing and alarming woman to prefer Strindberg to Ibsen.' 'I do, I do.' 'But how the hell do you know that he is preferable? That you should be right as well as – but we've sworn a truce about your other characteristics . . .' This last phrase in answer to one chapter in a running altercation. He had written a more than usually rhetorical letter about my beauty:

'Your beauty, it's only the insensate poverty of the English language and the feebleness of my imagination that prevents me describing it to you. Helen and Deirdre . . . names can only document it. How can one catch and preserve and pin down a living thing? Is it an insane chance that your features and attributes happened to meet?

> *So may your mighty amazing beauty move*
> *Envy in all women and in all men love.*

Oh most radiant!' This was followed by a few lines in Greek, from an ode to Sappho 'shining, throned, immortal Queen of Love . . .'

I had replied that I had a mirror after all and that I knew

what my face was like better than he did; that he must have
invented a kind of 'magical memory' mirror of his own; or
perhaps he was inclined, as Disraeli said of Gladstone, to
'become inebriated with the exuberance of his own verbosity'?
The reply came 'I am by the way insulted. You say I get drunk
on my own words. It is a thing that no lady should say to a
gentleman . . . I daresay Irish girls are very badly brought up
. . . I admit that being human I get drunk when I drink a lot of
champagne, and I get tipsy, when I see you, (sometimes it takes
me much the same way, once I couldn't walk) but, in my sober
moments, I say quite justifiably, *"This* is good champagne."
Damn it one must be allowed to comment on the facts of existence. I offhandedly throw off a few facts "This book is red",
"It is raining", "That tree is tall", "Consols are $73\frac{5}{8}$", "There
is no God", "Cathleen is incredibly, inordinately, devastatingly,
immortally, calamitously, hearteningly, adorably beautiful".
I will expand this some time. At present I am heated.'

How he let his pen run away with him! Once when I had told
him about Granville-Barker's theory that at moments of great
emotion the audience does not have to understand or even hear
some of the playwright's words, Rupert replied fiercely:

'I say, if your Mr. Barker says such damn silly things about
Shakespeare, I shall cut the last link with intellectualism and
become a Tariff Reformer, an anti-socialist and an admirer of
Mr. Lewis Waller. "Oh withered is the garland of the war!" etc.
Not mean anything indeed! The cad! The green-eyed cad! How
the devil dare he talk like that? Not mean anything! I could take
you, a mere woman and Irish at that and explain exactly what
it means, each phrase and line and sentence. And by God that
a man who wrote *The Marriage of Ann Leete* and some of
the darker portions of *Waste* should complain that *Antony
and Cleopatra* doesn't mean anything. The swine! The goat!
The actor-manager! The stay-at-home puking, God-forgotten,
grease-paint stinking, clod-pole! Were I by him, I should say:
"brother-in-law or the Hindu word for it which is a very terse
and compendious Indian insult; it implies (1) that the person
you are speaking to possesses a sister, (2) that the sister is of
light virtue, (3) that you, the speaker, have had personal proof
of it. Ingenious, isn't it? It reminds me of another compendious
insult I heard the other day:

A to B (a drunken looking lout): "I suppose you are Irish aren't
   you?"
B: "Irish, is it? No, bedad!"
A: "Then there must have been an Irishman on tour with your
   mother."

Again the triple insult you see: (1) You're Irish, (2) your
mother was an actress, (3) her virtue as we say in Canada
needed sandpapering.'

There were so many things to *do* together. I took him to the
American review *Hello Ragtime*, to which we both became
addicted. We saw it together at least half a dozen times. I think
he saw it ten times! I occasionally got a note from him saying:
'I cheated, I took someone else to see it because it's so wonderful
everybody should see it.'

Once when we had particularly enjoyed it, a letter was handed
in to me from the stage door that evening:

'I disagree with you about everything in the world except one
thing and that is the difficulty of getting an American accent on
paper. It doesn't matter between you and me because a quotation
from *Hello Ragtime*, and our letters have become little else,
brings its own atmosphere. But if one tries to explain it to
someone else? . . . Will you come with me and seek out a professor of phonetics and we will sit at his feet together – good
training for the stage – it might even help a dramatist.'

During the days, sometimes weeks, that we did not see each
other, we wrote to each other at least once a day – sometimes
twice, which accounts for our voluminous correspondence!
Sometimes, just nonsense, as when I wrote to him:

'Wouldn't this make a wonderful ballet, from the *Oxford
Book of Verse*:

> *They flee from me that sometime did me seek*
> *With naked foot stalking within my chamber:*
> *Once have I seen them gentle, tame and meek,*
> *That now are wild, and do not once remember*
> *That sometime they have put themselves in danger*
> *To take bread at my hand, and now they range,*
> *Busily seeking in continual change.*
> *Thanked be fortune, it hath been otherwise*
> *Twenty times better; but once especial*

Rupert Brooke, The First Four Months

In thin array, after a pleasant guise,
When her loose gown did from her shoulders fall,
And she me caught in her arms long and small,
And therewithal so sweetly did me kiss,
And softly said: "Dear heart, how like you this?"

Couldn't one have the words intoned, while lovely gazelle-like creatures, timorous nymphs and glorious bacchantes swirled round Nijinsky?'

And he replied:

'I thought your ballet very lovely – but you know, *allershönste*, it's not fair to put lovely words into their mouths, you couldn't do it on the stage. It's like Barker's stage directions. But you shall come to the studio – and show it to me, playing all the parts (you *do* dance?) and reciting all the words, till I catch you in my arms long and not small and say a truce to this waste of our precious time together.'

The studio was Albert Rutherston's. Rupert had written to say that he couldn't go on living at Rugby with his mother, and feared he'd been occupying Eddie's spare room in Gray's Inn too much, but that by great good luck Albert was going to Spain for two months and had lent him his Thurloe Square flat and studio. I remember going there one Sunday, rather protesting that I wanted to stay in bed because I had a toothache, a swollen face and was feeling ugly. But he insisted and tucked me up on the sofa, fed me on hot milk and aspirin, and lulled me to sleep; when I woke I was contrite to realise that I had been sound asleep for three hours and said, 'Oh darling – I have wasted your Sunday afternoon – I hope you found some time to read,' and he laughed and said: 'I have *written*' and handed me a sheet of Albert's notepaper with a poem on it, 'Doubts', which was printed in the book of poems published after his death. He had even written two copies – on mine was inscribed 'For Cathleen with a toothache'.

How quickly those four months seem to go by – I say four months, we met at the beginning of January and he went to America at the beginning of May. I must have had an ordinary life of acting, going to parties, reciting poems at the Poetry Bookshop, but all I can remember is that Rupert and I seemed to live in a world of our own. It's strange I can't clearly remember when it was that we really knew we were in love. Perhaps we had been subconsciously aware of it from the first. There was always that faint astonishment:

'I wonder by my troth what thou and I *did* till we loved?' in all our discoveries about each other. I think perhaps he was aware of it before I was.

There was a letter headed 'Rugby – the last time I wrote from here was before we *knew*. Or did we always know?'

We were continually delighted to find so many tastes in common especially literary ones. We had neither of us ever kept diaries, but we had discovered that in our extreme youth we had kept what I think were called 'commonplace books'. We both had had similar 'crushes' on Ernest Dowson, 'Cynara', of course, and 'To one in Bedlam' – 'with delicate mad hands, behind his sordid bars'. How we giggled when I showed him an earlier shaming choice of mine: 'Pale hands I loved, beside the Shalimar.' There was Masefield; and, with Rupert, Chesterton and Belloc and Noyes and Richard Le Gallienne; with me very early poems by that prolific author 'anon' including 'He came all so still to where his mother lay'.

I still have his little book which he must have tired of early. Half the pages are blank. How I wish I had done in mine, what he did so meticulously in his: note down the author, and the titles of the author's works from which he had extracted his favourite stanzas.

I had often forgotten that important notation, and I had one prose passage we never were able to trace. We loved it because we could have written it to each other.

'We should get together and comfort ourselves with the brave days I have known and wish for you; the same scenes strike us both, and the same kind of vision has amused us ever since we were born.'

He came to have supper with me one night to meet Sarah Allgood and Fred O'Donovan. Like me, in the days before we met he had been an assiduous visitor to the Court Theatre. I think it was listening to their 'singing' Irish voices that inspired the little 'song' he had written for me

'Oh love is fair, and love is rare;' my dear one she said,
'But love goes lightly over.' I bowed her foolish head,

77

And kissed her hair and laughed at her. Such a child was she;
So new to love, so true to love, and she spoke so bitterly.

But there's wisdom in women, of more than they have known,
And thoughts going blowing through them, are wiser than
their own,
Or how should my dear one, being ignorant and young,
Have cried on love so bitterly, with so true a tongue?

That evening we were busy laying out the food I had cooked in the morning, and setting the table for the visitors, when he suddenly flung down the empty tray he was carrying and put his hands on my shoulders and said, 'May I kiss you?' I can't remember why I shook my head, I know I must have longed for him to take me in his arms. Perhaps it was an obscure feeling of 'too soon', because I had only just finally broken with Ainley, perhaps a kind of shyness, a feeling of wanting to prolong the hush of dawn before the splendour of the day.

Whatever it was, he understood. He knew that it was a 'not yet', rather than a denial, and he left me and went into the other room.

I can remember still the strange swoon of delight that seemed to suffuse me, an 'exaltation' of mind and body, and yet I cannot remember when and where we actually did embrace. It must have been about then that he sent me my first love letter:

I adore you.

I was in a stupor all yesterday; partly because of my tiredness, and partly because of your face.

I'm gradually getting normaler again.

Why do you look like that? Have you any idea what you look like? I didn't know that human beings could look like that. It's as far beyond beauty as beauty is beyond ugliness.

I'd say you were beautiful if the word weren't a million times too feeble.

Hell!

But it's very amazing.

It makes me nearly imbecile when I'm talking with you – I apologize for my imbecility: it's your fault. You shouldn't look like that.

It really makes life very much worth while. My God!

I adore you.

RUPERT

I say 'must have been' for he never dated his letters, and so much seems to happen during our four months that much of it is blurred into one colourful kaleidoscope.

The country walks were what we enjoyed most. He would plan a cross-country trip, in the Chilterns or the South Downs or wherever, and we'd go by train to some little station in the real country and start from there.

Once I remember we got lost in a little dark wood, and suddenly came out on a clearing. Blazing in front of us was a field of hyacinths so intensely blue that the colour seemed to float out of them on the air. We lay down on the side of a bank and just held each other's hands without speaking. Then Rupert murmured some lines of Donne's 'The Extasie'

> *So to 'entergraft our hands, as yet*
>   *Was all the meanes to make us one,*
> *And pictures in our eyes to get*
>   *Was all our propagation.*
> *As 'twixt two equall Armies, Fate*
>   *Suspends uncertaine victorie,*
> *Our soules (which to advance their state,*
>   *Were gone out,) hung 'twixt her, and mee.*
> *And whil'st our soules negotiate there,*
>   *Wee like sepulchrall statues lay;*
> *All day, the same our postures were,*
>   *And wee said nothing, all the day. . . .*
> *This Extasie doth unperplex*
>   *(We said) and tell us what we love,*
> *Wee see by this, it was not sexe,*
>   *Wee see, we saw not what did move:*
> *But as all severall soules containe*
>   *Mixture of things, they know not what,*
> *Love, these mixt soules, doth mixe againe,*
>   *And makes both one, each this and that.*

We walked back hand-in-hand through the darkening woods still feeling that 'Extasie' that 'doth unperplex'.

I was too shy to quote some lines that were in my mind; Juliette Drouet, Victor Hugo's mistress, had written to a wealthy protector whom she had left, leaving all her furs and diamonds and splendour behind. 'Mon âme a des desirs comme mon corps et mille fois plus ardents. Si je trouverai un amant qui caresse mon âme comme tout autre caresse mon corps j'abandonnerai tout pour lui.'

There was such an exciting stirring of all the senses in just being together. Someone told me that in Mrs. Belloc-Lowndes's Diaries there is a description of her going up to Wycombe one Sunday morning in a train and finding a 'lover and his lass' in the compartment. They sat opposite each other and didn't either speak to each other or touch each other, but there was such a wave of 'almost magnetic attraction' moving between them that she felt like an intruder and buried herself in a book. Next day she chanced to go to The Pink and Lily and saw two names in the visitors' book, Cathleen Nesbitt, Rupert Brooke. 'So that's who it was, how I wish I had looked at him more carefully,' she wrote.

We didn't, of course, live in that 'exalted atmosphere' all the time; as I look back I remember him always in high spirits, inspiring me with a kind of vitality and gaiety which was not really in my nature.

We often spent a whole Sunday and Monday morning walking or lazing in the country. When we spent the night at a country inn we had separate rooms. He would come in and sit on the edge of my bed and talk almost till dawn, but strange as it may seem to anyone of this generation we never actually became lovers in the sense that he seduced me, as the contemporary phrase would have it. We both had very serious views on marriage and we both wanted to be very sure that we would have a good one. Then came the time for him to go. My first letter from the boat brought him so close that like a Victorian maiden I could have slept with it under my pillow!

'Dear love, you'll not take it in a bad sense if I tell you that there was never anybody so nice to go away from as you! *Really* my dear, I arrived solitary on the boat. After it started I asked at the office – more to show that I existed than in the dimmish hope of getting anything – were there any letters for Rupert Brooke. And out, astonishingly, came a letter and a telegram, both from divine *you*. And the letter you had been writing all those last good days secretly! Was there ever so nice a person? The fact that you had written then upset me more than I can say. And then the letter itself, I sat on my bed and laughed

1. Cathleen at about one year, 1889   2. Aged three with her mother, 1891

3. The Nesbitt family: Hugo, Terence, Cathleen, Anna, Thomas, 1898

4. above: [*top left:*] Helen Waddell with Helen Forbes;
   [*bottom left:*] Meta Fleming with Cathleen at Victoria College, Belfast, 19·

5. below: As Perdita in *A Winter's Tale*, 1912

6. right: Henry Ainley as Romeo

'He that hath the steerage of
my course, direct my sail!'

'Romeo.

THE PLAY PICTORIAL

№ 128   Vol. XXI.

Mary Ellen—
Miss CATHLEEN NESBIT.

Mary Ellen as an Irish Fairy.

7. 'Please do I have to be a fairy?' in *General John Regan*, 1913

8. right: As Phoebe in *Quality Street*, 1914

9. Rupert Brooke

10. right: As Jessica in *The Merchant of Venice* at the Court Theatre, 1920

11. above: Cathleen and Cecil Ramage's wedding, 1921

12. below: Mark's christening at the Chapel of the House of Commons;
from left to right: Cathleen's niece Prudence, Cecil Ramage,
Mrs Claude Johnson, Mrs Brooke, Cathleen with Mark, nursemaid Lily,
Herbert Asquith

and cried over it. And two hours after I went past again and there was a list stuck up called "Unclaimed Mail" (I thought it sounded as if a lot of knights who had promised to equip themselves for the quest of the Holy Grail had missed the train or married a wife or overslept or something) and at the top of the list Mr. Rupert Brooke! Good God, I thought, there *is* somebody else who has remembered my existence. But there wasn't! It was only that absurd Cathleen again, sending a silver boot of all mad things in the world! You can't think how it cheered me up, this string of communication with you. It felt as if your love was so strong it reached me all the way. I do feel as if there was a lovely and present guardianship all the time; my darling you give me so much more than I deserve. But it does make me feel so quiet and secure.'

The letter went on to tell me more about his life and his first unhappy love than I had known. I had a feeling that while he was away and while we wrote to each other, as we did sometimes twice a week, we would get to know each other very well indeed. And I think we did.

We vowed to 'amuse' each other in our letters during all the dreary months he would be in America. Towards the last weeks at home, he hated more and more the idea of leaving. But he felt he had to go, even apart from his contract. He had written to me about the unhappy love affair he had had to break: 'Oh it's bitter destroying and breaking things two have built together, intimacies and trusts and friendliness. It's like cutting something out of oneself – I feel so responsible for her. . . . Child, beyond a certain point men and women shouldn't go unless they marry. Not if they are people of human feelings, they pay overmuch in irretrievable ways. . . .

'I cling more and more to the peace and comfort, I find more and more in loving you and being with you. . . . My heart and my belief were so deadened before I found you. . . . You give me great riches, I pray you love good and keep away from the evil things of the world, for my sake and for your sake and for both our sakes.'

SEVEN

Rupert Brooke, The American Year
1913

I believe the year in America was very good for him. He had
such a very complex personality. Beneath the surface Rupert
that so many people found enchanting, the gay, witty, life-loving,
life-giving 'young Apollo', there was a deep puritanical, religious vein. I don't mean religious in the sense of a desire to
belong to any organised religious sect, or in an ethical or even
a moral sense, but just as some people have 'music in their soul',
he had religion in his soul, a need to worship, a belief in the
perfectibility of man, and, to use an old-fashioned phrase, a
sense of sin. I think that the dichotomy between that and the
sensual hedonistic side of him was what had caused the serious
nervous breakdowns he had had in the past. I could feel in his
letters, from the South Seas, a more relaxed view of his own
normal instincts, almost as though with Blake he could feel:
'Everything that lives, lives not alone, nor for itself.'

It took so long in those days to communicate by letters that
quite often we had to cable just to reassure each other that we
were still there, that we still loved each other.

He even had fun researching in newspapers, when he found a
city that had English ones:

'They said you were bewitching and gave a foolish part more
beauty than it deserved. . . . It's really a very good idea . . . I
have had plots for several plays which required that the audience
should know an immense deal beforehand . . . now I see all that
is necessary is to get Cathleen to come forward beforehand and
say: "Dear audience, in order to understand this play, you must

know that (a) four hundred years ago, the economic condition of Jutland was remarkable in roughly the following seventeen ways (1) the marginal value of cornland . . ." and so on. . . . It is absurd and offensive to human dignity to suppose that a stores catalogue read by Cathleen is better than Keats read by anyone else. . . . '

This was apropos a play in which I had to recount the plot of the drama being 'mimed' by the actors. Another time he wrote:

'I found an English paper that said Miss Snooks is to take Miss Cathleen Nesbitt's place in Chesterton's *Magic* at the Little Theatre. But what of Miss C.N.? *That* is what the public wants to know . . . it agitates me, are you dead or ill?'

I got a cable long before the letter, but, even before I answered the cable, he had reached San Francisco and seen that instead of doing *Magic* I was to play the lead in Barrie's *Quality Street*. He wrote wondering if Barrie was better than G.K.C.? 'Oh! oh! oh! I'm so exalted – so you deserted the very large man for the very little one?' and drew a little picture of a female, looking rather like a rat with a lot of hair, between a big, podgy man and a tiny square one both holding out large hands towards her, with a caption 'Miss C.N. being proposed to by Barrie on one hand and Chesterton on the other . . . hesitating'.

I'd had really no choice in the matter of *Quality Street*; I was under contract to Barker for four plays and this was the third. After telling me I was to play in Chesterton's *Magic*, he suddenly announced that Barrie wanted me for *Quality Street*. I was a little disappointed not to see Chesterton. He had written a polite note to say that he was glad I was to play Patricia in *Magic*, which had given me courage to write to tell him that I had great difficulty in reconciling the inconsistency of the part, to which G.K.C. had replied with Emerson's saying that 'A foolish consistency is the hobgoblin of little minds.' And I was having great fun trying to explain that if, for instance, an elephant should suddenly turn bright red it would be odd but consistent with his still being an elephant whereas if he were to turn into a rhinoceros he couldn't still be an elephant. I can't remember how I worked it all out, but I thought myself *very* clever in those days.

However I was now working for Dion Boucicault who was

directing, we called it producing in those days, and indeed he was producer and director and manager, and to me very terrifying.

I didn't know that he had argued in vain with Barrie saying that it was quite ridiculous to cast anyone so young and inexperienced with such a leading part. But Barrie insisted I was what he wanted, so Boucicault was against me from the first. He bullied me with sarcasm. He had an icy way of asking, 'Is that how you have decided to play this scene?' and one day when I stumbled once again over a passage which I always had difficulty in remembering, he said, 'I don't think it too much to ask that you should at least *learn your lines.*'

I burst into tears and stumbled through the morning trying to restrain them.

At lunch-time I found Barrie waiting at the stage door. 'You are coming home to lunch with me and relax,' he said. 'There's no rehearsal this afternoon.'

We went to his flat in the Adelphi. I was fascinated by the room which had a huge fire burning in one half, and a dining-table laid out in the other.

There was something very cosy about that great room which was a library as well with its book-lined walls.

'You must learn that one has to pay for every success in life often with tears,' said Barrie, as he sat by the fire puffing his pipe. 'Better to shed your tears before than after.'

After lunch he started to talk about my troubles. He told me that it was an actor's business to obey the director. If every actor wanted to go his own way the result would be chaos. ' "Dot" Boucicault is a very fine director but he can be wrong. He wants the Phoebe that Ellaline Terris played in the original production. It was enchanting, a little blonde delicious porcelain figure. And he is unconsciously trying to mould you into that. For instance when you cried real tears in the scene with Susan, he scolded you with "Real tears make you look ugly, your make-up would run and probably your lines would be incoherent." That is what *I* wanted and what *you* did, therefore we must compromise, you must restrain your tears at rehearsal and if they come unbidden when you *play – good!*'

That taught me one good lesson, never argue with a director, take the good he can give, and discreetly ignore the bad. And another lesson: on the whole 'Dot' is right; too many tears from the actor *inhibit* tears from the audience. And years later Barrie wrote me a letter I treasured when I was playing Jessica in *The Merchant of Venice*:

'Good girl, there were no tears in your eyes or in your voice when you said "I am never merry when I hear sweet music", but you moved *me* to tears.'

And the third lesson was one that recurred again and again, once when I heard Marlon Brando struggling with a 'phoney' speech in a film. If an actor who is conscientious and obviously reliable keeps on stumbling or forgetting certain lines, the author *is* sometimes responsible.

One day later, nearer the end of rehearsals, Barrie said, 'You say the lines in your scene with Godfrey Tearle: "my face was wet, you said you kissed me because my face was wet" quite admirably but I can *feel* you shying like a pony at a five-barred gate during the speech that follows. The words seem to stick in your throat. Why?'

It was the speech that Boucicault had bullied me about 'never remembering'.

By now I knew Barrie's kindness enough to venture: 'Well, I can't believe that Phoebe could have said all that. She has never shown "self-pity" in public, why should she show it to *him* of all people?'

I didn't quite know how to explain. I had never heard of Freud or the subconscious, but it wasn't a question of the words 'sticking in my throat', the block came from somewhere deeper than that. Perhaps for once I was reading, as Barker always said a good actor should, 'from his guts rather than his mind – what they call his instinct'.

But Barrie magically understood. 'A wise author will sometimes learn from his actors,' he said. 'We all let go to self-indulgence when our words run away with us.'

When we came to a run-through for possible 'cuts', I found to my delight that most of the speech that troubled me *was* cut. Strange, sad, devious little man, unpredictably kind at times, maliciously cruel at others, but a magician as a dramatist.

Even now when it is still much the fashion to deride him, as it was when Rupert Brooke lightly dismissed him as 'not as good as Chesterton', his magic holds. One reads his stage directions and shudders a little; one goes, usually unwillingly, to see

Peter Pan with children or grandchildren, and winces at the tasteless coyness of some of the Peter-Wendy scenes – but I defy anyone to sit through any of the plays without a sudden moment of emotion, when tears come unbidden to the eye, or a giggle of irrepressible mirth when a comedy line hits the bull's-eye unerringly.

He can't be classed among the great dramatists, but how few have given so many memories of unalloyed pleasure to the man in the street who goes to the theatre for a good laugh or a good cry and is doubly rewarded when he gets both in the same evening.

I suppose I *had* a life outside the theatre, during the time Rupert was in America, that I went to parties, or tried to get to the country for weekends, and had breakfasts with Eddie Marsh. Long afterwards I read in Eddie's Memoirs that he had written to Rupert:

'Luncheon at the Dunsanys, a beauty party – at tea here, Cathleen, Diana (Manners), Katharine (Horner), Ruby Peto, all looking their very best (Lascelles speechless with admiration he didn't know there *were* such people) . . . dinner with Gosse and Henry James with an adjournment to Cathleen's rooms to meet Sally Allgood and Maire O'Neill.'

How genuinely surprised I always was when people classed me among the 'beauties'. I was always too worried about the length of my chin and the width of my waist to be pleased with the rest of my looks. But I have no clear recollection of what was happening in London as I seemed to be living Rupert's life as those weekly, sometimes twice weekly, letters arrived, from New York, Boston, Vancouver, Samoa, and places north, south or west. We seemed to get closer and closer and yet as the time came near for his return, I began to feel a little nervous, and so I think did he.

'Letters are nothing. I wish I could *see* you. I realise sometimes that we know each other so little. I want to be with my head in your lap for a year and talk and listen. No, I don't want you to talk, or listen. I only want to feel you, your body and soul. Then after ages I should know you.'

Then at last came a letter with his sailing date:

'My dear, one thing I would implore you, it's *very* silly, but don't *tell* anyone the exact date I'm coming back. It's my fancy

to blow in on them unexpected. Just to wander into Raymond
Buildings, and hear Eddie squeak "Oh my dear, I thought you
were in Tahiti!" '

And in that letter, too, there was more talk of how little time
we had had before he went, but that he now knew more than
ever how he needed me and trusted me. That made me infinitely
happy. But when he would go on to say I was beautiful and
'divinely *good*': 'It is not possible that with those eyes and that
mouth you should be anything else. The body and the soul are
the same and when I have said you are lovely I have made a
statement about your most secret thought equally', my heart
sank a little. How *could* any one measure up to the dreams he
had fabricated?

However the next letter bubbled over with high spirits and
nonsense:

'I really ought to be able to write more poems about you or to
you. I tried one as I lay in bed this morning:

> *Cathleen! Loveliest creature! Nymph divine!*
> *Unhoped for, unapproachable, yet mine!*
> *Fount of all beauty, vision of delight*
> *Whom I love all the day and half the night;*
> *Child, and yet goddess, woman, saint and witch*
> (rhyme too obvious?) . . .

oh dear, I'm so sorry. I ought to be able to write to my beloved in
verse; for then it will come out in my "Life and Letters", and
they will all say: "How wonderful to write letters in verse and
how beautiful she must have been." '

Another time he sent me two nonsense verses:

> *There once was a lovely Cathleen*
> *The loveliest ever was seen*
> *Cleopatra and Helen*
> *And Deirdre, I'm tellin' you,*
> *Were not as fair as Cathleen.*
>
> *There once was a glorious Cathleen*
> *Her face when unswollen and clean*
> *Was so lovely and nice*

Quite a face not a fyce
I do enjoy seeing Cathleen.

I think it was Richard Church who wrote: 'To a man in love, the perfect poem is said to be the name of his beloved, repeated over and over again.'

Once Rupert just scribbled my name all over an entire page! As Shaw was to write so many years later, 'Stella, Stella, Stella, ah! Stella' twelve times, adding 'da capo – but perhaps you never copied orchestra parts and don't know that that means the same thing over and over again for a thousand times.' His verses to her were even 'sillier' than Rupert's:

Who'll be her man?
Why, he that can be
Apollo and Pan
I'll be her man.

Who kissed her toes?
Who d'you suppose?
And also her nose?
I kissed her toes.

EIGHT

Rupert Brooke, The Last Three Months
1914

∽∾∽∾∽∾∽∾∽∾∽∾∽∾∽∾∽∾∽∾∽∾∽∾∽∾∽∾∽∾

I think I was still playing in *General John Regan* when Rupert
came back. That also came in for his disapproval: 'A farce with
Hawtrey! Good God, what a waste of a precious year.'

But I had great fun as a little slut of an Irish servant daughter
of the local innkeeper, who when sent to the butcher for chops
dropped them in the dirty village street on her way back, picked
them up and wiped them on her equally dirty apron and went
on her way unconcerned. Her vocabulary consisted almost
entirely of two phrases 'oi moight' and 'and then again oi
moight not'. Except for one anguished appeal in Act III when
she came on swathed in yards of emerald-green tulle to play a
fairy at the village fête: 'Please, do oi haf to wear *wings?*' The
play was extremely funny and ran for almost a year, during
which, by standing in the wings watching Hawtrey every night I
learned a great deal from a great master about the art of acting
comedy.

Rupert had now decided to warn Eddie of the date of his
arrival ('to make sure of a bed') and wrote to me: 'I should get
in about midnight. I arrive at Plymouth . . . was ever so sweet
and droll a name? Drake's Plymouth . . . beyond which are little
fields, very green, bounded by small piled walls of stone . . .
by that the train shall go up – by Dartmouth . . . I will make
a Litany . . .' And make a Litany he did, a veritable Rosary
of lovely ridiculous English village names like Appledore
and Widdicombe and Dawlish, ending with 'oh noble train, oh
glorious and forthright and English train, I will arrive as I

was saying when I interrupted myself, on June 5th at midnight'.

Eddie Marsh took me and Denis Browne to dinner and a play to pass the time, till we went to the station at 11.45. 'The noble and forthright train, the English train' did not arrive till 2.45.

Rupert looked a little aloof, I thought, as he said to me, 'What are *you* doing here? You ought to be in bed.' And then his face lit up with the smile I remembered and he said 'I'm glad you came – I'm *never* going away again without you.'

He had to go to Rugby the next day to see his mother, and I had to go to Paris to play Viola in *Twelfth Night* for a hopeful impresario who wanted to establish a little 'English Theatre' in Paris. I think all he really established was the charm of the young musical comedy star who played Orsino, Basil Hallam, who afterwards became a wartime favourite with his song: 'I'm Gilbert the Filbert the Colonel of the Nuts' in a revue with Elsie Janis.

There we were, writing to each other again. But as Rupert wrote to Paris: 'We have time to "learn each other" again slowly. We have All Time before us.'

Soon after I came back I had to start rehearsing for Synge's *Deirdre of the Sorrows* for a short engagement at the Little Theatre. For once, Rupert was quite enthusiastic about my doing a play; he thought I should confine myself strictly to the classics and poetical drama: 'Now that you're away in Paris I have time to *think* more clearly and I'm finding it clearer and clearer how very important and glorious it is that you are going to be *Deirdre* . . . after all the rotten parts you have had.' I couldn't help smiling at that, since my début in Shakespeare, I had played leading roles in Galsworthy, Barrie, Boucicault and a comedy with Hawtrey. Nothing to be ashamed of there! However Rupert had a kind of obsession about it.

'I'm not going to see you in it. I couldn't stand the strain, and I should be mad jealous of O'Donovan . . . but I'm going to take charge of you till it's over. You are *not* to go to any parties. You are to come and sit in the big chair at Raymond Buildings, day after day, studying your part. While I cook you lovely food. And when you're bored with study, we'll discuss the world lazily and watch the fire and talk about *July*, or we'll go out and catch a train to some green fields – and you'll murmur Synge's Deirdre and I'll write sonnets, and you won't have a care in the world except your part, and I won't have a care in the world at all.'

We did go down to the country sometimes and lie in the sun and he would actually hear my lines. I don't know why he had this curious obsession about Synge's *Deirdre of the Sorrows* as it was not really a good play but just a series of quite beautiful poetic speeches, yet his letters were always full of it. 'Do Deirdre more nobly, more passionately than any other woman could. Burn into it as you learn it, live for it, wonderfully *be* it.' And now I can't remember at all whether I played it well or ill! I got a good press review, but I was a critic's pet in those days and what a complacent creature I must have been – I always expected good reviews!

Then I rather distressed him by accepting an engagement to tour, a long tour of a rather dreary drama called *A Butterfly on the Wheel*. 'It's so *unworthy* of you', he wrote, 'and you'll be doing it during *our* month.' We had planned to spend July together somewhere deep in the country.

But I had family responsibilities on my hands that I didn't want to tell people about; and I couldn't turn down the chance of making £5 a week more than I had ever made before. And playing Viola and Deirdre in the Little Theatre had *not* been financially rewarding.

I think Frances Cornford must have told him that I really *couldn't* turn it down. He took me down to Cambridge to stay with the Cornfords, and I stayed on for a day or two while he had to go on somewhere. She was a wonderful woman; I found myself confiding in her as I had rarely done in anyone. And after Rupert's death her letters gave me courage. However, Rupert and I had many good times together before the tour started, going to Drury Lane to see such ballets as *Les Papillons*, *Petrouchka* and *Spectre de la Rose*.

'Oh my darling are you *doing too much?*' he wrote: 'You looked so like a tired child last night at Drury Lane. If you knew how difficult it was for me not to take you in my arms, with Queen Alexandra and Bernard Shaw and George Moore and Eddie all looking on.'

Another day later on when I had had started my tour and was playing at Brighton, I came up for the day to go to a garden party at 10 Downing Street when the Asquiths were in residence; Roger Fry and Rupert and I were lunching at the Moulin d'Or and going on together.

91

Roger was correctly dressed in a cutaway coat and striped trousers and I in my very best summer dress. Rupert arrived in a grey flannel suit, a little crumpled, a brilliant blue-flannel shirt (coloured shirts were almost unheard of in those days) and an elegant little hat from the South Seas – the sort that Cecil Beaton often wears in the garden nowadays! He really looked magnificent, his skin almost honey-coloured and his hair bleached ash gold by the Samoan sun, his eyes extravagantly blue. He looked at us and he said, 'Oh my God, I've got the wrong clothes on! I didn't have time to go back to Rugby to get city clothes. I *can't* go like this.'

Roger Fry said, 'Oh nonsense! there will be lots of Labour Party members there, you'll pass all right.'

Rupert's Fabian socialist blood was roused and he retorted, 'I suppose the implication being that the Labour Party has no idea how to dress for any occasion', and they embarked on a political argument.

At the garden party he suddenly realised that everyone turned to look at him as well they might! Even I who had become accustomed to his looks had a sudden feeling: 'He really looks too beautiful to be true.'

But he took it for granted that it was his old flannel suit and his blue shirt that was attracting attention. He murmured to me, 'I can't stand this. I'm going to have some tea at Victoria Station. I suppose nothing will drag *you* from a party but you can join me if you like.'

I begged him to stay for tea and strawberries. He was adamant. I resolved to stay till the last minute, but of course couldn't bear to think of his sitting lonely in the Victoria Station tearoom – and soon followed him. He wasn't lonely at all! He was sitting with the *Westminster Gazette*, surrounded by tea and strawberries and buns and an adoring waitress hovering behind him. We stayed till it was time for my train to Brighton and at the last minute he jumped in beside me saying, 'I'll take you and see that you get to the theatre on time.'

We talked about Kipling. He had recently seen Siegfried Sassoon, who despised Kipling. 'He doesn't write poetry, just tub-thumping stuff,' Sassoon had said.

'Oh! hadn't he ever read *"Cities and Thrones and Powers"*?' I asked.

'But that's what I answered,' said Rupert. 'How did you know about that poem, Eddie put me on to it?'

'I discovered it for myself.' I was so proud of that I recited the whole poem to him there and then.

It was soon after that that we were sitting together in Eddie's flat when *The Times* rang up to say that Flecker had just died and to ask Rupert to write his obituary. It was Rupert who told me about Flecker. I had never read him. I started to learn the haunting 'Santorin' while Rupert wrote.

It seemed he had only just come back when suddenly war was declared. Rupert was torn every way. He loved the German people he had known, but thought Germany a world menace though not as bad, he thought, as Russia. He wished Germany to smash Russia; then France to smash Germany. 'France and England are the only countries that ought to have any power. If Russia prevailed, the future would be a Slav Empire, world-wide, despotic and insane.'

I kept on trailing round the country in my dreary play. Rupert was seeking some sort of war job everywhere till Eddie got him into Winston Churchill's new Royal Naval Division. He felt restless and I think was finding some distraction going about with Eddie, meeting people who might be helpful, a way of life that usually bored him.

'I've been having a sort of neuralgic headache. And in the intervals I've been dodging the young ladies who are in love with me. I wish I were a decent man. I suppose no unmarried man is decent and only 50 per cent of the married ones. My sub-conscious is angry with every dreary young woman I meet if she doesn't fall in love with me; and my consciousness is furious with her if she does . . . I wonder if young women behave like that?'

He was very happy and thrilled to finally get a commission in the 2nd Naval Brigade, and with his friend Denis Browne was posted to the Anson Battalion. He wrote in great excitement after he had lunched with Eddie and Winston Churchill. He said, 'Winston was very cheerful at lunch, and said one thing that is exciting, but a *dead* secret. You mustn't *breathe* it. That is that it's his game to hold the northern ports from Dunkirk to Le Havre at all costs. So if there's a raid on *any* of them at any moment we shall be flung across to help the French Reservists. So we may go to camp on Saturday and be in France on Monday.'

They were eventually sent to Antwerp and he sent me a thrilling description of the whole engagement in a long letter, one of the best descriptions of what the face of war looked like to a novice that I have ever seen.

The fact that he had seen that 'Dantesque Hell' and escaped unscathed gave us an odd feeling of security I think. The fact that there seemed no chance of their seeing any more fighting for a long time made it easier for him to get occasional leave. He wrote to tell me that he had a 'Sunday off' and asked where I would be. He seemed much entertained by the reply that I would arrive on Sunday at The Aquarium, Yarmouth. 'How *could* a theatre be called The Aquarium? But I will come to The Aquarium. Is thy servant a fish?' I hastily sent a telegram with the address of my lodgings, he had forgotten that the theatre would be closed on Sunday. He arrived in the late afternoon – after a hideous journey from Blandford. We had a supper of fresh bloaters – we had neither of us eaten anything but smoked ones before – and decided they were ambrosia.

Then he sat on the floor before the green-flamed driftwood fire, and put his head in my lap and said, 'Read to me something beautiful.'

I used always to travel with my Donne, my *Oxford Book of Verse* and the little volume of his own poems, so I read Donne's 'The Anniversarie'

> *All Kings, and all their favourites*
> *All glory of honors, beauties, wits,*
> *The Sun it self, which makes times as they passe,*
> *Is elder by a yeare, now, than it was*
> *When thou and I first one another saw;*
> *All other things, to their destruction draw,*
> *Only our love hath no decay:*
> *This, no tomorrow hath, nor yesterday,*
> *Running it never runs from us away,*
> *But truly keeps his first, last, everlasting day.*
>
> *Here upon earth, wee are Kings, and none but wee*
> *Can be such Kings, nor of such subjects bee.*
> *Who is so safe as wee? Where none can doe*
> *Treason to us, except one of us two.*

94

True and false feares let us refraine,
Let us love nobly, and live and adde againe
Yeares and yeares unto yeares, till we attaine
To write threescore: this is the second of our raigne.

He said: 'Donne is always the best. He knows about love and death. You left out the middle verse?'

'Yes,' I said. 'I don't want to think of graves and "coarses".'

I had a letter soon after in which he said 'I have, don't tell a soul, written a sonnet. If it gets finished you shall have it.' He seemed a little ashamed that a soldier should write verses, but comforted himself with the reminder that Sir Philip Sydney was no mean soldier.

Then came scrawled on a sheet of Hood Battalion notepaper, the sonnet

'Safety'

Dear! of all happy in the hour, most blest
He who has found our hid security,
Assured in the dark tides of the world that rest,
And heard our word: 'Who is so safe as we?'
We have found safety with all things undying,
The winds, and morning, tears of men and mirth,
The deep night, and birds singing, and clouds flying,
And sleep, and freedom, and the autumnal earth.

We have built a house that is not for Time's throwing.
We have gained a peace unshaken by pain for ever.
War knows no power. Safe shall be my going,
Secretly armed against all death's endeavour;
Safe where all safety's lost; safe where men fall;
And if these poor limbs die, safest of all.

Later he wrote when sending me a set of proofs of all five sonnets:

'My Muse panting all autumn under halberd and cuirass could but falter these syllables through her visor. God they are in the rough these five camp children. Four and five are good though and there are phrases in the rest. Forgive me if I include ours among them. . . . Only *we* will know, and it seems to belong with them.'

I noticed in the proofs, he had made two emendations in

Safety. In line six he had substituted 'morning' for 'freedom' and in line thirteen 'safe though' instead of 'safe where'. I liked the honesty of both replacements. And I was glad that he, like myself, thought the fourth sonnet the best; 'our' sonnet *Safety* was such a 'private' thing I couldn't judge it objectively. But I was always surprised that the fifth was the one that became famous.

It became fashionable later to decry all the sonnets and speak of them as false and sentimental. But I think they *did* represent the feelings of a great many of the young men who rushed to volunteer.

Cyril Asquith who was in Rupert's battalion was a great friend of mine (years later during the Second World War he rented my country cottage while I was on tour, to keep his children in the country) and he told me that they all felt almost as though they were crusaders and that they felt fulfilment and satisfaction in doing something necessary.

They all had something in them of public spirit. They felt in one way or another that they owed something to society, some gratitude for the good things that life had given them, their talents and fine education.

When Rupert wrote in March from the Aegean:

'What a thing it is to be a soldier and go lovely yachting cruises in the Aegean. We saw, they *said* we saw, very far away, Olympus. But I could not certainly see the Gods. However, its head was shrouded in mist. Also there was Parnassus even further away, and Shakespeare and the rest upon it. And my eyes fell on the holy land of Attica so I can die,' he was speaking for all of his friends who had had a classical education. When years later I went to Malta I knew what it would be like from his description:

'It's the *loveliest* place in the evening sun, softly white, grey silver white . . . like an Italian town in silverpoint, livable and serene with a sea and sky of opal and pearl around it. It was nearer than any place I have ever seen to what a Greek must have witnessed when he sailed into a Greek coast city.'

The next letter told of a pleasant little rest in Egypt, that he had sent me an amber necklace, and that he had had sunstroke and a touch of dysentery: 'It destroys all the harmonies of the body and the soul. I had the biggest headache in the world and a diarrhoea that was part of the cosmic process, even yet I am but a funnel through which arrowroot is poured.'

That letter was dated early April. There were no more. I was wakened early one morning by Eddie Marsh telling me that Rupert was dead; 'I did not want you to read it in the papers; he has left a letter for you to be given to you in case of his death.'

Then I had a letter from Denis Browne, the brilliant young musician who had been Rupert's friend during his Rugby and Cambridge days.

'It was after a divisional Field day, he was tired out. On Tuesday the 20th he stayed in bed. He was moved to the French hospital ship *Duguay-Trouin* and there he died. The end was very quiet and calm. He felt no pain whatever they said. For the last day and a half he was unconscious.

'We buried him at night the same evening, Friday, April 23rd, in an olive grove one mile up a valley leading from the sea – of all gracious and lovely places it was the loveliest I ever saw, delicious with purple flowering sage and thyme, an olive tree is over his head of which I send you a spray.' In another part of the letter he said he had always been in the best of health and spirits. 'He was the centre of a little group of six of us . . . once when we were discussing which of us would die and where we would like to be buried. He said that he would like to be buried in a Greek island and some of us wondered vaguely if he would be the first to be taken.'

Denis finished his letter by saying:

'I have tried to tell you all I can. I must write to Eddie and to his mother. Would you like me to write again? I will see you when it is all over.'

Denis himself was killed a few months later. Indeed of that 'little group of six' only Arthur Asquith and Bernard Freyberg survived.

After Rupert's death I was not even conscious of grief for a long time; I just felt stunned and empty, and a deep anger with myself for not having had a child by him. I never had felt quite sure whether he had drawn back from a complete union or whether it was I. I had seen how much he had suffered from his own 'inconstancy' to Ka, so much that in his last messages to Eddie he had said: 'She is the nearest thing I had to a widow.' I had wanted so much for *us* that it should be for ever; and so it seemed had he; why either of us thought that 'marriage lines' would have ensured it I don't know; we were both very unworldly for our age. Perhaps I crushed that vain remorse very soon, perhaps it remained buried for a long time. For many years I used to have a recurrent dream, two or three times a year, of having been lost in a strange town and seeing him come out of a tunnel and running away because I did not know how to tell him that I had betrayed him, that I had children that were not his. Then the dreams ceased, I don't remember when.

I took a job in the Censorship Office for I needed to do something and then Eddie Marsh told me that he was going to write a Memoir on Rupert to be included in a volume with all his poems. He asked if he might publish some of Rupert's letters to me. Somehow I couldn't bear the idea of anyone having them and seeing them, though I knew there were many that could easily be published with some passages removed. Finally we decided that I should take all my letters down to a friend's house in the country, whom Eddie and I both knew, and we should sit in the Library and I would read out to him what we thought would be of interest. We soon realised what a foolish idea that was – there was such an accumulation of letters that it would have taken a month of Sundays to put them into roughly chronological order. Rupert practically never dated a letter – only occasionally the day of the week, never the month or the year. We tried for a little, but what with laughing at some and weeping at others, we didn't get far, so I gave them all to Eddie and told him he could print what he liked but *not* the love letters. Poor Eddie had a very difficult time with Rupert's mother. At first she hated the idea of any Memoir being written at all, of Rupert being made into a Public Figure. She had never even heard of me, and asked Eddie, 'Who is this Cathleen Nesbitt?' I suspect she was mildly shocked when told I was an actress. However carefully Eddie had cut anything remotely resembling a love letter out of his selection, she quickly spotted that there seemed to be almost as many letters written to Cathleen as to all the other friends put together. So she insisted that all except a very few of 'my' letters should be headed 'To a Friend'. The result was that quite a number of people who read the Memoir wondered a little at the fact that everyone else's name was given. Who was this 'friend' who remained anonymous – could it have been a young *man*! Finally Mrs. Brooke felt she would like to meet me, and I went to spend a weekend with her at Rugby and from then on saw a good deal of her.

She was a remarkable woman, but I could see how Rupert must always have been trying to 'escape' not only from her, but from his own inheritance of a strong stubborn puritanism. She was a J.P., one of the powers of the local Liberal Party, and never appeared to give in to any weakness either emotional or physical.

Her youngest son Alfred had been killed soon after Rupert, and she had two easels in her drawing-room with large photographs of them both. When people who came into the room instinctively moved to look at Rupert's picture she always gently reminded them: 'Rupert was not my only son. This is a portrait of my son Alfred who also died in the war.' Once I brought a number of Rupert's letters to show her – the ones in which he spoke of *goodness* as the most important attribute of a man or a woman and talked of the virtues he wanted to cultivate.

She was very moved by them. I think she was deeply jealous of Eddie Marsh, and thought he was leading Rupert astray by introducing him to the social life of London and weaning him from the high-thinking low-living milieu to which he belonged.

We became great friends, and she was godmother to my son, and loved to have him toddling about her garden. In many ways she was more like Rupert than either of them imagined. She had a strong rebellious streak, and a wry humour. It was very entertaining to go to court when the magistrates were in session and see her causing a certain unease in some of her fellows, 'old fuddy-duddys' who thought they should leave all decisions to the clerk of the court rather than listen to the evidence. I saw her prevent several miscarriages of justice, and heard her chuckle with glee at her successes at lunch-time afterwards.

While I was working at the Censorship Office, I found my colleagues very irritating; I remember rescuing a letter from Margot Asquith (to a French friend asking her to make inquiries about the Asquiths' beloved old German governess) from my assistant who said, 'We can't let this go through – look there are messages in *German* to a *German* address.'

When I got an offer in 1915 to go to America to play a part I didn't much like in a play I didn't much like, I longed to go but felt rather guilty about leaving my 'job' such as it was, leaving my mother, even though she did have my sister with her, leaving my country in wartime. But when I talked to Barrie about it he said, 'Go my dear. Many waters cannot quench love, but they can help to quench grief. A few thousand miles of ocean is a great alleviation.' He asked me if I would arrange for him to meet Rupert's mother before I went, and I asked them both to lunch. It wasn't very successful, they were both overcome with shyness, and hardly spoke. I had such a touching letter from him afterwards saying he'd walked home all the way cursing himself for having stammered like a schoolboy 'when I wanted to talk to her about her wonderful son and what his loss meant to us all'.

So I set off once more for the United States. I didn't dream that I was going to stay there for four years.

NINE

The War Years
1915–1917

Why did I leave England where I had so many good parts, and perhaps would have had more, to be doing a bad part in a bad play and living, lonely, in a seedy little hotel? But I had brought a lot of Rupert's letters with me, most of those he had written from America to me, and found an odd comfort remembering that *his* letters had started with misery and grown happier and happier as the good things rather than the bad had begun to dawn on him. He had written, 'It's a beastly hotel, in a beastly room, over a cobbled street and there's a beastly noise . . . and I don't like the food and I don't like the people's faces and I don't like the newspapers and I'm going to be extraordinarily miserable here . . . I've signed my life away to the *Westminster Gazette* to do their beastly "Letter from America" for twelve months. . . . If I were in England I might be lying on a sofa in Thurloe Square, and my head in your lap and your face bent down over mine and your hands about my head. . . . This letter won't even get to you for ten days. I don't want to be alone, I want you. . . .'

I read to myself a letter every night. The next one started: 'You bloody woman. New York is so horribly much a place where *you* have been. Instead of admiring it and taking it in and elucidating and tasting it and generalising, which is what I'm being paid for, I keep thinking: "Now is this the place where the Irish policeman asked her when was her next night off?" or "Is this the place where she says 'Nice people live in studios'?" or "Is this the place where she perhaps once sat laughing in that

101

room high high up? . . . swinging your legs, smoking too much.''
Oh! I can *see* you talking your silly clever talk. What theatre
were you in that I may go and look at it from outside?' Another
began: 'I found myself at a table next to a man of fifty –
American with a humorous face and manner, shrewd with a
cold blue eye and a well-cut face. He seemed interested in
theatres so I gave him a short lecture on the drama, the art of
the theatre, the finance of theatres, music and drama, stage-
management, etc., and recommended him to see *The Great
Adventure*. "Very good entertainment," he agreed. "I've just
bought it for America." I began to feel uncomfortable. "Do
you *own* a theatre?" "In Noo York", he said, "I own 'The
Metropolitan', 'The Knickerbocker', 'The Noo Amsterdam',
'The Grand Opera House'. I have 900 in the States and several
in Canada." He turned out to be Klaw of Klaw & Erlanger. I *did*
feel a fool.' And then I came on a letter which reminded me that
I had dear friends in New York: 'I met your friends, Paul
Wilson and Frances Perkins at last. They sent messages to you
of infinite admiration and affection.' So I got in touch with
Frances Perkins, who was to become Paul Wilson's wife and
the first woman Cabinet Minister in American history. She was
Roosevelt's Minister of Labour, or Labour Commissioner I
think they called it. Whenever I was in Washington, I used to
stay with her. I always remember her beloved ugly face, rather
like a wise and humorous toad, wrinkling with a sudden grin as
she said, 'Sunday! My day for at least two double gins before
each meal. The only way to completely relax is to separate the
soul from the *body* for a while. My ancestors did it with prayer
and fasting, I haven't time for that, so it has to be liquor.'

Now to get back to Broadway in 1915, when my play closed
I had an offer to play Anne Boleyn in Sir Herbert Tree's production of *Henry VIII*. Sir Herbert was in California filming
Macbeth. 'Perched on a huge horse, weighed down by more
armour than any man could walk in, trying to pretend that it
was all a horrible nightmare from which I would one day wake
up with a groan of gratitude,' he told me later. I started rehearsals but found that not only Anne Boleyn's role was very
tiny in the play (which I would not have minded as I longed to
meet Sir Herbert) but that the director was merely a stage
manager without any talent for directing whatsoever, and was

without taste or understanding. I found it was misery to watch the play being mauled, cuts made not of a lot of the bad rhetoric which the play does display but of little odd scenes one felt must be Shakespeare's very own, such as the description of Anne's coronation by the Three Gentlemen; the Third Gentleman concluding a speech with 'So she parted, and with the same full state, paced back again to York Place where the Feast is held.'

FIRST GENT: *You must no more call it York Place, that's past;*
For, since the cardinal fell, that title's lost:
'Tis now the King's, and called Whitehall.
THIRD GENT: *I know it, but 'tis so lately altered that the old name*
is fresh about me.

When I received an offer to play opposite John Barrymore in Galsworthy's *Justice*, and in the only female part in the play, I asked our director to release me. I think he was glad to have me go, though he warned me that 'You are giving up what will be the season's success.'

But *Justice* proved, if anything, the greater success. It was beautifully directed and had a good deal of comedy in it, which was played delightfully. Every member of the cast was superb, and John Barrymore, himself, absolutely brilliant. He subdued all his own personality and became a sad timid little clerk with a cockney accent (quite faultless) and in a scene in the prison cell he gave such a picture of the searing agony of claustrophobia in solitary confinement that the play gave fresh impetus to a movement in favour of prison reform. In fact, wherever we went afterwards on tour we were invited to the local prisons (having already inspected the notorious Singsing of New York). In Boston we visited one of the few model prisons and were shown round one of the workrooms by a most charming and articulate young man. Jack was quite taken with him and asked if he'd like to come to see the play and have supper afterwards. We had taken him for a prison visitor or a head warder. 'I'm afraid', said the young man, 'I have two more years to do before I can accept any invitations.' '*You're* doing time?' stammered Jack. 'Whatever for?' 'Forgery,' was the reply. Ironically enough, forgery was the crime for which Falder, Jack's role in the play, was so cruelly punished that in the end he committed suicide.

I will add but one story to the hundreds that have been told about Jack. I read in some book about John Barrymore quite recently that 'No one knows just when Jack Barrymore met Michael Strange.' I do. It was I who introduced him to her. I had met Mrs. Leonard Thomas at a party and to my surprise she immediately asked me to lunch. I discovered that it was because she wanted to meet Barrymore and thought perhaps I could persuade him to come with me. When I told John that a Mrs. Leonard Thomas, who was very beautiful and very eager to meet him, had asked if he would come with me to one of her Friday lunches he exploded: 'Good God no! I never go to lunch parties given by society bitches.' However, I had promised to do my best and he finally succumbed.

When we arrived we were greeted by the charming husband, Mr. Thomas, who explained that Blanche was finishing some work in her studio. She dabbled in all the arts and had already I think published a book of poems under the pseudonym Michael Strange. Finally appeared a beautiful gipsy-like creature, dressed in a burgundy-coloured velvet teagown with long close-fitting sleeves, one of which had a large ragged hole in the elbow. I felt rather embarrassed for her and thought 'Surely her maid ought at least to have cobbled it up for her' and then added to myself, 'I suppose her maid is still waiting in her bedroom with a suitable dress for a lunch party.' However, she and Jack seemed engrossed with each other and after all the other guests had gone she suggested he should come up and see her studio – so I tactfully disappeared too. That night he looked in at my dressing-room. 'My God! that's a fascinating woman,' he said, 'where did you meet her? What eyes, and did you notice that cute little hole with her elbow peeping through? I do like a woman who doesn't get herself all tarted up like everybody else.' I had never heard of the elbow being an 'erotic zone' but I suppose when a beautiful woman is tightly encased from ears to ankles in wine-coloured velvet, even a tiny glimpse of flesh anywhere is seductive!

James Agate once remarked of an actor who had been acclaimed as a genius, that he would never apply the word to any actor who had not been seen in the great classic roles.

I agree, but there are exceptions to every rule. Anyone who has seen Laurence Olivier in *The Entertainer* or Edith Evans in

The Whisperers or John Barrymore in *Justice*, without having
seen them in anything else must have recognised genius immediately. I had to sit through the court scene in *Justice* every
night for months and every night I found tears welling up during
the prosecution's cross-examination.

The prosecuting counsel had asked him some question, to
which he replied, 'I keep thinking over and over again how it
was I came to do such a thing and if only I could have it all over
again to do different.' It was said very simply but the ravaged
anguished face and the desolate hopeless voice seemed to convey
the agony of every man or woman who had ever felt the utter
helplessness in the knowledge that 'what is done cannot be un-
done.' It was like Lear's 'Never, never, never'. I thought his
Hamlet the best I had seen except, of course, for John Gielgud
(no one in my lifetime has ever bettered John Gielgud's
Hamlet).

John Barrymore's great talent was dimmed early by a funda-
mental *boredom* with anything that needed a continuous discipline. 'Je m'ennui', 'I bore *myself*', something in him cried out
and could only be assuaged by destruction or simple mischief.
He loved to invent ways of teasing and trying to 'throw' his
fellow actors. At the final curtain of *Justice*, for instance, he had
to lie dead for a moment with his back to the audience, while I
threw myself down beside him weeping and Peter Heggie said
gently, 'Don't cry, my pretty. No one will touch him now, never
again. He's gone to Gentle Jesus.' It was a difficult line to say
and Heggie said it beautifully without any sentimentality. But
Jack started playing tricks – telling rather obscene stories under
his breath, sometimes pretending he saw a cockroach crawling
towards him or that he was going to sneeze; *I* could always
collapse on him and pretend that I was hysterical but it made
Heggie's timing impossible. After warning Jack several times,
he walked out of the theatre without waiting for the curtain
calls, and leaving a note to say that 'Unless Mr. Barrymore
apologised for his behaviour and gave a written oath to refrain
from any more monkey business Mr. Heggie would leave the
company for good and not return.' Jack thought he was joking
and said lightly 'Tell the old boy I'll be good next week', but
next week there was no Mr. Heggie. He stayed away for three
days till Jack, knowing how immensely valuable Peter was to

105

the play, had his lawyer draw up a contract swearing on his solemn oath to refrain from any misbehaviour and sent a copy to Heggie, adding 'I'll present it to you on my knees, with humble apologies, in your dressing-room if you'll only come back.' Heggie came back, Jack welcomed him with a bottle of champagne and kept his word. He never monkeyed about in any of Heggie's scenes again.

Peter Heggie was a beautiful actor, and a year later I played with him in Chesterton's *Magic*, the third play within a year in which I was the only female in the cast.

It was while I was playing in *Justice*, that I met Bridget Guinness. It was almost a chance meeting, but it led to a long friendship – indeed it was Bridget who, five years later, designed my wedding dress, and the dresses of my bridesmaids, one of whom was her daughter, Tanis.

I had had sad news from home, my brother Hugo, my mother's best-beloved child, had been killed in action, and within a week another cable came to say that Terence too was dead. Terence was almost more my child than Mamma's. She had had a serious nervous breakdown after his birth and though I was only about ten when he was born, I always regarded him as my baby. For a long time in the family my nickname had been 'Tassin' the nearest he could get to Cathleen. As soon as he could walk almost I pleaded to be allowed to take him out with me to church on Sundays; 'Church', I had always found excessively boring, but with Terence half-asleep on my knee a cosy excuse for not 'getting down when it was prayers' and 'getting up when it was hymns', I could dream the hours away happily. I always talked French with him when I returned from Paris, and instead of sending him to an English prep school, which Mamma longed to do, but which we could not afford, I managed to get him into the American Choir School in Paris. After three years, he spoke French beautifully. He had a great love of Latin and at Bedford Grammar School, where he went when he came home, he was regarded as having the makings of a great classical scholar.

But he got swept up in the fervour of patriotism that then seemed rampant. He had run away from school, aged sixteen and managed to persuade a recruiting sergeant that he really was eighteen.

I remember sitting on my bed all night, saying to myself, 'It's not fair, he hasn't had any life yet.' And thinking of all the mothers in Britain who must be feeling that same anger against the monstrous injustice of it all, was no comfort. It only brought back Mrs. Brooke, and my own desolation.

The next day Bridget Guinness happened to come to see the play and came round to Jack Barrymore's dressing-room afterwards. When she told Jack that she would very much like to meet Peter Heggie and Cathleen Nesbitt, Jack told her that he did not think I would really want to have any strangers to talk to, and explained why. She asked whether I lived alone and Jack said he thought I did; whereupon she came straight up to my room, put her arm around me and said: 'Dear child, won't you come and stay for a few days?' You need not talk to anyone, my house is in Washington Square, it's very peaceful.' I had heard of Mrs. Guinness as a famous hostess who had a famous house in Washington Square, but somehow hadn't till then realised who she was. She simply swept me up, 'Don't bother about toothbrush and nightgown, we have always got spares. Come now.'

She wouldn't even let me take my make-up off, her maid did if for me, while she herself got some hot soup and left it in a thermos by my bed with a sleeping-pill.

Bridget. What a rock of comfort she was during all the years when I lived in New York. She was a very remarkable woman, a 'patroness of the arts' in a real way. Like Sir Edward Marsh in London, she was unerring in spotting new talent. Young musicians, young painters, young actors, she encouraged them all. At her house I met the Washington Square Players, an enthusiastic group of ambitious young amateurs and semi-professional actors, Helen Westly, Teresa Helburn, Philip Moeler, Lawrence Langner. Four years later, they became the Theatre Guild, the company which made such a terrific impact on the American Theatre. Bridget had a great house in Washington Square and a studio nearby where she studied lacquer work under an elderly Chinese gentleman. I used to love to watch her at work. I had always vaguely thought that 'lacquer' was just a good piece of wood painted red or green or amber and then varnished. I began to realise that the wonderful bloom of good lacquer is obtained by innumerable coats upon coats of delicate colour and clear varnish, each layer rubbed and smoothed till it was like glass. It seemed to me that the same precision, delicacy and patience went to it as to the cutting of a fine diamond. She gave wonderful parties, when Le Grand Monde and La Haute Bohême mingled enthusiastically. It was there that I first heard Cavalieri, and Frances Alda and Maggie Teyte sing. It was there that I first saw Arthur Rubinstein. I don't know whether he was already famous in 1917. I saw him one night, a tall, rather ugly and unimpressive young man I thought, and wondered whether he was one of Bridget's painters or musicians or perhaps actor protégés? When he sat down at the piano, there was an immediate hushed attention from all the guests; one had a feeling that something wonderful was going to happen. I, who know nothing about music, was awed, not only by his playing, but by the miraculous beauty that had transfigured what I had taken for an ugly face. He looked like an archangel. I got to know Bridget intimately when I stayed with her while she organised one of her many war charity matinées.

She thought it would be fun to have a children's performance of Barrie's *Quality Street* in a setting that could be fitted on to a platform in the Washington Square Ballroom and wanted me to produce it. She had seen me play in *Quality Street* in London before the war and had always loved the play. Her three children, Loël, Meraud and Tanis, were to play the principal parts (when I said how I liked their odd names she sighed, 'I might have chosen something less Welsh if I had foreseen how their friends would pronounce the names – 'Lole, Mur*ode*, Tan*iss*'.). The production was a great success. I must admit that Loël 'stole the play' as the dashing Captain Browne, Meraud and Tanis looked delicious in their Regency dresses and all their little friends danced the polka in the ballroom scene with great *élan*.

It was at another matinée for the Belgian Relief Fund that I met Sir Herbert Tree and had the thrill of playing Viola to his Malvolio in a scene from *Twelfth Night*. Bridget took us both back to lunch with her and on the way he looked at me quizzically: 'So you are the little girl who wouldn't be my Anne Boleyn? If I'd got back from Hollywood in time I would never have released you.' I quickly replied that if he had been playing Henry instead of Wolsey I should never have dreamed of going, which seemed to amuse him. Bridget happened to mention Constance Collier and I said I'd always hoped to meet her, and Sir

Herbert invited me to a little supper party he was giving for her
and Lillie Langtry next evening. It was an entrancing evening
with Tree at his wittiest and the two splendid ladies, still
beautiful, in their maturity, vying with each other to keep up
with him. As he drove me home, he asked which of them I
would like to meet again. I replied, 'Constance Collier. I don't
know why. They are both beautiful and amusing, but honestly I
felt every now and then I wished that Constance Collier would
talk more and Miss Langtry less.' 'Quite right, my dear,' he
said. 'Constance and Lillie have both met all the famous and
interesting people of their day. Constance remembers what they
said to her. Lillie only remembers what she said to them.' A
great lesson to those of us who are not born with great wit or
wisdom: 'Cultiver nos prochains.' One of the pleasant things
about being English in America is the way the English get
together in New York. I should probably never have met Sir
Herbert in London, unless I had been a member of his company,
but while I was in New York he became a dear and stimulating
friend. He was always good company and always had a quick
answer, usually a witty one, to everything. He used to take me
every Saturday 'between the shows' to have dinner at a restaurant in Central Park called The Claremont.

How the faces of my contemporaries in New York light up at
a mention of The Claremont, just as they do in London at the
mention of The Carlton Grill. The first time he took me there
I lit a cigarette; a waiter *en route* with the menu produced a
large square card and laid it in front of Sir Herbert, who read it,
smiled and said to the waiter, 'Could you possibly find me a red
pen or pencil please?' The waiter looked puzzled but went in
search. After quite a time, red pencils not being on the menu, he
returned and triumphantly presented the pencil. Tree wrote a
few lines on the card and showed it to me. The card read:
'Ladies are not allowed to smoke in public in this city. Would
you kindly ask yours to refrain.' Tree had underlined the word
'yours' heavily with his red pencil and added as a footnote:
'Alas! the lady is *not* "mine" but I *will* try gentle persuasion.'
I then began to realise that one rarely saw a woman smoking,
except in her own drawing-room, and even then it was considered rather 'fast'. To smoke Players as I did *was not done*, it
had to be Balkan-Sobranie or Egyptian or Turkish. Now that I

think of it I believe that even in Britain until some time after the war no hostess liked anyone, male or female, to smoke anything but Egyptian or Turkish 'because of the smell'!

After a few weeks, Herbert was joined by his lovely daughter, Iris, with whom I became very friendly though she was much younger than me. We both thought ourselves too fat and were always exchanging diets. One day Iris telephoned. 'Let's lunch together, there's a *wonderful* new diet guaranteed to take off five pounds a week. You eat *nothing* but baked potatoes.' That sounded good to me. I have always loved baked potatoes. We discovered, however, that the potatoes must be eaten without salt or pepper or butter or indeed any addition of any kind. It was a cunning recipe: try eating nothing but baked potatoes 'au nature' three times daily; you end up eating nothing and naturally lose weight fairly rapidly. Iris wrote poems which I loved. She gave me a book of them and I treasured that little book in its yellow cover for years, and then I lost it.

I think providence intended that I should never have possessions – I was always moving from one town to another or from one continent to another and would take with me my most favourite possessions. Invariably most of them ended up lost, stolen or strayed. I say favourite rather than valuable because they were valuable only to me: books, letters, photographs. I don't think that I have ever in my life owned anything – furs, jewels, silver – of real commercial value. I have always been like the lady in Dorothy Parker's famous poem.

> *A single flower he sent me since we met*
> *All tenderly his messenger he chose*
> *Deep hearted, pure, with scented dew still wet*
> *One perfect rose.*
> *Why is it no one ever sent me yet*
> *One perfect limousine, do you suppose?*
> *Ah no, it's always just my luck to get*
> *One perfect rose.*

If I had ever been presented with a 'perfect limousine' I would have probably parked it somewhere and forgotten where.

Even when I was with the Irish Players doing one night stands, there was always the odd bedroom slipper left in the hotel or the odd glove left in the train. I remember Kerrigan, looking out of the window one morning when the train stopped in the middle of nowhere, shouting 'Be God! Cathleen must have passed this way some time, there's a petticoat lyin' in the middle of the tracks.'

But one loss still grieves me when I let myself think of it. It was a large envelope containing, most precious of all, a sheet of paper headed 'Hood Battalion Royal Naval Brigade' with the sonnet 'Safety' in Rupert Brooke's own handwriting. (Now I have only the galley proof with three corrections in that sonnet and one in the 'The Dead'); a letter from Sir James Barrie written after meeting Mrs. Brooke at my house and saying with a most un-Barrie-like simplicity what meeting 'the mother of such a son' had meant to him; a letter from Ellen Terry saying I had given her pleasure to look at and listen to because I was 'honest' in my work. Into this precious envelope I had put the little yellow book of poems by Iris Tree. All the things I wanted to keep for ever, to look at in my old age were in that old envelope.

I don't know how I lost it or where, I sometimes dream that I have found it again but I always wake before I have opened it. I must stop thinking about it and go back to Iris. My most vivid memory of her is of waking up one morning and looking out of the window of the country house of George Moore (not *our* George Moore – an American tycoon of the same name) and seeing Iris in a white jumper and in white jodhpurs and boots riding on a white horse up an avenue of trees, her 'cap' of bronze hair shining in the morning sun; all her life she wore it in the same way in a page-boy crop with a straight fringe across the forehead. Her hair was quite striking, sometimes bronze or reddish-gold, sometimes a curious clear yellow – 'buttercup colour', Haddon Chambers called it.

Haddon Chambers, at that time the most successful playwright in London, was a great friend of Tree. I remember writing to tell him that I had last met Sir Herbert and how delightful I had found him. Haddon replied by next post, 'I'm not surprised that you have fallen in love with H.B.T. Indeed I uneasily suspected it. That man has injured me in my affections through the best years of my life. "I never loved a dear gazelle who charmed me with her mild brown eye but she would wave me a farewell when Beerbohm Tree came tripping by!" I was so interested and pleased to have your letter yesterday. But why are

you all so happy without me in that 4th Avenue joint? Sir H. and
John B. are too lucky. I should be there to stir up a little strife
and set their complacency atremble. Tell Iris with my love that
on Sunday last I lay for two hours near Marlow in a field of
buttercups the exact tone of her hair.' After a description of
London in wartime, 'dark o' nights, but the church bells ring as
of old – no excuse for idleness for the ungodly,' he continued:
'I'm delighted at the continued success of *Justice*, more particularly perhaps for your sake. I've never seen or read the play but
seem to have gathered the knowledge generally that it is an
earnest, honest and worthy work.' Haddon believed that the
theatre was for entertainment! He was the only friend I ever
talked to when dark fits of depression came on me; sometimes I
would write to him to apologise for being such a bore and he
always wrote back at once. 'It delighted me to get your letter,
you appealed to me more humanly than ever. I was pleased and
touched by your Donne quotation: "And now as broken glasses
show a hundred faces, so my ragges of heart can like, wish, and
adore but after one such love, can love no more." I know why
it lingers in your memory. I remember, in a happily forgotten
old melodrama, making a woman say: "You have broken my
heart but the fragments belong to you." That does not entitle
me to claim even an obscure literary kinship to Donne. . . . No,
my dear, I don't find "Life awfully long", I find it awfully short.
So will you in the time to come.'

Broadway was booming during the early war years and I was
seldom out of work. When the theatre closed down because of
excessive summer heat, which sometimes killed all but the big
musicals, there was usually a summer stock season going on
somewhere.

There was a wonderful summer season at Milwaukee, where
we were promised 'a feast of classic and poetic drama'. And
indeed I had a chance to play in Masefield's *Nan*, which I had
longed to do ever since I had seen Lillah McCarthy in it. We
were financed by a young beer tycoon, one of the Pabst family
I believe, as a tribute to his mother who was avid for 'culture'.
We opened the season with *Nan*, and Lionel Atwill and I had a
very passionate love scene in it. We were much intrigued to hear
that 'Pabby', as our sponsor was called by the locals, had
promised that he would guarantee us an extra three weeks if we

would promise to put *Nan* into the repertory three times a week
through the summer. Sure enough he came, usually only for
Act II, and sat in the back of a box. There were many ribald
suggestions as to just what it 'did' to him, but it became somewhat inhibiting to Lionel and myself and we were glad when the
poor man went down with pneumonia and did not come any
more. The Milwaukee public did not share his enthusiasm, so
we only played *Nan* once a week thereafter. The only other
plays I remember were *The Pirate* and *The Little Mermaid*. The
pirate was played by a tall gangly young man, Alfred Lunt, who
lived on a farm at Tennessee Depot nearby. He would eat an
enormous Spanish onion during one of our scenes. 'Oh! Alfred,
couldn't it be a large apple?' I moaned, as I was allergic to
onions. 'The script says an onion,' said Alfred firmly, and an
onion it was every night. I didn't feel sympathetic then, but in
after years I realised that he must have found it as tiresome as I
did, that he had to eat an onion, and that I didn't like it! Then,
as now, he had the most enchanting and courtly manners of any
actor I have ever met.

The Little Mermaid, written by the then very successful playwright, Edward Sheldon, decorated by two up and coming stage-
designers, Norman Belgeddes and Mamoulian and boasting of
'The most fantastic and terrible shipwreck ever seen on any
stage', was a success and the company decided to make it all
bigger and better and move it to Chicago, rather drowning Hans
Andersen's *The Little Mermaid* in the process. But I have one
happy memory. I had to make my first entrance coming up from
the sea, which stretched wide and blue from a little line of
broken rocks. I had to crawl, clad in a scintillating tail and a
cloud of Lady Godiva hair, under the 'wave cloth', to one of the
larger rocks, behind which was an opening from my tunnel,
gaze with longing at the Prince's Castle, and disappear under
the sea again. Dennis, an Irish stage-hand, was always waiting
to extricate me. 'Ah be gob!' he would say every night: 'Easy
now ye poor wee thing! Ah begob! it's the first time I ever seen
a leadin' lady make her entrance on her belly and she crawlin' like
a worrum.'

When there was no summer play for me I would go to the
Peter Heggies. I had played with Peter in *Justice* and *Magic*;
how I wanted to tell Rupert that I did finally play in *Magic* and

found that Chesterton, as I had suspected, *was* inferior to Barrie.

Peter and his wife had a cottage by the sea on Great Island opposite Hyannis Port. It wasn't *quite* an island, being connected to Hyannis Port by a narrow isthmus, but it was a world in itself. It belonged to a millionaire friend of Peter's, Malcolm Chase, who in spite of much pressure refused to allow anyone but his family and friends to set foot on it. He absolutely refused to build a hotel on it, but if a visiting friend or relative showed a passionate love of the island or better still an obsession with cat-boat racing, Malcolm would build him a cottage. There were no roads on the island, a rough track was made from one house to another by driving a car on it up and down day after day. Most of the children over ten could drive and it was their great treat to be allowed to form a procession of family cars to make a path and end up chez Malcolm with home-made ice-cream. There were no policemen to inquire about licences. Indeed I seem to remember there were no licences in those days. You just bought a car and learned to drive – some went to driving schools and some were self-taught. Nobody kept statistics about accidents either. Then back to Broadway to do a play for Belasco. I can't remember anything of the play but I remember the rehearsals vividly. Belasco was an imposing figure with snow-white hair and piercing eyes. He loved to keep his cast together. We didn't even go out to lunch. It was served in the downstairs dining-room in the theatre. He told us he didn't want us to break the 'magic of the theatre' by going forth into the outer world in the middle of rehearsal. I think he gave us a very good lunch for the pleasure of having a captive audience. There was no doubt that he was a talented director, with even a spark of genius occasionally. But I had worked with directors in London, who had talent and genius and *taste*, a quality that to my mind Belasco seemed to lack. He was incidentally a very fine actor.

The first great actors' strike was called by Equity, while we were working. We were told by our Equity representative that we were 'on strike' even from rehearsals. Belasco really impressed me when he came on the stage and spoke with real tears in his eyes and a quiver in his voice. He begged us to remain loyal to him: 'I am, I always have been, a father to my actors. I have always paid them more than any manager in this town . . . I have never broken a contract. You have eaten of my bread – brought me your problems' on and on it went. And so moving was it that, had it not been for the restraining hand of our 'dowager', the imposing Margaret Illingworth, I would have flung myself on him and cried, '*I* will never never desert you, Mr. Belasco.' Miss Illingworth waited till his oration was finished and then said firmly, 'Sorry, David, we must take a vote on it. All hands up in favour of the strike.' All hands were raised, Belasco stood still for a moment then drew his watch from his pocket, stamped on it and groaned: 'A plague upon you all' and made a magnificent exit. I was told afterwards that he had several times in his life played the watch trick. Not very often, but he always kept a Woolworth 'gold' watch in his pocket *in case* occasion should arrive.

So I became a founder-member of American Equity. I have benefited very much from it as an alien during all the years I have been in America, and out of a sense of duty I have always staunchly supported my union both in Britain and America. And yet a small rebellious part of me said, 'Actors have no business with unions' – when I took part in the great Broadway March.

I think it was soon after that that I went on a tour playing opposite an elderly matinée idol, who was still a big draw outside New York. The small-town folk are more loyal to their old favourites. In one scene he sat relaxed, speaking a very long monologue, while I standing behind him tenderly stroked his hair. Having to look down on it so often, I became aware that something was happening to it. Was I dreaming? Were the auburn hairs really slowly turning to mousy brown flecked with grey? Was that beautiful soft wave losing its curl? But on opening night in Washington, I was startled to see it in all its erstwhile glory curling gently on his forehead reflecting glints of auburn in the spotlight. Naïve as I was, it had never occurred to me that men used dyes and had permanent waves, and that a week of one-night stands where there were no good hairdressers might be as distressing to a man as to a woman!

We had two weeks in Washington, an utterly delightful two weeks. A beau from New York, Henry Hooker, who was Franklin Roosevelt's friend and lawyer, was staying with Roosevelt who was then assistant Secretary to the Navy. With

Henry Hooker as guide, I saw everything and went everywhere. He took me to lunch once or twice with the Roosevelts. Each time the five children seemed to be tearing around under our feet. One day as Henry and I were talking with Mr. Roosevelt, a secretary tiptoed in: 'The Ladies' Delegation from Peoria are out in the hall. They say you promised to see them – I'm afraid you did.' 'Holy smokes, did I? Why did you allow me? Tell them . . . tell them . . . I'm detained at the White House on important war business . . . ssh! I hear them in the hall,' and he promptly dived behind a huge sofa, surrounded by a gaggle of giggling children. The secretary managed to placate the ladies from Peoria who were peering into the room, empty but for Henry and myself, and they went away. 'You can come out now' called Henry and they all emerged, flushed and triumphant. What a handsome man Roosevelt was. I fell in love with him at sight.

'Love.' Love? I was always falling in love in those days. 'Love or the word "love" abused under which many childish desires and conceits are excused.' It wasn't ever really love but a desire to *be* loved, a kind of 'addiction'. I became passionately 'addicted' to a Russian called Boris Soldadenkov (he taught me to pronounce Russian names correctly!). I was attracted to him by his looks, which were rugged and superb, and by the fact that he was the only one of the White Russians who were pouring into New York fleeing from the Bolsheviks, who did *not* claim to be a prince of the blood, or a duke, or at least a baron. 'I was the managing director of a travel company, now I sell tickets *for* a travel company. I am lucky man!'

He thrilled me by saying he did sculpture in his spare time and wanted to do a head of me: 'You have face of beautiful lioness – no – lioness cub.'

I loved him at once for guessing that *that* was the face I had always wanted to have – all the faces I have ever thought beautiful – Tallulah Bankhead, Gertrude Lawrence, Lauren Bacall, Vivien Leigh, Audrey Hepburn – all had lovely 'cat faces'. I have always had, if anything, a fox face, or should I say a vixen? jaw too long, eyes too small. How I have longed all my life to have a different face. I know that people have often called me beautiful, and of course it has always given me great pleasure to hear it, but something in me deep down always answers with a little shock of disbelief. 'Beautiful?' I say to myself, 'oh no,' and then the old saying always echoes in my mind: 'Beauty is in the eye of the beholder.' I have never liked my face very much, it's not a 'shape' that I admire. In short, as Alec Woollcott once said of a generally acclaimed play that he did not like, 'Even if it *was* good I wouldn't like it.'

Boris couldn't really see a cat face when he tried to sculpt my head. But I still clung to him. I would waste long Sundays, taking trains and buses to God knows where and watch him patiently for hours while he played chess, just for the sake of a few hours in his studio when he made love to me. 'Is true you are a virgin? No? Yes?' he said one day.

'Is true,' I confessed, ashamed of it and half hoping he would take me, not quite knowing exactly what that meant actually, half fearing that something would happen that would get me with child. I knew nothing about birth control – did anyone in those days? Even married women? But of course they must have. I just had been so stifled by my upbringing that I don't think I could ever have dared to inquire. I dimly remember saying, or did I only 'feel', 'I'm sick of being a "virgin", it's ridiculous at my age.' 'You want me to take you?' said Boris. 'Oh, you nonsense-talking baby, you do not, you would not like it, you would not like me, you would not like yourself. You are not a true "amoureuse", I think now it a good time to say goodbye.' So he kissed me goodbye and I thought I was very unhappy.

But there was always work, blessed work. I discovered the other day looking in a theatrical 'who's who', that between 1915 and June 1919 I played fifteen different parts including tours and summer stock, so there can have been very few weeks when I was not either playing or rehearsing or both. Then I found a man again. An aviator who fell in love with me from the stalls and found someone to introduce him, after he had seen me several times. I thought that rather romantic. He was tall – he was good-looking in his uniform. He had enlisted early, hoping America would 'come in' and he could get over to help. He took me dancing and I loved to dance. He showed me something even more exciting than dancing – flying! Discipline must have been non-existent in the Air Force in those days, or he would never have dared to take me up in his little plane when practising landings on the Long Island beaches. Young people of today who have only stepped off a ramp on to a 'Flying Hotel de Luxe' can have no idea of what excitement there can be in actually *flying*, strapped into an open plane with the wind blowing in your face and the sudden breathless realisation that you are actually up in the air. I remember the first time I went up I seemed to hear a strange screaming noise in the wind. 'How funny the wind sounds up there, almost like screeching,' I said when we landed. 'That was *you* screaming, baby,' he said. 'Me? *Me?*' 'Yes you! at the top of your voice. We all do the first time up. It's sheer excitement.' I hadn't even realised that I had opened my mouth. It was a glorious sensation, but it only happened once again. Somehow, a rumour got to the top brass that some young officers were taking their girlfriends for rides. Dire threats of 'dishonourable discharge' from *any* branch of the U.S. Forces were promulgated. I don't think anyone ever dared to risk it again. I was rather hoping I would fall in love myself: 'Perhaps this time I will get married, have children and settle down?' Then, of course, I discovered that he had a wife and children. He explained that he and his wife both wanted a divorce, but they were waiting a while to see if her father could be placated; father strongly disapproved of divorce, and would cut her off from a handsome inheritance. Once I went down to spend a weekend at their place in the country. His wife's lover was staying there too. She ushered me into a spacious room with a large double bed: 'I expect you like to share, or do you prefer twin beds?' I stammered something, and I think she realised that we were not sleeping together, for she sat down on the bed and laughed. 'Well I'm damned! He told me he hadn't been to bed with you yet but I didn't believe him. You really are the first girlfriend he's had here that *hasn't* shared this bed with him.' I didn't enjoy the weekend. She and her lover seemed such nice normal people, what was the matter with me I thought, was *I* abnormal? 'Did your wife sleep with you before you were married?' I asked him as we drove back. 'Sure,' he said, 'but I'm not sure it wasn't a mistake. I guess it's fun getting to know people quietly first, let's just be "engaged" for a while, baby, shall we?' I think I was as nearly being in love with him at that moment as I ever was. I'm not going into the boring details of an affair that dragged on for a long time with me clinging idiotically to my 'much prized virginity', which I didn't 'prize' at all, and he, not unnaturally, alternately attracted and repelled and, at last, obsessed with the desire to 'break me down'.

But I learned some very interesting things from it, the most important being how very important it is to come to terms with oneself. I had always been so eager for people to like *me* without really considering whether *I* was likeable or not. I was now startled and shocked to find that I didn't like myself. It's difficult to live with other people when you dislike them – it's almost impossible to live with yourself when you dislike yourself. I think for a time I became neurotic and everything I read or heard seemed to apply in some vague way to *me*. I read in a French novel a scornful phrase about a 'jeune fille' who had 'led a man on' almost to madness. 'Ca, c'est une espèce de demi-vierge – une Taquineuse; quelle type dégôutant.' 'Ca, c'est moi', I thought. I was unhappy in love in those days because I was not generous in love.

I can remember (with astonishment and incredulity as to how I could ever have felt like that!) looking out of my window one night and being so 'out of love' with myself so overwhelmed with misery, that I had a powerful urge to throw myself out of the window – anything to put an end to thinking. 'Nothing good or bad but thinking makes it so, makes it so, makes it so' I found myself muttering as I backed away from the window, slightly overcome by the vertigo that always attacks me when I look down from a great height. 'Gas would be a cleaner job . . .' at which moment I caught my foot in a hole in the rug and fell forward against the radiator. 'Oh *damn* that rug!' I shouted, 'I might have killed myself' and rushed to a mirror to see if I had broken my jaw. By this time I found myself laughing, giggling hysterically, and went to bed and slept. I have had periods in my life since then when I have felt suicidal, but Dorothy Parker has put the whole thing into perspective:

Razors pain you:
Rivers are damp;
Acids stain you;
And drugs cause cramp;
Guns aren't lawful;
Nooses give;

Gas smells awful;
Might as well live.

Something happened to distract my attention from myself, always one of the best remedies for unhappiness. My mother wrote to tell me that my sister, Anna, was suffering from consumption, as dread a word then as cancer is today, and had had to give up her ballet lessons. I don't know whether leukaemia had been diagnosed in those days. Anna's doctors had decided that her illness was tuberculosis of the stomach but they had hopes of a cure in a dry climate, so Mamma was proposing to come out to live in Pasadena in California. I knew nothing about the geography of California, nor I suspect did Anna's doctor! I have since thought that he confused it with Palm Springs, where the desert air is always hot and dry, or perhaps Mamma, who had a friend living in Pasadena, had thought that the climate was the same everywhere in California, and it would be comforting to find someone she knew. So I got busy, writing to the friend in Pasadena, asking her to find a little flat for them if possible with a garden. Anna had to have lots of fresh air. I gathered that she was apparently quite well so long as she didn't overexert herself, which meant no dancing. I was desperately sorry for her and racked my brains to think of what I could do to keep her reasonably happy. Then I remembered a letter from Mamma, written some months ago, saying, 'Anna has been losing weight and the doctor thinks she has been practising too much, so she is amusing herself having driving lessons, though I can't see what good it will be to her as we are never likely to have a car.'

A car, a little car of her own! I set about having one ready-parked at her front door to greet her on her arrival. It gave me a vicarious pleasure to choose it. I had never owned a car and didn't think I'd ever have the courage to try to drive one in New York!

How reviving to a heart, a little soured by concentration on *itself* and its 'splendeurs et misères', is a sudden awareness of the honest truth of the maxim, 'It is more blessed to give than to receive.' Having got into an egocentric habit of thinking continually of me, and taking things for myself, it was quite exhilarating to be giving for a change. To be waiting on

Mamma and Anna, cooking American delicacies for them, buying pretty summer dresses for Anna and real silk stockings – 'Milanese' was a thick silk stocking that was the ultimate in chic, and to be richly 'opaque' rather than transparent was the mark of a luxury stocking. And to buy Mamma a white fox fur, something I knew she had secretly coveted all her life (and which she lent me for my wedding five years later). And more fun still to take her to a hat shop, and say, 'Choose a hat for the California sunshine and *don't ask the price.*' How I laughed at myself only the other day when I went to buy a hat and tried on solemnly one after another, looking for one that would be kind to my face, and remembered that day when I had smiled somewhat patronisingly at Mamma, thinking to myself, 'Fancy caring that much about whether a hat is becoming when you are *sixty.*' Here am I, more choosy about hats now, at eighty-four than I was at sixty!

Finally they set off on the long train-trip to California, and it was all I could do not to leap on to the train with them; strange I never remember having actively missed any of my family before – perhaps it was because I had always been the one to 'go away'.

My dear friends the Guinnesses and the Trees had all gone back to England. I half thought of going back to England myself when I got a request to call on Mr. Alf Hayman who had been Charles Frohman's partner, and since Frohman's death on the *Lusitania*, had been managing all the Frohman Enterprises.

I had been warned that Mr. Hayman was rather eccentric, and that for some reason he kept a huge wooden Indian in his office of the kind that used to be a mascot outside barbers' shops. Sure enough there it was larger than life, a very *Red* Indian with splendid feathers on his head and baleful eyes. Mr. Hayman kept me waiting for some time, and I was just getting the creeps from the glassy eye of the wooden Indian when his secretary led me in: 'Siddown, dear! Siddown,' he said. 'I have a play here, maybe you would like to play the ongeenoo?'

'The ongeenoo?' I wondered. 'Was there an Indian maiden in the play?'

'Haddon Chambers writes me to take a look at you. He's coming over with Cyril Maude. An' we have this little play, an' we have that grand woman Laura Hope-Crews, an' there's a boy an' a girl in it and that's it.' I could have embraced him; a play by Haddon, and with Cyril Maude and the incomparable Laura Hope-Crews; the whole set-up promised bliss. And bliss it was!

How we laughed during rehearsals. There was a scene at a dinner table during which the four of us ate and drank steadily. We had long discussions as to what form of ersatz menu was most easily chewed and swallowed.

'Sliced bananas for the "filet de sole",' said Haddon. 'No, *no*! Sliced canned pears', said Cyril, 'slip down much more easily – the right colour too.'

'Harder to eat,' said Haddon. 'Let's have a bet on it,' said Cyril, 'who's got a stopwatch?' The stage manager obliged. There was an eating dual on as to who could get down what in the shortest time; with everyone cheering on the sidelines. 'Go it Cyril, one more bite and you're home!' 'Haddon's cheating, he dropped a bit on the floor.'

Then there was the question of who should sit where – one person *has* to have his back to the audience at a table for four.

'Let's toss for it,' said Cyril, always ready for a gamble.' Let's all change places once a week,' suggested Laura. 'I always find it so *restful* to get my eyes out of the footlights.'

At the last rehearsal but one Cyril brought a huge bottle of champagne for the dinner scene: 'Mop it up children, we will be drinking nice fizzy ginger ale for the next year, once the curtain goes up.'

We were all sure the play would succeed, and for once the actors were justified in their hopes – it ran from September 1918 to April 1919 – an unheard of success for those days.

I sometimes think there is an odd imponderable which makes one play more popular than another, which may be an equally good play and equally well cast. And that is the harmony and affection existing between the members of the cast. If all the actors like each other, respect each other, and enjoy each other, it somehow *does* add to the enjoyment of the audience. It certainly was so with *The Saving Grace*. Even our impresario, Alf Hayman, who came to look at us during our three-day try-out, had no criticism to offer. He sat in a box without moving a muscle, chewing a big cigar, and when he came back-stage afterwards he had one solitary comment: 'I think Miss Nesbitt's shoes are too fancy for an English girl.'

122

Haddon nodded gravely: 'Of course, you've said something Alf.' And Cyril added equally solemnly, 'Why don't you take her out tomorrow morning and buy her some *quieter* ones.' For a moment I thought they were in earnest and trembled for my lovely pink satin pumps, cross-gartered like a ballet dancer's specially chosen by Lucille, the famous dressmaker. It was the first time in my career that I had had elegant clothes to wear – it had either been 'costume' or 'peasant' up till then!

I discovered that, like myself, Cyril and Haddon clearly loved a party. They naturally had many more invitations than I had, but very often they took me with them and Cyril and I always stayed till the very end. 'You two,' grumbled Haddon, 'you wait till you get swept out with the empty milk bottles!' 'We ride home with the milkman,' said Cyril, and Haddon christened us the 'Home with the Milk Kids'.

One night I actually outstayed Cyril at a dance. When I got to the theatre the next evening, I found a picture of Cyril. A self-portrait drawn in ink by himself inscribed to 'Home with the Cream,' from 'Home with the Milk'.

Cyril used to love illustrating any communications with little pencil drawings. I have had three 'correspondents' in my life who had that charming habit – Rupert Brooke, Cyril Maude and Douglas Fairbanks Junior. Of them all Douglas produced much the wittiest!

My troubled love affair with my aviator was beginning to crop up again. He had been away in a training wing for some time, and was eager to 'set up house', as it were. I poured it all out to Haddon one day. He asked if I *liked* the man, as much as I *loved* him. I thought seriously and confessed, 'Sometimes I don't *like* him at all, and often I don't like myself when I'm with him.'

Haddon handed me his *Oxford Book of Verse* and opened it at 'The Holy Land of Walsingham' and said, 'Just read the last four verses.'

> *Know that Love is a careless child,*
> *And forgets promise past:*
> *He is blind, he is deaf when he list,*
> *And in Faith never fast.*
>
> *His desire is a dureless content,*
> *And a trustless joy;*

He is won with a world of despair
And is lost with a toy.

Of womenkind such indeed is the love
Or the word love abusèd,
Under which many childish desires
And conceits are excusèd.

But true love is a durable fire,
In the mind ever burning,
Never sick, never dead, never cold
From itself never turning.

And he said he thought I was behaving very badly to myself and to my young man: 'You don't really *love* him,' he said. 'You just like to play hot and cold. Give the whole thing up. If you haven't the willpower to do it here then go back to England as soon as the play is over.'

Haddon was a very wise man. I wonder if anyone remembers his plays nowadays? *Passers By, Captain Swift, The Saving Grace.* I must go and look them up in the drama library to see if they are as good as I thought them then.

He was a wonderful companion. His memory was a never-ending source of amazement and delight to me. He had, like Herbert Asquith (Lord Oxford), practically total recall. I doubt if there was a sonnet of Shakespeare or a favourite poem in the *Oxford Book* that he couldn't quote at will. To me, who could learn a poem by heart with tremendous speed, and be unable to quote a line of it within a week, his memory seemed God-like and his wisdom infinite. I knew that his advice was always good. I must get out of New York.

TEN

The Halcyon Summer, Sunninghill Park
1919

I cabled every London manager I knew to ask if one could give me a job. The only one who replied was J. B. Fagan, who wrote to say that he was doing *The Merchant of Venice* at the Court Theatre with a great Jewish actor, Moscowitch. He could offer me the part of Jessica but the role only carried £15 a week. By that time I was getting $150 in New York, which then equalled £75. As usual when there is a decision to be made, my two selves were at odds, the cautious one saying, 'Don't start running away from things again, don't go back to London to earn one fifth of your salary and be overshadowed by everyone else in the cast.' The reckless one saying, 'I *must* go, I can't trust myself to stay, one must take chances in life.' So I cabled 'Yes' to Mr. Fagan and booked a passage home in July 1919. On the ship I spent the first day looking miserably at the ocean. It was nearly four years since I had crossed it in the opposite direction, running away from myself both times. I was told later that I had said 'Oh hell!' in a tone of such despair that the solitary woman taking her exercise on deck had stopped and sat down beside me. 'Is it really as bad as all that?' she asked. Her name was Ruby Ross. She had a funny face and a funny voice, and wore enormous glasses long before anyone else thought of horn-rims. 'I guess what you really need is a drink,' she said and hauled me down to the bar. She told me she was an interior decorator and was going to Paris via London to visit Elsie de Wolfe. When I returned to America thirty years later, she had become the most famous woman decorator in the States. From Boston to Detroit, the status symbol was to have your house 'done' by Ruby Ross. She had an enormous talent for making a house or a room look as if, like Topsy, it had 'just growed'. When she married a wealthy stockbroker, Chalmers Wood, she built a house for themselves in the shape of a crescent moon, all on one floor round a patio. I saw the foundation stones laid and within two years there it was, looking as if several generations had lived there, all of whom had left their own mark, so that when one first saw the great living-room one said 'Oh! how cosy' rather than 'Oh! how elegant' or 'how luxurious'. One discovered the latter qualities later.

Ruby was my salvation on the boat, bubbling all the time with sheer enjoyment of life – a real 'life-giver'. As we neared home, she asked me where I lived. 'Nowhere as yet,' I answered. My mother and sister were still in California, my father was building bridges in India. My brother, Tom, had a little house in Brompton Square – I had cabled hopefully to ask for a bed and had no answer. If it turned out that he and his wife were on tour I should go to a hotel. 'Well, if there is no one home when you arrive, just come straight to the Cavendish in Jermyn Street. Rosa Lewis always has a little suite for me and, if you don't mind sharing a room, the bedroom always had two beds in it.' I had never heard of the famous Cavendish or of Rosa Lewis, but found that the house in Brompton Square has been let for six months while Tom was on tour, so off I went to the Cavendish. It was quite an experience! Ruby and Rosa greeted me warmly. There was a delightful courtyard full of blossoming shrubs, out of which a corridor led to Ruby's little suite. We all drank champagne. Rosa said she'd have some dinner sent right to our room and while she was away Ruby told me what a famous character she was – in her day the best cook in London. King Edward VII, it was said, 'could always be tempted to a dinner party if his hostess could say, "Rosa is going to cook it"'. 'I'll get her to show you her picture gallery some day in her little office – framed photographs of all the aristocracy with affectionate inscriptions. They do say that all of them, from Edward VII to Lord Ribblesdale, have been her lovers too, at one time or another, and during the war she nearly bankrupted herself serving champagne "on the house" to any young officer in uniform. Some of them always came, and slept, on the courtyard

floor if there wasn't a bed free, on their last night of leave; and
Rosa was always up at dawn to see that they didn't miss their
trains.' After dinner we had a bath and sat in the sitting-room in
our nightgowns finishing the rest of Rosa's presentation champagne. There was a knock at the door and without waiting for
an answer Rosa sailed in with another bottle of champagne and
two young Guards officers in full regalia. We fled to the bedroom, Ruby to don a dressing-gown, I to take refuge in bed. I
was tired and not in the mood for a party, but Ruby was wide-
awake and more than ready! I heard sounds of merriment and
finally fell asleep. When I woke, as I often do in the small hours,
Ruby's bed was still unoccupied. I asked her in the morning if
she had had any sleep at all? 'I had a *wonderful* night; make what
you like of that,' and she winked at me behind her horn-rimmed
spectacles. She died years ago, but the memory of her still
glows; and so many lovely houses bear traces of her influence.
None of the houses she did ever looked as though a decorator
had been at work. She never had that passion for seeking out
period pieces to go with each other in every room till in the end
every room looks like a museum. She was delighted when I told
her a story of Lord Dunsany, when someone was questioning a
curious long table in a room full of Queen Anne walnut valuable
pieces, he replied, 'That table was made by my own carpenter,
from my own wood, that I brought back from Malaya. It blends
beautifully with everything. All good pieces can live together
and it *is* good – a period piece, my period.' Even during the last
few years when I have happened to go into a house only a few
months after it had been 'settled into', Mary Rodgers' house in
Connecticut, or Mary Lee Fairbanks's in Palm Beach, for instance, I've found myself saying, 'How Ruby Ross would have
liked this. The furniture seems to belong to the house, it's all
mellowed so quickly.' The reply has come eagerly, 'You couldn't
have paid it a greater compliment – Ruby was a real genius –
she taught me a lot.' Oddly enough, both these ladies of enormous taste had realised the value of those lovely new Portuguese
carpets in a country house. How Ruby would have approved!

To return to London in 1919. The Guinness family were now
living in Carlton House Terrace and when I telephoned Bridget,
she at once asked if I'd like to come down and spend the summer,
till I had to start rehearsing, at Sunninghill Park, on which they

had taken a long lease. She was somewhat shocked to hear that I was staying at the Cavendish. 'It is not a place for a young girl, in fact it is not a hotel for ladies at all.' As a matter of fact, I have met several real ladies of immensely conservative and proper families, both English and American, who always stayed either at Brown's or the Cavendish while in London! Indeed, I occasionally stayed there for an odd night or two myself. The *old* Cavendish, that is. The present one is such an architectural monstrosity I can hardly look at it. I am glad that my son saw it in its original shabby splendour. I thought it would amuse him while he was on leave from the Second World War to see where the young officers of the First World War had so often spent their days off. When my son and I went in, there Rosa was sitting in the hall as usual in her white coat and skirt. Her golden hair had been allowed to go white at last, and she was confined to a wheel-chair, but her eyes brightened at the sight of a young man in uniform and a split of champagne was brought at once to wish him good luck. She pretended to remember me but she quite obviously didn't. Even the name of Ruby Ross didn't ring a bell. She tired easily as her secretary had told me, so we left very soon. Just as we left, she looked at me with dawning recognition: 'I know *you*', she said with a bawdy chuckle. 'You were Lord Wimborne's piece, his little bit you were.' I hadn't the heart to explain that I had never even *seen* Lord Wimborne, let alone met him, so I left her chuckling over her memories.

It was June 1919, when Bridget took me down to Sunninghill Lodge. Such a splendid house it was, with a lake in the grounds and an island in the lake. Bridget once gave a party, at which the Covent Garden Ballet gave a performance of *Swan Lake* on the island, the audience sat on the lawn that sloped down to the lake and watched the ballet by moonlight.

The very first weekend was enormous fun. Bridget had organised a party of young people to clear the drawing-room of all its 'horrors' and take them to the attics or the cellar. 'No one is to dress tonight, we'll all dine in our oldest clothes. I want all the strong young men to volunteer to carry these hideous chairs to the attic. Would you believe it I have found twenty-four quite exquisite painted Hepplewhite chairs just "stacked" in the attic! And Cathleen, you must organise all those ghastly china ornaments. Give out labels – they are to go on shelves in the basement; each one must be labelled saying which room it came from as someone may want to put them all back one day.' And what fun we had, writing out labels to stick on the 'horrors' – 'China Dog. Place – Library Table'; all vying with each other as to which had found the most hideous ornament or the most incredible lampshade. Even the children had been allowed to stay up – Loël and Meraud and Tanis – and their step-cousins, the beautiful Jungman girls, Zita and Baby.

I had read many laments while in America about Britain being so changed after the war: 'All the splendour and luxury of the Edwardian era is no more,' they said. It seemed to me that there was plenty of luxury left at Sunninghill! I don't know how many servants there were. Housemaids were invisible – one only saw the butler and the footmen and occasionally the housekeeper or an odd parlourmaid or two. There was a maid called Rosemary, deputed to look after the ladies who had not 'brought their own'; I remember her name because the housekeeper had firmly insisted that it was too 'fancy' a name – she must choose to be called 'Rosie' or 'Mary'. 'My mum called us all after plants' she said; 'Olive and Ivy and Myrtle and Iris and then she started on 'erbs – if there'd been another girl I bet she'd 'ave been called Parsley – but it was a boy so 'e was Basil.' I would love to have met Rosie's mother. Rosie was a splendid girl; any odd garment that needed washing or ironing was whisked away and returned before one had time to miss it. And she was very helpful as to which dress to lay out for dinner. 'I should save that for to-morrow, Miss, it will be white tie,' which meant that there would be guests. Sometimes she would have two or three ladies to look after but she could always find time to sew on a button or even deal with recalcitrant hair.

How I loved to sit on the corner of Bridget's bed while she organised the weekend parties with the housekeeper. Someone had told me that the Guinnesses had the best chef in the country and I'd always imagined the chef as a man but Bridget's cook was a woman. She was a superb cook, and when some special guest was coming she could invent the most fantastically decorative puddings with spun sugar of every colour twisted into flowers and fantasies. But mostly she liked to be 'interviewed' about menus in her own domain, the kitchen. Bridget and the housekeeper would go down the lists. 'Mr. and Mrs. H. . . .

I can't remember. Do they like separate rooms?' 'Oh no, ma'am, they like to share and Mrs. H. can't bring her maid this time – Mr. H. is bringing his man.' . . . 'Well perhaps Rosie can fit her in with the young ladies.' . . . 'Lord and Lady B. . . . They *do* like separate rooms, don't they?' 'Yes ma'am – his Lordship snores very heavy.' . . . 'Let's see, we can't very well put him in the bachelors' wing – he wouldn't like the stairs.' . . . 'There's the blue room now, ma'am – you remember Lady C. telephoned cancelling?' 'Of course, I'd forgotten. Thank you, Mrs. Manton.' And so the organisation went on, the visitors placed carefully in position according to their rank, temper and preferences.

Then there were the days when the Duke of Connaught came for lunch and tennis. He was a really serious player and remarkably agile for his age. Cook always surpassed herself – when His Royal Highness was expected. He had a great liking for one of her famous dishes 'pigs' chitterlings'. One day he had consented to open a fête in the grounds that Bridget had organised for charity. He disappeared after the very early lunch and towards 3 o'clock everyone was getting a little nervous – where *could* he be? Surely he hadn't forgotten the fête and gone home? Finally he was tracked down to the butler's pantry where Hughie Green, a famous music-hall comedian who was assisting at the 'entertainments', was teaching him card tricks with the appropriate patter. His Royal Highness could only be persuaded to leave on condition that they could be reunited later. 'I'll do my turn and you do yours, and then couldn't we meet here at 4 o'clock say, and get on with it.' They went on with it till 6 o'clock when Hughie Green had to depart to the Shepherd's Bush Empire.

That time was before the days of baths to every room – I think there was just one to the four rooms in the corridor where the unmarried young ladies slept. Irene Curzon and I were waiting our turn in Irene's room when out of the bathroom came Diana Manners. She took one's breath away: the rosy baby skin, the pale golden silky hair, damp from the bath, the great blue eyes like jewels. I had met her once or twice but never at a time when I could just sit and stare. 'So might thy mighty amazing Beauty move. . . .' The line rang in my mind like a clarion when I looked at Diana.

I saw so many beautiful women at Sunninghill that summer.

There was Mary Curzon, Lady Curzon of Penn, blonde and radiant. There was Lady Irene Curzon, daughter of the great Lord Curzon of Kedleston, dashing, handsome, glowing. There was Generis Mainwaring, not really as beautiful as the others but with an aura of magnetism that drew everyone towards her. 'She's a real Welsh gipsy,' said her husband, Sir Harry Mainwaring. Harry Mainwaring was a whimsical man with a fund of good stories about everyone. One about Lady Curzon I still remember. It was the time when London was full of royal refugees such as King Alfonso of Spain and King Manuel of Portugal. Lady Curzon was known to be having a little affair with King Alfonso. One evening at a ball, a friend peered knowingly at a little scar, suspiciously like tooth bites, on Lady Curzon's shoulder. 'Spain?' she inquired. 'No, Portugal,' replied her Ladyship, placidly. 'One mustn't show favouritism.'

Bridget said to me one day, 'Harry seems to be very devoted to you.' 'Oh, no,' I cried. '*Not* another married man' I thought to myself instinctively. 'Oh yes!' said Bridget laughing. 'Do start a little flirtation with him while they are here. Generis is so naughty, she really doesn't care about anything but hunting. She neglects him quite shamefully and now if we could make her feel a twinge of jealousy it would be *so* good for her.' So I carried on with general approval a delightful flirtation with Harry. I don't think Generis even noticed it, she was planning her autumn weekends for the hunting season.

At weekends, there was often a group of schoolgirls, Alice Astor among them, dressed like a princess on Sundays, on Mondays sent off on an early train to the Notting Hill Gate Girl's High School, a fad of her mother's, frowned on by her stepfather, Lord Ribblesdale, snorting at her dreadful school uniform – '*must* she be dressed like that? Can't she wear human clothes even at this school?' Poor little Alice, what a cheerful start to the day it must have been for her. How she must have longed to have a darling governess like Meraud and Tanis.

Another memory. The great American star, Laurette Taylor, who had taken London by storm in *Peg o' my Heart*, was sitting disconsolately on the terrace, unaware that everyone who didn't go to Church on Sunday morning either stayed in bed or went for a walk or for a ride. 'Hartley (Hartley Manners, her husband) has gone to see if there's anyone around – we haven't seen a human face since we got up,' she moaned and then with an impish grin, 'and me in my best frock all ready for a kill'. Odd the things one remembers – when there is so much one forgets.

Why should I remember sitting in the library when Benjy Guinness rang the bell to ask for more logs? The butler appeared, picked up the empty log-basket and went out; Bridget and Benjy looked at each other rather sternly, I thought. The butler returned with the basket, put some logs on the fire and departed. Bridget shook her head, 'I'm afraid that settles it, he'll have to go, he'll never be really satisfactory.' 'Has he done anything wrong?' I ventured to ask. 'My dear child, he ought not to have brought the logs in, *or* put them on the fire – that's a footman's business; he should have sent Peter with them.' Seeing my astonishment, she added 'No butler can possibly have authority over his staff if he starts doing their work for them.'

How strange the whole class structure of those days – especially among the older generation who had been taught to 'abide in the station God had given them' – seems nowadays. Sometimes it did even then. I remember a charming American woman, who was staying while Lord Charles Beresford and his wife were there, saying, 'I've just written home, Lady Charlie, to tell them how absolutely *medieval* your village is – all the old ladies on the village street curtsying to you when you go for a walk and even that nice young woman at the lodge doing her "bob" when she opens the gate.' 'And why not? They *enjoy* curtsying to me just as I *enjoy* curtsying to my King. I mean it's part of the *order* of things. . . . *And* I like going down on my knees in Church,' she added unexpectedly. 'You did till your knees gave out on you,' chuckled Lord Charlie. 'Here comes my old craft in her new coat of paint,' he would say as she appeared on the terrace in her full warpaint. Her eyesight was no longer what it had been, so one eyebrow was often nearer the hair line then the eyelid, the mouth rather garlanded with lipstick than actually outlined, the neck quite a different shade from the face. But there was something so life-giving, so warm and generous and gallant, so 'imposing' in an odd way that I always felt I would enjoy curtsying to *her*. She was a 'lady of quality'. A 'lady of quality'; it used to be defined as a 'member of the nobility'. What do *I* mean by the phrase? Let me think of all the women I have known whom I have instinctively thought of as 'my betters', to whom I have often found myself making an invisible obeisance. Everyone of them has a vastly different personality from all the others – each one is for me 'a lady of quality': Rosina Filippi; Bridget Guinness; Mrs. Brooke (Rupert's mother); Lynn Fontanne; Sybil Thorndike; Mrs. Patrick Campbell; Lady Diana Cooper; Enid Bagnold; Margot Fonteyn. All of them women of character. They all had or have in varying degrees warmth and wit and widsom, kindness and generosity and, being human, the occasional 'défauts de leurs qualités': arrogance, egotism, shyness, irascibility, eccentricity, the imperfections that give spice to the dullness of perfection. Yet there are people who appear to have all these qualities without having that curious quality which compels respect as well as affection.

Perhaps it is simply that in all of them one senses a real *person* behind or underneath the personality, 'the persona'. There is a solid core, a virtue, I don't mean in the ethical sense but in a practical sense – the sense in which the Greeks spoke of a sword having *virtue*, a 'nobleness' in the practical sense again, as one speaks of a building or a tree being *noble*. I think most of the ladies, indeed all of the ladies, on my little list would laugh at me if I called them 'noble women'. But to me they are – and so I'm back where I started. A lady of quality *is* a noblewoman.

As all summers must, the Halcyon summer came to an end. I began to be restless, I had had nearly two months off, a longer period than I had had for years. I had found a place to live in London. Miss Elizabeth, whose surname I am ashamed to say I have forgotten, was P.P.S. to a member of the Cabinet, and she had a dear little house in Pelham Street, of which she rented me the upper half: bedroom, sitting-room and bath – I shared her kitchen. She was out all day, I was out all evening. We never got in each other's way and she was more like a kind hostess than a landlady.

But I confess I had enormously enjoyed the luxury of Sunninghill Park. To have one's tea brought to one's bed by a smiling housemaid, early in the morning, so that one could awake from sleep (something I have never been able to do without hot tea or coffee) without having to go down to breakfast. To have two delicious meals a day without having to think about them, to shop for them or cook them for oneself. To find, oh beloved luxury, one's bed turned down for the night and a dress for dinner laid out, beautifully pressed and with the right shoes, how I enjoyed it all – and how at times I decided I really did understand why people 'married for money'!

I wondered if ever again I would meet so many stimulating, and intelligent and beautiful people as I had met at Bridget's famous Sunday lunches. But once in London there was no time for repining – I was all wrapped up in Jessica.

Life 'alone in London' was a wonderful blend of work and fun. London seemed so relaxed after New York. No hectic 'What do we do tonight? Where are we going tomorrow?'

Two or three nights a week I went dancing, with some of the young men I had met at Sunninghill. I don't suppose I should ever have been considered a good dancer had I been young today. From visits to discotheques, I have gathered that you have to be really inventive and practically a ballerina. But in those days, being by temperament a follower rather than a leader, I was in my element. 'Gee! I could dance with you all night! You follow like a bull moose,' said an American beau one night. I didn't know what a bull moose was, but I knew I had received an accolade. With dances like the Charleston and the Quick-Step you had to follow your partner's lead, almost anticipate it, or you'd both miss a beat and, as for a Tango, that was very tricky indeed.

However, as time went on I became less and less inclined to go out. Rehearsals were so fascinating that nothing else interested me. I was wrapped up in Jessica, from her first passionate outburst: 'My father's house is hell', to her last strange line: 'I am never merry when I hear sweet music.' I watched Moscowitch intently, partly because he was such a tremendous actor, partly because I wanted to make my Jessica, every inch of her, Shylock's daughter. I have always been fascinated by the strange mixture of arrogance and humility that is the birthright of the Jew, even from the beginning of time, when he walked *not* free in his own land, bound by the strict Laws of his terrifying Jehovah. I wanted to make Jessica *look* as like Shylock's daughter as possible, from the glossy black ringlets that escaped from his turban, to the gorgeous oriental colouring of his raiment. When she cries: 'Alack! What heinous sin is it in me to be ashamed to be my father's child', that sense of sin comes from the very depths of her consciousness. And when she confesses her shyness at the thought of her lover seeing her in boy's clothes: 'I'm glad 'tis night, you do not look on me; for I am much ashamed at my exchange', it is not, as it might be coming from a Gentile maiden, a pretty *minauderie* but the genuine modesty of a strictly brought up Jewish girl. Bernard Shaw wrote in one of his Prefaces: 'The "modesty" of a British Miss is often due to a lack of passion; in an Irish or Jewish girl it may be more often an excess of passion.' There was some splendid casting – Miles Malleson as Lancelot Gobbo did truly, as some of the critics said, 'make history'. Lancelot Gobbo has for long been regarded as one of Shakespeare's most tiresome clowns and the most unfunny. For the first time in dramatic history, 'young Gobbo' almost stole the play from Shylock – Miles Malleson kept the audience in such roars of laughter that they began to applaud his entrances as well as his exits. What a help he was to Jessica! Teaching her the 'merry word games' that his masters were so addicted to themselves. There were some bad mistakes in the production: Portia was sadly miscast; heavy-handed, ponderous, with 'no music in her soul'; Edith Evans equally miscast as Nerissa. It wasn't that the part was too much for her – she was too much for the part! Years later, when I read a review of Sarcey's, condemning one of his favourite stars of the Comédie Française: 'I cannot say that Madame Plessy is indifferent in her role. With her intelligence, her natural gifts, her great position, her immense authority over the public, she cannot be indifferent in anything. She is, therefore, not indifferently bad. She is *bad* to a point that cannot be expressed'. I remembered Edith as Nerissa! She and I shared a dressing-room at the Court Theatre, where we gave tea-parties in the intervals on matinée days, to which we sometimes (strictly against the rules) invited friends who were 'in front'. Nigel Playfair was there one afternoon. While we were engaging in shop talk, Edith said, 'If I am not a star by the time I am forty, I shall give up the stage and try something else.' When her call came and she left the room, Nigel sighed, 'Star? Star! Poor girl, poor girl, what a hope!' Within a year he had to eat his words.

There was a Sunday night Phoenix Society's production of *Venice Preserved*. I played Belvidera, one of the famous tragic roles of the Siddons era. Without hoping to emulate Mrs.

Siddons, I thought I was going to be rather good, but from the moment of Edith's entrance, Belvidera was completely eclipsed. As Aquiline the Courtesan, she swept everything before her with a kind of insolent splendour that left the audience gasping. She became a star overnight. What good days they were in the 1920s, when young actresses could play in a commercial success and earn their steady bread and butter, while, thanks to the Phoenix Society and the Stage Society, they could play Sunday nights and Monday matinées and stretch themselves in the great classic roles: *The Duchess of Malfi, Marriage à la mode, The Faithful Shepherdess, Venice Preserved*. I played them all, some well, some ill, within the space of two years.

One could never go away for weekends, so on Sundays there was time to see friends, a lunch party with Bridget at Carlton House Terrace, a lazy day at the Mainwarings. Generis was usually away hunting so I could browse in Harry's library and discover Walpole and wondered how I had lived without him for so long, look at some of Harry's treasured letters: one, fading and yellowing behind its glass frame, from Charles II in exile, begging his good friend, Philip Mainwaring, to lend him in his dire need £100, promising a reward and recompense 'should I regain my rightful place'. Charles had kept his word, Philip was given a Baronetcy and a gift of land in Cheshire. 'Baronetcies cost a bit more today,' said Harry, 'but think what it would have been if only old Philip had been one of his bastards. I might be rich and a Duke.' Poor Harry, he was the last of his line and as he had no son to inherit, the title fell into abeyance. I wasn't in love with him, but I sometimes wished that Generis would leave him for a Master of Hounds and let me marry him and have a son! I longed to be married, to have children, but no one ever asked me, or if they did I didn't like them.

I was also kept busy flat-hunting for my mother. She had written to say that my sister, Anna, was not really deriving any benefit from the Pasadena climate and felt homesick, so they had decided to return to London. Mamma hoped I could find a flat with three bedrooms somewhere in the Earl's Court neighbourhood where she had friends. My heart sank – she seemed to take it for granted that I would want to live *en famille* when they came back. I thought Earl's Court a horrible neighbourhood, Tregunter Road and Trebovir Road have since become better known as have Blomfield Road, and Maida Vale, which has now become 'Little Venice'. Fifty years ago, they were dreary 'outposts of civilisation' as Arnold Bennett called them. However, I finally found a *two*-bedroomed flat in Trebovir Road and wrote to Mamma that it would be just right for her and Anna, and that I would be happy to stay on in Pelham Street. 'You see it's so convenient I can *walk* to the Theatre.'

During the early weeks of *The Merchant of Venice*, I seemed to be always having my photograph taken. One sitting had an odd sequel. I was wandering about the studio and happened to pick up a stuffed bird that was lying among the photographer's props. 'You look more like Juliet than Jessica at the moment,' said the photographer and added idly, 'I would I were thy bird'. 'Sweet so would I,' I replied promptly. 'Yet I should kill thee with much cherishing.' I looked tenderly at the bird and he called, 'Hey, that's a good pose. Hold it,' and so it was taken. Eddie Marsh liked the picture and I gave him a copy. A few years later, he asked if he might lend it to some young Canadian who was writing a biography of Rupert Brooke and also give him some of the letters which had already been published, after which I forgot about it. Many years later, when I was in America, I was sent a rather sickly sentimental book about Rupert called *Red Wine of Youth*. In it was the photograph of Jessica with the caption:
'This, Rupert's favourite photograph of Cathleen, was carried by him to the Mediterranean and was found after his death off Skyros among his effects. It was sent with his other possessions back to England.'

A number of young Rupert Brooke fans cut the picture from the book and sent it to me begging me to autograph it. I did so and sent them back, adding a friendly warning. 'This caption is not true – the photograph was taken *after* Brooke's death.' One irate gentleman was annoyed. He even took the trouble to buy another copy of the book and sent me another picture. 'Please just autograph it. What do you mean *"not true"*? If you turn to page 262 you will find absolute verification.'

On page 262 I found an equally apocryphal paragraph.
'Dennis and "OC" had the sad task of gathering up their comrade's belongings . . . his treasured photograph of Cathleen, her black gloved hands [*sic*] holding a dove, and an equally

treasured bundle of her letters had to be assembled and despatched to Eddie.'

Since then I am never surprised – when I see historians arguing among themselves in print about the 'authenticity' of someone's account of something that has happened centuries ago – to notice that the gentleman who says, 'I realise that this account was written fifty years after the incident, but the *details* are so *meticulous*, it must be correct,' always thinks he has clinched the argument. I am no longer surprised when I find that stories about myself or about people I know well are accepted as truth once they have appeared in print, even if they have no foundation in fact whatsoever.

Quite a number of people wanted to paint Jessica, her clothes were splendidly colourful. I say Jessica rather than me because several people, Wilfred de Glehn among them, got such a firm picture of *her* in their minds that they couldn't quite reconcile it with *my* face! I seemed to be having an inordinate number of sittings, he wanted to send it to the Royal Academy, but suddenly had to go to France, and I don't know whether he ever finished it.

My great joy after sittings was to hide myself behind some great red plush curtains on the halfway landing down from the studio to peek at the next sitter – who came for her portrait the same days as I did. It was Karsavina the great Russian ballerina. I had only worshipped her from afar from the pit of a theatre. It was thrilling to see her so close, especially as she sometimes paused for a moment on the landing and threw her head back and closed her eyes. How they seemed to blaze when she opened them.

Years afterwards I told Lynn Fontanne this story while I was looking at her portrait by De Glehn. 'I'll tell you something,' said Lynn, '*I* used to hide behind those very red plush curtains to peek at *you* going up to your sittings.'

'*Me?*' I gasped. 'If I'd only known.'

'Oh!' said Lynn, 'you were a real live actress by then, I was still only an ugly duckling *aspiring* to the stage.'

By this time Lynn was a great star, to me the brightest star in the firmament. I felt like poor Sir Andrew Aguecheek 'et ego in Arcadia' . . . to think that once *I* had seemed romantic to *her*.

ELEVEN

Antony and Cleopatra
1920

～～～～～～～～～～～～～～～～～～～～～～～～～～～～～～～～～～

As the run of *The Merchant of Venice* was coming to an end, I
was looking forward to having more time to finish the flat in
Trebovir Road and everything ready for welcoming my mother
and sister. Mamma had written to tell me that they were staying
at Staten Island for a week on the way home as Anna had been
tired by the journey from California. Then came a cable from
my friend Russell Loines with whom they had been staying.
Anna had died suddenly and Mamma was sailing home alone
on the S.S. *Cedric*.

I was heart-broken for my poor mother. It had been a shattering loss for her when Hugo was killed. I think he had been her
best beloved because he had always been 'the delicate one' of her
children. But now she had transferred all her affection to Anna
when Anna became 'the delicate one'.

Of course there was no question of my not living with her in
Trebovir Road. And I lived there till I married; my father was
in India, bridge-building, and indeed did not return till after my
marriage. I think I was on better terms with Mamma than I had
ever been, I had always sensed the incompatibility between
them, and had always been instinctively on his side. Mamma,
too, had mellowed and even her attitude to 'sex' had softened. I
had started rehearsing a new play, *The Grain of Mustard Seed*, by
H. M. Harwood, and I rather feared that Mamma would be
shocked by the part I was playing and the very passionate love
scene that I had to play with Jack Hobbs. As a matter of fact it
shocked some of the critics as being rather 'violent'. I remember

one paper remarked that 'at one point Mr. Hobbs seemed about to remove Miss Nesbitt's dress, it went so high above her knees.' But that was before very short dresses came into fashion and to see a lady's knees was still 'suggestive'. It was before the days of *Oh! Calcutta!* I imagine that in a play produced today the actors in that scene might well have been asked if they had any objection to playing it in the nude.

The effect it had reinforced my firm belief that 'suggestion' is infinitely more exciting than 'representation' in the theatre whether it be sex or violence. I remember seeing Tallulah Bankhead and Glen Anders playing a love scene in *They Knew What They Wanted*. She was sitting near the footlights, dressed in a kind of frilly peasant skirt and a long-sleeved high-necked blouse. He came from outdoors and stood in the doorway for a moment. He walked slowly towards her and she lifted her head and looked straight in front of her. They generated between them so much intensity of passion that when he finally put his hands on her shoulders and a little shiver went through her, the entire audience shivered too as the curtain went down. A man sitting behind me in the stalls said to his companion, 'That curtain went down just in time, or we *would* have seen something!'

Neither Jack Hobbs nor I were in the least in love with each other but we had what Ellen Terry used to call 'les paumes sympathiques'. 'You can tell if you could have an affair with a man when you clasp his hand, palm to palm, a holy palmer's kiss! There is a sympathy of the skin . . . You may never meet the man again but if you do meet him again and have to play a love scene . . . it works!' It apparently worked very well with Jack and myself. What the audience thought they were seeing you may gather from a contemporary caricature done by the artist E. Kapp, who at that time – some fifty years ago – was earning his living by doing caricatures for the *Sketch*. I'm sure I would have remembered it if Jack had really clutched at my behind in the way it appears in the cartoon, but obviously that was the impression given to the audience.

But what I started out to say was that I'm sure Mamma would have been shocked if we'd really been *doing* something shocking! Or perhaps she was just thrilled by the whole evening not least by being taken out to supper by Ned Latham (the

Earl of Latham). He had invited me to Ciro's and as he had
the most enchanting manners, good manners born of a good
heart, he had insisted on Mamma's coming too. I'm afraid
Mamma had daydreams about my ultimately becoming Lady
Latham. She was still so innocent about many of the facts of
life that I couldn't set about explaining to her that Ned was
practically married already to a devoted boy friend who lived
with him.

I renewed acquaintance with Somerset Maugham during the
run of the play. He was a friend of Harwood and loved to tease
him: 'You know, Tottie, you think you have written the most
brilliant political comedy of the day, and pride yourself on keeping the audience quiet with all that "talky talk". But what really
draws them in is that illicit passion in Act II.'

I first met Maugham in New York when he had come out with
Syrie Wellcome to decide whether they should get married or
not. Syrie was staying with a friend of mine who rang me up one
morning saying, 'Well they have decided! it happens this week,
they are going to Atlantic City for the honeymoon! There is a
doomed entanglement if ever there was one.'

I thought they looked very contented with each other when
they returned to New York; and he seemed quite enchanted
when I told him about the Marquis de Polignac walking very
slowly round a dinner table, where all the ladies were extremely
décolleté, and finally taking his place beside Syrie saying, 'I
have come to the conclusion that Syrie Wellcome's back is the
most beautiful back, not only in this room but in the world,'
whereupon everyone got up and solemnly inspected Syrie's back
which indeed did stand up to inspection. It was quite exquisite:
satin smooth and pearl white.

When I had come back to London, I had stayed with them for
a week in their house in Dorset Square and I confess I was rather
astonished by the courtesy with which he accepted the constant
change of surroundings!

Syrie was starting her decorating business, and for a time
used her own house as a show place for precious pieces which
were always being snapped up and removed by eager clients.

One night when he came down to dinner, he found that his
sacred writing desk was gone from his study, and all his papers
and manuscripts laid out on a table. I say sacred as I imagine a

professional writer's desk must really become a 'Holy of Holies'. When Syrie said cheerfully, 'There's a magnificent new desk coming tomorrow, darling,' I almost expected him to knock her down but he merely said, 'I see,' with a tight face and closed the door.

I sometimes wonder whether the continual 'battering down' of the normal rages and resentments and 'psychic wounds' that any hypersensitive man is prone to had not etched the haggard tortured mask of his old age.

He was a very sensitive man and had a great deal of sympathy. I shall never forget how once several years later, and at a time when I had quite lost touch with him, he came to the opening night of a play called *This Marriage* in which I was appearing. It was soon, rather too soon, after the birth of my son and I was more nervous than usual. I actually 'dried up' completely during Act I. I sat 'bouche bée' helpless and had to be prompted loudly by the stage manager. It had never happened to me on stage before, and on a first night! I gathered myself together and got through the rest of the play giving a very uncertain performance. I rushed back to my dressing-room longing to be at home to cry myself to sleep. To my astonishment Mr. Maugham was standing there, he who never came back-stage. 'I came through the pass door', he said, 'to catch you before the crowd arrives. I came to congratulate you on your performance,' and seeing the tears in my eyes he added, 'that little fluff in the first act didn't matter a damn. You soared above it and gave a very moving performance.'

I knew that he could not really mean it but his stammer made it sound absolutely sincere and I went home relieved. If he had been preceded by all the kind friends who had come round to reassure me that I shouldn't worry too much about that dry up: 'It was really quite amusing, darling, to hear the stage manager reading your line', I really *would* have cried myself to sleep and had a trauma about it for the rest of the run.

Incidentally it was to my baby son that I owed the privilege of having the star dressing-room for myself. Tallulah Bankhead and I were co-starring in the play and the stage manager was rather perturbed as to who should have the star room. I said that Tallulah as a 'visitor' to London should have it. Tallulah with equal politeness insisted that I, as a resident, had every right to it. In the meantime at rehearsals it was used as a green room by the company, and by me, when the luncheon break came, as a retiring room to feed my baby. One day Tallulah decided not to go out to lunch and when Nanny brought Mark down for his 1 o'clock feed, she was absolutely fascinated. She had never seen a baby breast-fed before.

When Nanny had picked him up replenished and gurgling and he had departed, 'What happens when the play opens?' asked Tallulah. 'Oh, I'll have lots of time to do it at home even on matinée days. And I've worked out that the last interval does not come till 10 o'clock and I have ten more minutes before my entrance so Nanny will bring him down every night.' 'That settles it!' said Tallulah, 'I will not have that lovely baby going upstairs. This is *your* room. No arguments.'

I don't think it occurred to her that it was Nanny's feet and not the baby's that would have to negotiate the stairs.

She tells the story in her autobiography *Tallulah*.* 'In *This Marriage* I was the seductress and Herbert Marshall was my prey. I was trying to steal him from Cathleen Nesbitt. . . . Cathleen had just had a baby and I insisted that she have the star dressing-room. My motive in giving it up was not as noble as you might guess. I was fascinated by babies and on matinée days when I was off stage I spent most of the time in Cathleen's dressing-room anyway playing with her youngster. The baby was infinitely more amusing than anything we said or did on stage.'

It was in 1920 while *The Grain of Mustard Seed* was still running that I had begun to make friends of my own age. While I had been in New York all my real friends – I don't count dancing partners or lovers – had been male or female, older than myself. And even in London during the first year I was only really intimate with Bridget Guinness. Elizabeth Pollock was my first friend and she introduced me to all hers: Joan Capel, Violet Campbell, Moyra Goff. I felt a little shy with them all at first. They were all richer than me, and lived in fine houses to which I thought it an honour to be invited. I discovered later that they all thought it rather grand to be invited to tea in my dressing-room as I was a leading lady in the theatre. Betty Pollock was on the stage, too, and shared a dressing-room with Violet (always known as Bunny). Joan's mother Lady Essex gave wonderful

* Tallulah Bankhead, *Tallulah: my Autobiography*, Gollancz, 1952.

parties in South Audley Street, where Joan and Betty introduced me to the really exciting stage stars like Gladys Cooper and Gertrude Lawrence and Gerald du Maurier and delightful young men like 'Cys' Asquith and Ned Latham. Ned Latham was mad about the theatre and he ultimately died almost penniless having poured all his wealth into backing plays, always losing on a disaster more than he had made on a success. He was a beautiful dancer and took me often to Ciro's or the Embassy. And 'Cys' introduced me to another world – the Downing Street and political set.

Betty was regularly in demand as a 'curtain raiser'. It was becoming more and more difficult to find good one-act plays or good actors willing to act in them. But Betty's brilliant imitation of all the most fashionable stage stars drew all the most fashionable audiences to be punctually seated at curtain time rather than half an hour later. Betty's father, Sir Adrian Pollock, an imposing handsome gentleman who reminded me of Lord Ribblesdale, always allowed Betty to invite her actor friends to Sunday lunch at their house in the Boltons, and in the summer for weekends in their country house.

I remember Lady Pollock confiding to me that she was sometimes a little perturbed at the thought of what Betty might produce! To my great delight Gladys Cooper came to lunch that day and Sir Adrian fell for her 'hook, line and sinker' as he declared. To be as beautiful as she was, and yet be so forthright and natural and running over with abounding vitality seemed to be almost too good to be true. I remember her holding out both hands to Sir Adrian and asking 'Is that as you like it, Sir?' and him bowing over them, kissing both hands and saying: 'Refreshing! Refreshing!' Betty explained that the last time she had lunched, Sir Adrian had been holding forth on the 'horrible fashion of blood-red lacquered long finger-nails . . . that made all females look like harpies,' and Gladys for fun had removed every spot of colour from hers this Sunday. Betty told me once that she had been just a little nervous about inviting a rather odd young man called Noël Coward down for the weekend. 'I was rather afraid Daddy would think he was a bit bumptious, but my dear, he was so much Daddy's cup of tea that no one else got a look in. Daddy didn't even have his sacrosanct six games of Sunday tennis. He was so fascinated by Noël's conversation.'

It was just about then that I met Noël for the first time. He had sent a play called *The Rat Trap* to 'Tottie' Harwood, who had given it to me to read. I remember I'd admitted to Tottie that there was a part I'd like to play in it, but I had to admit I didn't think it a very good play. Tottie replied, 'Neither do I, but I do think he has a great talent.' I said I'd be thrilled to meet him and Tottie said I might take the script back to him to Ebury Street. I can't remember exactly what I said to him, or more important, what he said to me, but I was immensely impressed by and envious of his studio, which was a huge room at the top of the house, and vowing to myself that I would turn my bedroom at Trebovir Road into a bed-sitter where I could entertain my own friends. What a snob I was in those days, longing for a 'good address'. I don't suppose Ebury Street where Noël lived was really much more chic than Earls Court in those days, but it seemed so to me! And when I started to decorate my room and change my bed for a divan, I remember saying to myself rather dismally, 'Who would come out to *Earls Court* to see me!'

The Grain of Mustard Seed ran for eight months, a most unusual success for anything then, except for a review or a musical.

Then I went into a charming little comedy called *The Romantic Age*. At least I had thought it a charming little comedy at first, and welcomed a romantic heroine as a change from a hard-boiled one; but I soon began to feel as Julie Andrews once said to me about certain scenes in *The Sound of Music*, 'I feel as if I were pushing a load of treacle up a hill.'

How I welcomed a Mr. Charles Morgan who came to see me at the theatre, about coming to Oxford to play with the O.U.D.S. Mr. Morgan, President of the O.U.D.S. (and later dramatic critic of *The Times*) asked if I would like to play Cleopatra in the O.U.D.S. production of *Antony and Cleopatra*. In my career I can only remember one other time when I felt so absolutely dizzy with delight at the idea of playing a part. The other time was when I was asked to play in Enid Bagnold's *The Chalk Garden*.

The O.U.D.S., the Oxford University Dramatic Society, was a very famous club indeed – it still is, but no longer offers such splendid opportunities to professional actresses. In those days

Oxford undergraduettes were not allowed to act with the O.U.D.S. In fact I don't think they were allowed to act at all, and certainly not allowed to invite the undergraduates to their colleges even for a cup of tea.

What a change when I went to visit my daughter at Oxford some twenty-odd years later, to find a cocktail party going on in her bed-sitter, with Ken Tynan, Sandy Wilson, Frank Hauser *et al.*, eagerly discussing rehearsal dates for plays they were putting on.

I knew I was too young to play Cleopatra and that I hadn't really enough 'temperament', but I had treasured for a long time Edward Shanks's notice of me as Jessica saying that I should be playing Cleopatra, and naturally I wanted to see if I could!

The O.U.D.S. cast was unusually good. I had been a little uneasy at the thought of what it would be like to play with 'boys' and amateurs at that. But I had forgotten that this was a much older generation than usual, who had come to the University after five years of war which had given them unusual maturity and authority. Some of them had even commanded regiments and most of them at least a battalion.

'Captain' Cecil Ramage (M.C., Order of the Nile, etc.) who played Antony was, I honestly think, more impressive in his role than I was as Cleopatra: he was very handsome, very tall, 6ft. 3 in., graceful in his movements and had both a 'rich' voice and a natural instinct for phrasing. Before the run had ended he had been approached by several London managers with offers of stage jobs. But he wanted to pursue law and became a barrister with political ambitions.

The same year that he played Antony he became President of the Union, Oxford's famous debating society.

Not all Presidents of the Union become Prime Ministers but most Prime Ministers have been Presidents of the Union – if they have been Oxford men at all.

From the first rehearsal we had been aware of what Ellen Terry called the 'sympathy of the skin'.

We played well together as lovers on the stage. Off-stage I don't think we had even met alone. On the last night there was a farewell party and we danced together continually. I think we would have been dancing 'cheek to cheek' as the popular song has it, but he was so tall that I could not reach up so far. During the last dance he kissed the top of my head and said: 'Will you marry me?' and I answered: 'Yes. Oh! *yes!*'

Next morning when we met at The Randolph for lunch he asked: 'Did you say you would marry me? Or was it a midsummer night's dream?' I, too, had begun to wonder if it was a dream, but now it was morning, and a dream come true.

In a 'profile' that Sir Cecil Beaton wrote of me for *Vogue* a year or two ago, he said of me, 'When she went to Oxford to be Cleopatra for the O.U.D.S. she not only married her good-looking Antony who at that time was President of the Union but she created a legend. Lord Avon, Lord David Cecil and George Ryland still consider her the best Serpent of the Nile they ever saw'.

I was very moved to read that. It confirmed what I had often felt when men came up to me and said, 'I saw you as Cleopatra,' or 'I was a Roman soldier in the O.U.D.S. production of *Antony and Cleopatra*,' and they told me what a tremendously romantic evening it had been. I had always thought, 'What a wonderful play to see after five years of war!' Whoever played it would spell romance. I am sure that many of the people who came to see it had had very little chance to see any Shakespearian plays, and having gone away as boys and come back men, to see such a splendid tumultuous saga of love and war must have been thrilling and the fact that the Antony and Cleopatra were obviously powerfully drawn to one another must have added an extra colour! I say obviously, because, as I found out later, everybody seemed to have known it before we did ourselves.

We wanted to keep our secret to ourselves as people do when 'new in love' but some daily tabloid came out with pictures and headlines 'Cathleen Nesbitt and Cecil Ramage to wed', 'Cleopatra to marry her Antony'. Such consternation it aroused in our respective families! We started by denying it; Mamma, suspicious, I suppose, because of my secrecy about it, asked all the questions I had never asked myself, 'Who is he? Has he any money? A barrister? Going to be one? But they can barely support themselves for years I believe.' His parents were aghast. 'An *actress*! What are you going to live on? You haven't even a profession yet.' They had lost most of their money in a family business crisis, and could only just afford to make him a small allowance.

Even Bridget Guinness joined in the chorus: 'Darling don't *rush* into matrimony. Do just become engaged for at least a year. Why you haven't even met his people yet.'

Finally I made a trip to Edinburgh where his people lived; and he came and talked to Mamma. And I said to Bridget, 'I know you think we are behaving like impatient children, but I am thirty-two. I want to have children. I am older than he is. . . . Oh! I can't wait for ever. Why waste years that could be beautiful?'

So with somewhat grudging approval from everyone a 'marriage is announced' notice was sent out to *The Times*.

I used to subscribe to a press-cutting agency in those days and sent all the clippings to my father in India. I was amused to see, when a couple of years later he brought them all home pasted into a large book, that there were more little paragraphs beginning, 'The formal announcement of the betrothal of Mr. Cecil Ramage to Miss Cathleen Nesbitt disposes of denial that followed *our original statement* etc. etc.' or 'The engagement of Miss Cathleen Nesbitt to Mr. C. B. Ramage, President of the Oxford Union Society, *although denied when we announced it* last March', etc. than there had ever been reviews of my acting in any play.

The *Western Mail* and the *Anglesea Record* chatted about my Welsh ancestry, the *Belfast Telegraph* and half a dozen Ulster papers talked of my Irish origins, the *Glasgow Herald* about Cecil's Scottish descent. I was even greeted, when I went to spend a weekend at Ned Latham's house, Blythe, in Lancashire, with a bundle of papers from a little Lancashire weekly with a photograph of Antony and Cleopatra embracing. Mrs. Patrick Campbell and I went to Leeds on the same train and Ned met us at the station with copies of the paper. Stella was in one of her 'mischief' moods that weekend. 'I've met Cathleen's young man,' she said, 'I don't approve of him.'

'Why?'

'Because he does not approve of me! He sees through me!' And she took the papers and threw them out of the car window.

In the hall when we arrived there was a great corner cupboard with shelves of wonderful scent bottles. We were invited to try them all and choose our favourite perfume. After tea we found toilet water and soap and bath essence to match the scent laid out in our bathrooms. I was enchanted. Stella said sternly: 'All this vulgar luxury. I'm surprised you indulge in it. But your father was only the *second* Earl wasn't he? Where did your grandfather make his money, I wonder?'

'It's so ostentatious all this out of season food' she remarked while enjoying a second helping of everything. But after dinner she gazed at the Sargent picture of the *Ladies Pleydel-Bouverie* and suddenly turned to Ned: 'Darling Ned, what a bitch I've been all evening, you know what it is of course? Sheer envy. I envy you your riches, I envy you your title and most of all your Pleydel-Bouverie Blood,' with such comic emphasis that we all laughed and then she set herself to 'amuse'. She had a talent to amuse that was very endearing, when she was in the mood.

When I was in bed she suddenly appeared at the door, 'I smell so heavenly with Ned's heavenly perfume. I must have someone sniff at me. Now tell me, aren't you beginning to regret marrying into no money, don't you want a little luxury?'

'Shall I tell you why I'm going to marry Cecil?' I said, not quite truthfully, 'because he is the first person without any encumbrances in the shape of another wife, or *something* in the way of a "let or hindrance" who has ever asked me. And as for money, I have just signed a three-play contract with Norman McKinnel. We can live very comfortably on that till he makes a fortune.'

Stella was off at a tangent at once, 'Norman McKinnel, that great heavy man who played in *The Grain of Mustard Seed*? My dear he'll crush you; and I hope you saw the plays before you signed the contract! You may think he is a good actor but I assure you he has no *judgement*. He wouldn't know a good play if he saw one – and as for *three*! . . .'

Stella was right as usual. She was as shrewd about the making of money as she was reckless about spending it. I didn't have a contract, just a sort of gentleman's agreement with Norman McKinnel to co-star in three plays with him. I felt quite happy about the first one, *The Love Thief*. I had seen it in New York with John and Lionel Barrymore playing two brothers. Set in Renaissance Italy with romantic scenery and the heroine 'dressed by Botticelli' with long fair hair and flowing robes, it had been a great success. The plot of the play concerned an Italian nobleman going off to the wars – and his younger brother slipping into the nobleman's bed pretending to be his brother.

The first-act curtain fell on the young brother watching the door through which the lady had gone to her bed and moving towards the door as soon as the light was extinguished.

The second act rose on the lady coming from her bedroom exuding contentment like the cat that has swallowed the cream and suddenly freezing in horror as she sees her true wedded lord coming through the great outer door clad in all his armour; when she looked back in anguished amazement to her own bedroom the audience as well as the lady gasped when the younger brother emerged slim and elegant in tights and tunic. I forget what ensued and who killed whom, but the audience in New York had loved it. However, from the first rehearsal I knew that we were doomed – McKinnel himself, 'that great big burly man', was playing the elder brother. In a moment of wild aberration he had cast Ernest Thesiger as the handsome honey-voiced young Don Juan. Ernest to put it mildly was not handsome, he was quite painfully thin (the costume of the period demanded better legs), he also had rather a thin voice – and no one could possibly imagine him in anyone's bed, except perhaps that of a very good looking young man. On the opening night when he crept towards the door in the half light almost invisible behind his great hat and flowing cape, I imagine that the audience, not knowing the plot, must have thought he was going to assassinate the lady. After the intermission the lady floated out, obviously enjoying the aftermath of an enchanted evening, Norman entered, looking larger than life in his heavy suit of mail, and promptly out of the bedroom came Ernest, in scarlet wig and tights, looking perilously like a favourite actress of the time, Violet Vanbrough. There was a moment of silent stupefaction from the audience until a giggling voice came from the gallery: 'Lor! how *could* she?'

The laughter that followed from the whole house was long and loud. The play did *not* survive!

TWELVE

The Married Woman
1922

∿∿∿∿∿∿∿∿∿∿∿∿∿∿∿∿∿∿∿∿∿∿∿∿

Once the banns were called I began to feel a little nervous. Was it all 'too rash, too ill advised, too sudden'? Oh! dear! Could I never make an important decision without unleashing an immediate state of internal warfare between 'Kate the Careful' and 'Kate the Cautious'?

But there were some lovely letters that warmed and comforted me. One from Mrs. Brooke wished me great happiness and said she would like to be godmother to my first child. And one from Barrie saying he didn't go to weddings but wished me well. I wrote to thank him for his wedding present, and said that Mrs. Brooke didn't want to go to the gathering afterwards, but was coming down from Rugby, just to come to the church. He at once decided he would meet her at the station and take her back to her train after the ceremony. I was very proud to see them there.

Just to take me down a peg, George Moore wrote me a very grudging letter. 'I don't wish you anything but good of course, but in case you should consider inviting me to the wedding, I shall most certainly refuse. I agree with G.B.S. it's a barbaric ceremony. For a moment I really thought you were going to marry an actor, and then read in another journal that he is destined for politics! That is even worse. Come to luncheon and talk it over.'

I had met George Moore a year or two before when he had asked me to come and talk to him about playing the heroine of his play, *The Coming of Gabrielle*, which had Nigel Playfair as producer. All the young women of my generation regarded George Moore as a genius and his famous novel *Esther Waters* as one of the world's great books. I found him repellent to look at, but extremely entertaining to talk to. 'Do you like to have long speeches in a role you play?' he asked. 'The longer the better', I replied, 'if they are really about something. I just like the sound of words.' 'I too; I am so tired of these modern realistic dramas. I recently saw a play of Galsworthy in which the characters were so strangled by their own emotions that they played the whole scene in monosyllables, less articulate than parrots.'

Then he gradually turned the conversation to love, his favourite topic. He never during the course of any conversation attempted to 'make a pass at me' but how he loved to talk about other people's love affairs, with surreptitious hints about his own. When he asked how many 'serious affairs' I had had, I could not resist murmuring with a complacent smile, 'I'm afraid I've lost count,' and shifted the conversation back to the play. In later weeks I had to draw heavily on my imagination to keep up the myth that I was a *grande amoureuse*!

We duly started rehearsals at the Little Theatre. The play did not quite work. Mr. Davenport, the hero, an elderly novelist whose 'great work of genius, *Elizabeth Cooper*' had been read by the whole female population of Europe, was obviously based on George Moore himself. This gentleman suddenly bored at the prospect of attending a great festival in Vienna celebrating a production of a play he had written based on a famous book, sent his handsome secretary to impersonate him. There was a lot of complicated plot with the secretary finally marrying the Lady Gabrielle, Countess Von Hoenstadt.

One morning we were startled during rehearsals by a voice of thunder from the stalls: 'Stop it! Stop this travesty,' and on to the stage bounced Mr. Moore, who had looked in by chance. He had not been consulted about the cast and did not like what he saw. He threatened to withdraw the play at once if all the male members of the cast were not fired immediately. Playfair, furious, said it was quite impossible, they all had contracts, and offered to resign himself. And we actors crept away quietly and left them to it. The next morning I received a letter from Mr. Moore.

121 Ebury Street

Dear Miss Nesbitt,

I hope you didn't think me too rude in my opposition, but I am sure you didn't for you must know that you could not struggle through the scenes with that 'mute at the funeral' young man constantly out of key, and to escape the spectacle of a disheartening struggle, I left the theatre. But there are plenty of young men able to play a secretary whose lightheartedness pierces through his sense of responsibility. Mr. Hannen would not be an ideal Davenport for he lacks force, he is finicky and Davenport is a man who has made his way in literature and to do that requires force, his gait and every gesture should imply force and there are plenty of actors who can do this, and overdo it. Norman McKinnel, for instance.

I hope you will not disappoint me on Monday, but come to luncheon, for the pleasure of seeing you will help me to bear my disappointment and we shall be able to talk over how much I shall have to accept so as to avoid a public scandal. How Playfair could have done it! and what luck that I came down to rehearsals!

Always sincerely yours,
George Moore

I suspect that whoever played the part of Davenport would not have satisfied Moore. Nicholas Hannen was an actor of infinite charm and Norman McKinnel an actor of infinite force. To find an actor who could modify the force with the charm and live up to Mr. Moore's sublimation of himself would not have been easy. In another letter he said that a Mr. Hackett now wanted to do the play.

I have lost confidence in Mr. Playfair. It seems incredible but he does not seem to know anything about a play, how to rehearse it, how to cast it, I shall not forget seeing him in all complacency lecturing to 'Sebastien'! If you are doing nothing tomorrow come to luncheon and between ourselves we'll decide if it would be as well to throw in our lot with Mr. Hackett.

Yours as ever,
George Moore

The play never was produced. I have as a souvenir a very

elegant 'presentation' copy of the play, thickly annotated with many alterations and cuts by the author. I re-read it the other day and thought what fun it would have been to do, especially as Gabrielle, Countess Von Hoenstadt, really had all the best lines in the play. However it did bring me a delightful acquaintance with George Moore with whom for several months I had a regular luncheon date. He had a gourmet cook and beautiful pictures and an insatiable curiosity about one's love life. I confess that I began to think that mine was rather tame by his standards, so I used to invent rather shocking stories about my 'vie amoureuse' in New York. I remember telling him a story about the day that Prohibition finally became law. An enormous number of even sophisticated New Yorkers really believed that a drink of any kind would henceforth be unobtainable. Some had been laying in enormous stores for months but those who hadn't the space or the dollars for such foresight were out on the town saying a 'last farewell to liquor' and seeing how much they could consume. The Ritz Roof was the fashionable resort and I was there with my current boyfriend. 'Which one?' he inquired eagerly. 'The Russian,' I replied quite untruly.

'Ah! They have good heads and stomachs for unlimited liquor.'

'I have neither, so he drank my share. We stayed till 5 a.m.' said I, then I proceeded to recount and indeed it was scarcely an exaggeration, how by 4.30 a.m. practically everyone in the restaurant was on the floor, including the orchestra. The lift was out of order and one had to pick one's way down the staircase which was littered with recumbent bodies.

'Those who had any life left in them were clutching at my ankles,' I said. Actually one very old gentleman had tried to pull me down on top of him! But I couldn't help embroidering a bit, it seemed to give George such vicarious pleasure, especially the finale with Boris and myself locked in a fond embrace in the ladies' cloakroom. The truth had been far different. My 'aviator' and I had had a violent quarrel and he had stormed out, probably catching the last lift while I sat in tears. On normal nights a lady sitting alone in tears at a table on The Ritz Roof would have drawn many disapproving comments. That night no one saw me and I finally picked my way among the bodies on the stairs and walked home to a solitary bed.

After a month or two our weekly luncheons seemed to have 'talked themselves out' and I think Mr. Moore must have been delighted that some business called him to New York. He would have been incapable of telling a lady that she bored him! His manners were impeccable to what he called the Fair Sex. I notice that the presentation copy of *The Coming of Gabrielle* was produced in 1921 in New York by Boni and Liveright, so I suppose he must have returned just in time to see the publicity about my engagement, hence the invitation to talk it over. I did go to lunch with him and he was in one of his 'wise and serious' moods and talked much about the inadvisability of any man of talent devoting his life to politics: 'It's a dog's life, it cannot but corrupt a man and it is a cruel profession. If a man follows a decent trade like a carpenter or a plumber or a decent profession like medicine or law or literature he will only be struck down by natural causes such as illness or death, or by his own negligence or evil-doing. In politics he may rise to the highest position, Prime Minister or Lord Chancellor today and nothing, less than nothing, tomorrow, for no better reason than the idle vote of the idle populace who imagine that a change of government will better their lot.'

I of course do not remember his actual words except certain phrases like 'Nothing, less than nothing' and 'the idle vote of the idle populace', because of the force of his delivery. But I couldn't help thinking of these words when I saw the newspaper pictures of Mr. Heath entering 10 Downing Street in glory and Mr. Wilson retreating bag and baggage from the back.

Mr. Moore spoke very accurately of the proportion of G.O.M.s of literature expiring in a blaze of acclamation compared to the number of G.O.M.s of politics. How he would have disapproved of G.O.M. for 'Grand Old Man'. He had been very disapproving of the young man who had rehearsed in his play saying RADA instead of 'Royal Academy of Dramatic Art'. What would he have made of SEATO and NATO?

I think I started talking about my wedding before Mr. Moore cropped up. I had had to play Elena in *Uncle Vanya* for the Stage Society the week before my wedding and received wonderful notices for the 'magnificent burst of hysteria' with which I brought down the curtain in Act II. I did not deserve them. What looked like a fine performance of Elena by the actress was

155

merely the outpouring of Miss Cathleen Nesbitt's own nervous exhaustion. I doubt if I could ever have recaptured it; but for one performance only it must have been stunning.

When the day came I was almost in tears with fatigue. Mamma was worn out with preparing to 'receive' so many people and a final small infuriating detail, my 'period' which was not due till two weeks later suddenly burst upon me.

Inside the church I felt that baby Zara Mainwaring with her ethereally lovely little face and her aureole of pale golden hair was the cynosure of every eye, and outside the church the little mob of onlookers that always collects for a wedding, was really giving a little cheer for the white Rolls-Royce, lent by a friend. I almost began to wonder whether Cinderella hadn't felt like that at the ball! But as the ceremony went on I regained my sense of proportion. Cinderella had never driven away in a chariot like mine with Prince Charming at her side. And no Prince Charming could ever have 'taken over' the whole party with such charm and gaiety and good humour as Cecil did or have made every-body feel that they were having such a good time.

After a week at St. Margaret's Bay we came back to the little flat we had found and furnished in Great Ormond Street. I had three weeks before starting rehearsals, and life was very gay and 'social'. Betty Pollock and Bunny and Joan all seemed to get married about that time. Bunny had married an actor, Nigel Bruce, and like ourselves had no money. Betty and Joan had both 'married rich'. Betty was the best hostess and the worst housekeeper imaginable. I remember once she had invited two very elderly royal princesses, Princess Helena-Victoria and Princess Marie-Louise, who shared a grace-and-favour house at Kensington Palace. Dinner consisted of canned tomato soup so watered down that it was pale pink and tepid at that, some rather greasy and underdone chops and chips and a leaden apple pie soaked in a rather revolting custard.

But the two old ladies were obviously having such a glorious time meeting Bea Lillie and the music-hall comedian Hughie Green, that everyone had a glorious time too. Betty rang me up the next morning and said 'The dinner was rather filthy wasn't it? But I had cook trouble. She got drunk at lunch-time, and Madge (the parlour maid) and I had to concoct something. I didn't mind for the princesses, they don't really get asked out much except to very dull parties, and they must have eaten so many ghastly official dinners they are used to bad food – but they rang up as soon as they got home and said they had not had such a delightful evening for months.'

We gave little dinner parties ourselves occasionally – but we liked to make the most of the time alone together before I started work again. Great Ormond Street was very convenient for work for both of us, Cecil was in Sir Geoffrey Lawrence's chambers in the Middle Temple, and theatre land was very accessible for me.

At night we would wander round the Bloomsbury squares, and plan which one we would live in when Cecil was Lord Chancellor, or even Prime Minister. We even amused ourselves by deciding on a title to take, when he would be offered an earldom. Lord Ormond we decided would be appropriate, or even a resounding double title, 'Earl of Ormond and Gower'. The world was our oyster, and we savoured it with gusto.

In the meantime the rent had to be paid; and I started rehearsals – *The Love Thief* as Stella had foretold was a resounding flop.

Then I went into a curious melodrama called *The Eye of Shiva* in which I strolled about the stage with a tame leopard on a leash; I can't remember *why* a leopard but one critic wrote that we both 'promenaded with equal grace'. I did not have to suffer it long, for very soon I had a thrilling offer to play in Basil Dean's production of *Hassan* with Henry Ainley and Basil Gill. To be in a verse play by one of my favourite poets, James Flecker, music by Delius, a sumptuous production. I could wish for nothing more and wickedly concealed from the management the fact that I was pregnant!

I somehow managed to persuade myself that 'it wouldn't show' for months. After all, some people 'got away with it' – look at Mrs. Siddons! All those children! and never missed a performance in her life. But, of course, the children helped. She boasted proudly, 'They all managed to be born on Christmas Day or Good Friday,' and of course her costumes were a help; no nonsense for her about dressing Lady Macbeth in twelfth-century hessian, or Cleopatra in Graeco-Roman draperies – she wore her own magnificent ample skirts for every period. She *was* her own period and her ever-adoring audiences asked for no better.

But as Yasmin, I wore flimsy Turkish trousers and a bolero that revealed quite a lot of Yasmin. I *was* quite lucky, though, even at the sixth month I could say to Hassan, 'There are rows and rows of fair young girls in the Caliph's harem but none with a shape like mine,' without acute embarrassment. And I longed to stay till the last possible moment. It was such an exciting colourful production, and the Delius music was haunting, especially the last chorus of the Pilgrim's 'We take the Golden Road to Samarkand'.

Ainley was 'Hassan the Confectioner, rotund, moustache, turban, greasy, grey dress, about forty'. How wonderful it was to suddenly hear from that 'dumb domestic bird', the magical voice of Ainley called his serenade to Yasmin.

> *But when the deep red eye of day*
> *Is level with the lone highway,*
> *And some to Mecca turn to pray,*
> *And I toward thy bed Yasmin.*
> *Shower down thy Love O Burning Bright!*
> *For one night, or the other night*
> *Will come the Gardener in white,*
> *And gathered flowers are dead Yasmin.*

Unfortunately, by the seventh month, although I was willing to go on, there were two tricky moments. One, when Hassan flung me to the ground in rage: 'Oh, thou stupendous harlot! Get thee gone!' and would murmur under his breath, 'For God's sake mind the baby, that child will pop out on the carpet one night moaning Allah! Allah!' and another when Yasmin was lying on the ground semi-conscious, and Masrur, the African slave put his hands under her and carried her aloft up a flight of stairs. I remember the difficulties we had with that 'lift' at rehearsals, we had practically decided that it was impossible to lift a woman from the ground without her 'clinging on', when Basil Dean suddenly had the idea of sending for Anton Dolin from the Sadler's Wells Ballet and begging him to show us the secret of levitation, the balance and breathing on my part, and of using the right muscles on his. But though there never had been a stumble, we both began to feel nervous, so sadly I took my leave.

But there was another excitement to compensate, my husband

had been chosen as Liberal candidate for Newcastle-on-Tyne
and I went up to help canvas for him. Newcastle had been tradi-
tionally a Labour seat and seeing the dreadful poverty, the
unemployment, the deplorable housing situation, I was not
surprised. I felt ashamed to go knocking on doors and saying,
'Please vote Liberal,' knowing that every candidate whether
Liberal, Tory or Labour would make the same empty promises
to 'do something about it', when nothing short of revolutionary
action could do anything. I compromised by just saying, 'I wish
you would vote for my husband because I would like him to
become your Member' and as by that time my condition was
apparent, they would invite me to come in and sit down, and
have a cosy obstetric chat: 'Now when do you expect your
increase, Hinny?' they would inquire. 'Oh, that's none far off,
February, you be careful, this be a hilly town.' A hilly town it
certainly was; San Francisco is the only city I know to equal it
for practically perpendicular streets. The excitement of the
'count' was breathtaking. Now I always think of the waiting
wives when I'm anywhere where an election of any kind is going
on. Everyone had thought of it as a hopeless seat to fight for,
but it turned out a triumph for Cecil as he won by a big majority.
One thing made an enormous impression on me during that time
in Newcastle. Lord Grey and Lloyd George both came down to
a big meeting in the Town Hall to speak for the candidate and
the Liberal Party. Lord Grey gave, to my mind, a very articulate, well-thought-out and documented speech on Liberal
policies and was politely received. Lloyd George gave a great
'performance'. As a piece of sustained oratory, it was superb,
and was received with roars of approval and a standing ovation.
Next morning I read a verbatim account of both orations in the
daily press. There was absolutely no comparison between the
two speeches, Lord Grey's was telling and literate and made one
think, 'There is much to be said for the importance of a Liberal
Party if you believe in democracy.' Lloyd George's was just an
emotional *cri de coeur*, a sheer visceral appeal to the fighting
spirit: 'Let's keep the other beggars out.' 'It made one frighten-
ingly aware that the bigger the democracy (in the sense of the
size of the population) the more it is at the mercy of the
demagogue, not that I had anything against Lloyd George who
was one of the world's great 'charmers'. (At that time I hadn't

anything against him. But in later years what he did to Asquith made me distrust him deeply.)

We returned to London joyfully. Gilbert and Sullivan's shrewd observation that every child alive is born a 'little Liberal or else a little Conservative' was fulfilled by all the Liberal newspapers, greeting my baby's arrival with pictures of the 'Liberal baby of the Year'.

Photographs with his mother at three days, with his father, the new M.P. at the age of three weeks! He took a very long time to come into the world, there were moments when I had a panic certainty that the end would be a healthy baby and a mother untimely dead! I was told by my doctors that my language during the intervals when they stopped giving me an anaesthetic was quite a shock to the nurse! But when he finally arrived and they showed me a fine baby boy I almost swooned again with rapture. I don't think that ever in my life I felt such utter bliss and contentment as during the hours when I fed him. In fact I think I overdid it. There was a time when he cried in piercing wails all night, till I became desperate, and when the doctor said, 'There's nothing wrong with him. He's gaining weight splendidly,' I betook myself as a last resource to a baby clinic in Bloomsbury. 'He's gaining ounces every week', I wailed, 'so there can't be anything wrong with my milk.' 'How many ounces?' asked the sister. When I told her, she said, 'Poor little thing, no wonder he cries! He's trying to tell you that he is suffering from acute indigestion. He's being stuffed like a prize goose. Surfeit of mother's rich milk, that's all he is suffering from.' So I was given a strict timetable of how often and for how long I should feed him. After a very short period of misery for both of us when he was sure he was hungry, and I had to refuse to listen, he settled down and flourished. How I looked forward to those moments when I sank into a lethargy of bliss and murmured the ancient Rosary, slightly misquoted: 'Sainte Marie, Mère de Dieu . . . je suis bênie entre toutes les femmes.'

So many friends said, 'You'll call him Antony I suppose' that we said 'No!' and called him Mark. He was christened in the House of Commons chapel, his godmothers being Mrs. Brooke and Maud Johnson and his godfathers, Mr. Asquith and Sir James Barrie. I think Bridget must have been abroad or she certainly would have been there as godmother. One of Cecil's friends

afterwards told me that a photographer had been asked by
someone, 'Who is the little girl holding Mr. Ramage's hand?'
and been told 'Prudence Nesbitt'. The inquirer raised an eyebrow. 'Oh, has Cathleen Nesbitt got another child?' and looked
quite disappointed when told that it was Mrs. Ramage's *niece*.

I nursed my baby for nine months. Once I took him on tour
with me, and as there were no bottles to wash and diet and
'formulas' to be coped with I didn't need a nanny. I took a little
maid, Lily, with me who pushed him around in a pram when I
had a matinée and brought him down to the theatre every night
for his 10 o'clock feed. Fortunately I only had one short tour in
a play called *The Blue Peter*. It wasn't very good and I think it
would have folded after a few weeks if it hadn't been for the
visit from King George and Queen Mary during our first week.
We were naturally delighted, a royal visit meant a great deal
to the box office, but we did wonder why? I was told later that
'the Sailor King' had been attracted by the title, and must have
been very disappointed to find that the play had nothing to do
with the Navy!

I had determined not to have another baby for a few years,
but accidents will happen, and the following year again I had
to leave one of my favourite roles, the street-walker in *Spring
Cleaning* by Lonsdale. Basil Dean, who directed it, thought I was
quite unsuitable for the part, but Freddie Lonsdale insisted that
no one else should do it. How he laughed at me one day when
he asked, 'Where did you lunch? I came to take you and Ronnie
Squire out to lunch at The Ivy but we couldn't find you.' I explained that I had found a little 'joint' in Greek Street that was
as far as I could see patronised exclusively by 'Ladies of the
Town'. It was fascinating to have a seat by the door and watch
a girl's face suddenly unwind from her 'street face', pouting
mouth and 'come hither' eyes, and start a conversation with a
girl friend; very domesticated it was, the usual female chat
about the inadequacy of chars and how difficult it is to get a
reliable baby-sitter. I only once heard bad language, and that
was during an angry discussion about the bad luck of 'Pore
Liza! Fourteen days they give 'er and you know why, that
fuckin' dog's-body of a copper! She 'adn't given 'im 'is weekly
nugget, 'e wanted double from 'er because 'e thought she was
doin' extra well that week and she'd 'ad a drop and told 'im to

put it you know where, so 'e just hauled 'er in, dirty bastard.'

'Poor bitches!' said Freddy, 'what with their pimps and their weekly bribes to the police, they don't keep much to themselves.'

Sitting next to Shane Leslie at a dinner party a few days later, I found he took a deep interest in the subject of prostitution and the history of its existence. When I told him how shocked I was at Lonsdale's story of how they had to buy police protection I added, 'I thought our police were supposed to be above corruption, the most honest in the world. Do you think they are *all* corrupt?'

'No, but no policeman anywhere is above "corruption" when he has to administer a law that no one believes in,' said Shane Leslie. 'You couldn't bribe your way out of murder or rape or grand larceny if you offered them £1,000, but prostitution and gambling . . . they know as well as you or I that no ordinary member of the public believes you can stop it by law.' And he went on to say that the law would finally have to recognise that if a man can't gamble lawfully he'll do it unlawfully. One would have thought that the lawmakers would have learnt a little from the American experiment of Prohibition, but apparently not – America's dismal aftermath has been forgotten.

Mona in *Spring Cleaning* was such a good part that I had a wonderful time with it; and as always when one has a really good part, good reviews and many fan letters, one of which I can't resist inserting, from Sir Shane Leslie:

'I came up from a Sussex farm and return after seeing your superb performance. It was interesting after that half hour I had talking to you about the part to see how you improved upon every thought or suggestion. You have either studied the part by going among the "filles de joie", "Ladies of Lucifer" or whatever irony we use to denominate or you have improvised a wonderful artistic guess. I was enthralled by your performance on which the success of the play hung from your difficult entry to your delicious exit. The gallery loved you for your humanity and the intellectuals for your art. A lady next to me greeted your name with disdain but was overwhelmed by your performance. It was an amusing conversion. In a week or so the rest of the cast will be acting on your plane and we shall have the success of the season. You have given us a great spiritual lesson. I salute you.'

But once again I was to be denied the joy of a long run. I had hoped that this time I could get at least five months out of it – however, my 'front' began to look very prominent at the end of three, and again I reluctantly had to give up.

I didn't know then that a large protuberance doesn't necessarily mean a large baby, and was rather dreading the birth pangs, but the baby more than made up for everything.

She slipped into the world very quickly and easily at 9.30 p.m. I was making coffee for some friends who had been dining with us and at midnight there she was, and doubly welcome because she was a girl.

I could only feed her for six weeks as a strange gland suddenly appeared in my neck. At first as large as a nut, then a plum, and by the time they operated as big as a tangerine. The doctor said it was tubercular which sounded ominous but they successfully removed it. They were not so successful at plastic surgery some fifty years ago! They left some nasty scars which are still faintly visible. At the time I became very depressed about them, great red ugly weals, how was I going to disguise them for my next part?

I was to start rehearsals as soon as I left the nursing home for Granville-Barker's *Madras House* directed by himself and they had sent me sketches of the tailored suit and dinner dress I was to wear. I remember lying in bed, in the depths of depression, slow tears rolling down my cheeks when the door opened and in burst Mrs. Pat Campbell, pushing the nurse aside, 'She told me you were leaving on Saturday, but you weren't seeing visitors yet. Sheer nonsense! now run away my good girl, and bring us some tea.'

What a friend she was! And such practical friendship. Within ten minutes she was drawing little pictures on the dress designs showing me that this frock could have a chiffon scarf with little 'bones' under the ears like those Edwardian ladies stiffened their collars with so that it shouldn't slip down; and with the tweed suit: 'A Chinese neckline to the blouse, you know, like a mandarin's collar. You might even have it made of Chinese brocade, what colour is the suit, let's get some paper and write a letter to the dressmaker to get the materials.' By the time we had written the letter and had our tea, I was as happy as a lark. Suddenly she said, 'Should you go back to work so soon?' 'Oh yes, I must, and anyway I wouldn't miss a Barker production for anything.'

She rummaged in her bag, and thrust four £5 notes into my hand. 'Now, now! I know that "must" is partly financial, I've been through it myself. I wish I were rich but this is just a little present to my godchild, for her mother to take taxis to rehearsals.' How *giving* Stella always was. I remember when I was still nursing Mark, she came to visit me in Brunswick Square. We were living in the upper half of the old Georgian house and when I apologised for the stairs, 'Nonsense I've always lived in houses with stairs. You look thin, are they getting you down? . . . No, I'm sure they are not, it's that great baby, no wonder you are thin.' Then she disappeared for a few minutes and returned as mysteriously. 'Just giving a message to my chauffeur.' Fifteen minutes later the door bell rang and up came the chauffeur panting under the weight of a great case of 'Ragget's nourishing stout for nursing mothers as supplied to her Gracious Majesty Queen Victoria'. 'And you know how many children she had!' said Stella, 'and *she* got plumper and plumper! So get that inside you.'

Before I went into the nursing home, I had acquired a great treasure, Nanny Dumble. Miss Dumble had come to me as a mother's help. She told me she had had very little experience with children. But I soon discovered that she was a born nanny. She took as much trouble bullying the doctor, seeking advice from the baby clinic, experimenting with a formula to replace mother's milk as if Jennifer had been her own child. There was nothing that she would not do for the children. I had brought a large twin pram for her to take them out to Brunswick Square and the environs for airings. The square was green and spacious but nanny decided it was town air, and took them all the way to Regent's Park at least three times a week. Once on her day off Cecil and I embarked on the same trip; almost before we reached Euston Road he was moaning: 'Oh! Oh! My back is breaking.' It's only fair to say that from his height he had a long way to bend. Nanny and I being short women could cope better. I think that was the occasion when having shown Mark elephants, kangaroos, monkeys, hippopotami and finding no sign of amusement or interest, we decided he didn't like animals. As we crossed the road outside the gates an old tabby cat jumped from

the wall and crossed with us. The baby clapped his hands glee-
fully: 'Pussycat,' he shouted, 'Pussycat'.

Cecil was never good at pushing a pram, but he was wonderful
with children. From the first he insisted that if they wanted to
talk at table, their conversation must be reasonably intelligent.
If they started to gabble and stutter, as small children so often
do when they are full of something they want to say, he would
advise 'Just stop stuttering, *think* over what you want to say
and then say it so we can enjoy it'. If they didn't understand a
word or struggled to use one they couldn't pronounce, he'd say
'Let's get a dictionary and be *quite* sure'. He was a marvellous
inventor of games and could organise treasure hunts for their
parties that became famous. Between us we taught them both to
read by the time they were between four and five. In those days,
before TV, books were blessed baby-sitters!

THIRTEEN

Two Houses

1933

Sometime during the years that followed we moved from Brunswick Square to a dear little house in Drayton Gardens, and we learned the joy of gardening, from trying a few bedded-out wallflowers under the brick wall at the bottom of the garden, to achieving a long border of roses and delphiniums and phlox. Cecil became infinitely knowledgeable about hoeing and pruning and mulching, and organising little forays after dark into the road outside. Mr. Burgess kept a riding stable up the road, and, as the horses clip-clopped home during the afternoon and evening, they dropped quite a lot of valuable manure which the whole family swept up with little brooms and carried in a pail to the compost heap. A door at the bottom of the garden led into Thistle Grove which was, and still is, a perfect little passage between two long brick walls, where children could cycle happily and safely from Fulham Road to Brompton Road, and dogs could be walked in the evening under flowering trees whose branches strayed from the gardens behind the brick walls.

What fun I had with that little house. I painted the treads of the stairs and the banister, all five flights from the attic to the basement. I really went mad with the paint-brush, and even tackled the piano! A mahogany baby grand. I felt it jarred with my sea-blue and green room, and I painted it very pale blue and put a little green in the varnish with which I 'antiqued' it; it really 'went' beautifully with my long blue-green shot-silk curtains. It was only by the exercise of will-power that I trained myself to stop whatever I was doing at 5 o'clock every day and rest for two hours before going to the theatre.

'Ou sont les neiges d'antan?' Then I paid rent of £250 per annum for a house with a drawing-room and a dining-room and a large nursery and a large kitchen and four or five bedrooms and two bathrooms, and then there was always the 'little man' to do the odd papering and painting one couldn't do oneself. Now, I pay three times as much for two rooms, kitchen and bath; and now, one waits and waits, and pays and pays to have a few bookshelves put up.

But now the years have brought patience and an eyesight that is kinder to all things if one removes one's glasses before looking at them – even one's face, Dieu merci!

And furniture that in my forties I longed to change for something better, now in my eighties has become friendly and cosy.

During the years from 1926 till 1935 I played in thirty-five productions and usually when I had a part I did not enjoy, as in *The Constant Nymph* or *Children in Uniform* it ran a year; when it was a part I did enjoy, like Lady Myrtle in *Fame* with Gerald du Maurier it ran only three months. Gerald had decided that he was bored with always playing himself, he'd like a part in which he really had to act, and chose for himself the role of an unhappy, frustrated violinist manqué who in the end committed suicide. Unfortunately, Audrey and Waveny Carten who wrote the play didn't succeed in making the poor violinist convincing, but they wrote extremely funny dialogues for Lady Myrtle and her country-squire fiancé, played by Nigel Bruce. The scene when he tried to persuade Lady Myrtle that a bracelet of 'elephant bristle plaited together' was infinitely better than a diamond one 'because an elephant is so lucky', was so funny that Gerald used to double up with laughter and then shout, 'Damn it you two, get off the stage, you're having all the fun: I've got all this bloody emotion to do.' Superbly he did it too, but his public wanted their Gerald to be himself, and it only had a short run for a du Maurier production. I enjoyed myself enormously getting slightly drunk on cherry brandy in a ravishing riding habit made by Gerald's own tailor, fittings supervised by Gerald himself, and wearing a shimmering evening dress made entirely of crystal beads hand-sewn by Norman

Hartnell's wonderful embroiderers. It looked like a moonlit waterfall and gave great point to the line '*Elephant's hair?* With *this* dress? One night I was a little slow on the line so Gerald nipped in and said it for me, naturally getting a bigger laugh than ever I did. Which so enraptured him that he announced the news to me 'I'm going to keep that line for the rest of the week just to "learn" you to be on your toes.' But he suddenly realised that it was really a bit out of character for him, which made him hesitate. 'He who hesitates is lost,' and the laugh didn't quite come off that night. 'You can have it back,' he said with a noble gesture as of one producing a jewel, which indeed it was to me. We had only been running six weeks when I had to have a mastoid operation. I thought I had flu and struggled through the matinée but I looked so ill that Gerald bundled me into a car and took me to his doctor who said at once, 'Did you say your ears ached?' 'Just my right ear.' He made me walk up and down the carpet-line and other odd things, 'testing for balance' I was told afterwards. 'Can I play tonight?' I asked. 'You are going to King's College Hospital now. It's Taylor's hospital; we'll see if he can operate tomorrow.' And operate he did. 'Just to see that man with a scalpel is like seeing a great dancer,' said a little nurse to me afterwards, 'you were lucky to get him. He's the King's surgeon, and no wonder. The tops that's what he is.'

I've had three serious operations, and a very difficult child-birth in my life, but oddly enough I cannot remember any pain except the mastoid one. I remember lying awake saying to myself 'It's coming, it's coming, a great stone foot . . . *stamp*, oh *no* I can't bear it again . . . it's coming . . . it's coming . . . a great *stone* foot . . . *stamp*, always in the same place, always in the same place.' I think perhaps it is the recollection of that dreadful weight of monotony in real pain that makes me unable to endure films or books or even newspapers reporting violence or torture.

I am not the stuff that martyrs are made of. Could I stand up to torture without betraying another human being? Thank God I have never been put to the test. I discussed that with my doctor once and he said 'You have an unusually high "tolerance" of pain physically, so I'm afraid it would take an unusual severity of pain to cause you to lose consciousness which can sometimes be the salvation of people suffering.' We were discussing this during an illness I had in 1931 while I was playing in Edgar Wallace's ingenious melodrama *The Case of the Frightened Lady*. We were making the film of the play in the Beaconsfield studios, and in the thirties, in British films anyway, the lights caused a terrific heat in the studios. One dress had to be taken off and dried between every 'take', I sweated so profusely. Going up to the theatre one night when there was snow and frost I suddenly began to feel ill. I got through the play but collapsed on the stairs on which I made my last exit. The audience thought it an excellent piece of 'business'. But in the dressing-room the doctor found I had a dangerously high temperature and I was hurried back to bed. Next morning I still had a raging fever and my stomach was so swollen that I looked as if I might have triplets at any moment. I don't think that anyone has ever had more specialists at her bedside. The insurance company for the film (they couldn't continue shooting without me) and the insurance company with whom Edgar Wallace always insured against the illness or departure of a star (and I had the authentic star-billing of 'name in lights' over the theatre) both sent experts to try to diagnose the trouble. No one seemed to know quite what it was, but everyone by now having brought in a second opinion wanted to open me up and see. 'Was it acute appendicitis?' 'Was it an inflammation of the colon?' 'Was it', as one gentleman said, 'a conception in the Fallopian tube?' But my own doctor kept them all at bay. 'It's a very severe chill', he said. 'If she keeps warm and lives on hot lemon juice and water at frequent intervals she will be with you in seven days.' And he was right, I was back at the studios within a week, though Edgar insisted my understudy should hold the fort at the theatre till the film was finished. My doctor and I used to have a little chat every evening. 'I must have an injection tonight,' I wheedled, 'one little shot of morphia and I can sleep'. 'It's for you to say,' he answered, 'you know it will remove the present pain, you know also that it will make gas in your stomach and in the morning you will burp and burp and each burp will be agony.' Tomorrow seemed a long way off. 'I'll have it now,' I would say and when morning came I would regret it bitterly and warn him, 'Don't even come tonight, then I cannot have it.' I can't quite remember, but I think as the pain lessened my will-power strengthened and I would say proudly, 'I can do without it tonight.' The games people play with themselves. I'd be very bored with myself if I found myself so dependent on sleeping pills that I had to have one every night of my life; on the other hand if I get overtired or overstrained I immediately suffer from insomnia and take a pill at once. Then each night I have a little argument with myself. 'It's much worse for you to have a sleepless night at your age than to take a pill,' and so I go on taking them for a week or sometimes more than a week and one night I get immersed in a delicious bedside book and forget all about the damned pill and sleep splendidly and without a dream. I never understand the experts who assure us that a completely dreamless sleep is much less restful than one during which one dreams a great deal. I find dreams exhausting and I nearly always do have dreams and rather unpleasant ones at that, when I have been taking pills for a time.

When I started to try to write this book I swore to myself that I would never write down the list of the plays I've played in or print a press notice that has pleased me. It may be interesting for me but how boring to anyone else. And yet for an actor the plays he has played in do constitute a very sizeable part of his life; a writer can put down his thoughts, and there they are printed, bound, standing on the shelf giving pleasure to generation after generation; a painter can put down his thoughts about life on canvas and know that someone a hundred years hence will understand them; a musician, but why go on? We all know that acting is an ephemeral art, if art it is, but it *is* using one's creative gift while one is doing it. Even a bad writer, painter or musician has something that he himself can look at and say, 'Yes, that's it, what I felt or saw or heard at that moment.' But an actor has nothing, he has put fifty or sixty years of himself into doing something as well as he can, but it can only live as long as the people who have seen him do it live. Sometimes there is a writer there who can put it down. What idea would we have of Garrick if Charles Lamb had not seen him, or Coquelin if Henry James hadn't seen him, or Bernhardt but for Maurice Baring. When I have seen a really tremendous performance and felt that thrill of 'recognition': '*Of course*, that's how it is, that's how it should be.' Laurence Olivier's Macbeth for instance, how I have longed to have a Henry James or a Charles Lamb or a Hazlitt beside me to write it down. I can only say 'I know now I have seen Macbeth as Shakespeare must have seen him during every moment of his creation' or having seen John Gielgud as Hamlet I know I have seen Hamlet as Shakespeare must have dreamed of him. But I have no winged words with which to share my knowledge. I myself have never attained the heights but I have sometimes done things well and I treasure it mightily when a writer like Rebecca West or Shane Leslie or a poet like Edward Shanks has written something that shows that I have 'got across' what I wanted to say. Perhaps I will quote some of them in a separate chapter so that no one needs to read it.

To be done with the 'stocktaking', the only play to excite me except Galsworthy's *Loyalties*, which did give me a mild pleasure, was *The Taming of the Shrew* at the Old Vic. To play in Shakespeare again was bliss and to play Kate had always been my ambition. Like everyone else I would have liked to play Juliet and Viola but I didn't think I had the equipment; with Kate I could cope. I enjoyed every moment, even the bruises inflicted by the roistering Petruchio who was played by Maurice Evans with to me quite unexpected strength and humour. I say unexpected as I had only seen him as Richard II. How one scorns managements that go in for type-casting and how often one finds oneself doing it.

I loved Kate's last speech starting with a silken irony, teasing and mocking, and suddenly finding herself dreaming of an ideal world where every woman's husband would be her 'Lord', her 'Life', her 'Keeper', who for her sake 'commits his body, to painful labours both by sea and land, to watch the night in storms, the day in cold,' while she 'lies warm at home secure and safe'. Adam and Eve in the Garden of Paradise – 'He for God only, she for God in him'. What a merry exciting marriage it could have turned out 'When two raging fires meet together, They do consume the thing that feeds their fury.' I wasn't sure that anyone but me would like my Kate, but W. A. Darlington in the *Daily Telegraph* said it was the best he had seen since Ellen Terry's, so my cup was full.

Miss Baylis asked if I would like to be her leading lady at the Old Vic next season. I wanted to. Oh how I wanted to but I made the 'Esau choice'.

I thought I could not afford it. £20 a week was the highest

salary they could pay. I had just acquired a little house in the country, my children were at expensive schools, my husband had had an illness, so many spurious excuses. I say spurious, because if the theatre had been the first thing in my life, as it *ought* to be if one wants to scale the heights, I could have found a way. The really great ones, such as Sybil Thorndike, Gielgud, Olivier, have always, if there was a clash put the theatre before the money-bags. Anyhow I was never very sure that I had any valuable talent and I had never had very much money dangled before me! So I probably made the right decision and went back to the good old Walter Hackett melodramas in which all I had to do was slink about in elegant clothes as the wicked lady who was out-manoeuvred by deliciously funny little Marion Lorne as a comical simpleton.

Not that I have anything against a melodrama, when like Edgar Wallace's thrillers it is superbly plotted and skilfully written.

I thoroughly enjoyed the long run of his *Case of the Frightened Lady*. My role was that of one Lady Lebanon who was fanatically proud of her ancient lineage: 'One of the Cedars of Lebanon I presume?' said Emlyn Williams, who played my son. Young Lord Lebanon was a criminal lunatic, and to protect him from the law, Lady Lebanon was up to every kind of mayhem, including trying to dazzle the police force with her distinguished ancestry, and long speeches on heraldry and the importance of family crests and mottoes. Edgar was delighted to find that I could rattle off esoteric phrases like: 'Two eagles regardant ducally gorged bull's head argent with chevrons argent and sable' or 'Gules charged with a bend vair.' I confessed that as a child I had spent many hours poring over what Mamma called her family tree.

Mamma liked to remind us that we were all, like herself, descended from that great Welshman Owain Glendyr (she despised the English spelling of Glendower). His motto was 'Not Us From Kings, But Kings From Us' and Mamma could, to her own satisfaction, trace the descent to centuries back! She had inherited a splendid legacy from her great-uncle William Bulkely, or was it Bulkely William? He was a rural dean with a passion for genealogy. He had plenty of leisure for his hobby; the sermons he preached to his contented parishioners had been once delivered by his own great-uncle who had them printed in a book. There were sixty of them, I had heard, and preached in rotation over and over again, they lasted his lifetime.

The legacy, which he must have spent many many years concocting, was a copy of his family tree. What a labour of research it must have been, going all the way back to Owain Glendyr, with the mottoes and crests of the families involved, penned in bright colours all about the banner.

For, to my great disappointment, it was not a tree at all – I had envisaged one with great spreading branches. But it was wrapped round a rod like a window blind and unrolled when pulled by a little golden tassel – at least five feet long, it was.

'There!' said Mamma triumphantly: 'You see right up at the top *Owain Glendyr* and look, there is great-uncle's name, and great-grandpapa's, and right down at the bottom, see, here we are.'

Catherine Hughes-Parry *m.* Thomas Nesbitt

Cathleen	Thomas	Hugo	Anna	Terence

On the right-hand portion of the scroll were much more illustrious names than the Hughses and Williams and Parrys and Bulkelys of our branch (very few crests among *them*). From Glendower's daughter, Lady Mortimer, came a splendid bevy of earls and barons, with here and there a dull patch (when you had sixteen or seventeen children there were· sure to be some who didn't marry well!). Right near the bottom, on that side, were Earls of Radnor, and one of them had a family of five, like Mamma's. His children were called Pleydell-Bouverie.

'What a *beautiful* name' I said wistfully, 'are they really our relations?'

'Well, yes. A long way away but they came from the same roots. The founder of that strain was a Turkish merchant called Bouverie.'

That conjured up even more romantic thoughts about those distant relations. Were they dark-skinned, the Turkish? Or was that only Indians, I wondered.

Father, of course, scoffed at it. 'Right back to the time of Henry II? Rubbish. Hard to trace one family that far, let alone dozens, anyway I bet the old humbug just dreamed most of it up out of his own head.'

I fear I was rather wickedly pleased when I was older and had started to read the historical plays of Shakespeare, to be able to confront Mamma with *Henry IV* Part I and ask solemnly, 'Darling how could you be proud to claim descent from that arrogant loud-mouthed old rascal?'

But Edgar took Mamma's banner quite seriously, to her great delight.

He insisted on coming to tea with her and having a look at it. He loved to say wistfully that he had never known *where* he came from, he had been 'found abandoned on the front steps of a lodging house in the East End, and picked up by the milkman's boy'. It was a good story, so long as he remembered not to tell it in front of anyone, like me, who had already been regaled with another story that his great-aunt had been a famous female Hamlet, and that he had inherited his love of the theatre from her.

How romantic Edgar was; he insisted on borrowing the banner to hang in my dressing-room at Wyndham's. It was Edgar who conceived the idea of having a plaque made to hang on the wall; a kind of role of honour, with the names of everyone who had occupied the star room since the theatre had been built. So many illustrious names – Charles Wyndham, himself, Weedon Grossmith, Mrs. Patrick Campbell, Seymour Hicks, Charles Laughton, Charles Hawtrey, Cyril Maude, Gerald du Maurier, Marie Tempest, Leslie Banks, Vivien Leigh – all gone now. Some died in their prime like Leslie and Gerald and Vivien – others lived to a ripe old age.

How proud Mamma was when Edgar gave a little party in the dressing-room the day my name was painted on the plaque – to do her justice she had never shown her family tree to anyone outside her own family, but I think she was very thrilled by the idea that any of my visitors could see it!

It was about then that I bought a little cottage at Penn. It was really two cottages made into one. Some of the villagers swore that they had been built for Anne Boleyn to house her grooms in but I don't think it was as old as that. There was a rose garden with brick paths backed by a glorious old rosy brick wall on one side and an old barn attached to it on the other side, big enough to let one slice a garage out of it, and still have enough room for the children to have a playroom, some stables that we turned into a tool-shed and a greenhouse. And behind we had three and a half acres of paddock.

What an everlasting temptation. 'Suppose we take in a bit more for another kitchen garden? What about that bit for more currants and raspberries?' The fencing that separated garden from paddock receded further and further. We didn't have to mow the grass; the local farmers always wanted to graze cows or sheep on it, or the local riding mistress her ponies in return for which she mounted Jennifer for any local gymkhanas. As a matter of fact there was always a pony for either of the children but Jennifer was going through the horses period which many female children go through, when it is bliss to be allowed to groom the horses, clean the harness, work harder than any stable-boy just for fun, and love of horses!

We ripped layer after layer of red linoleum from the living-room floor, and found a delightful flooring not of parquet but of solid oak blocks. Oak cut in the size and shape of bricks and laid square to square. It could be scrubbed white like a ship's deck. With thick white rugs strewn about it was one of the prettiest floors I have ever seen. Ruby Ross came to visit us during one of her London trips, and was so taken with it she begged a couple of blocks to take back to America to have them copied for an old farmhouse in Maine. We looked about for a place where it would not show. 'You'll never move that great sofa under the window, there's nowhere else in the room you can put it.' So we dug under the sofa and the village carpenter filled in the hole with any old wood.

We stripped away the hideous little Victorian fireplace and found an ancient cottage stone fireplace that was at least six feet wide with a brick oven let into the wall one side and a little wooden bench against the wall, on the other a seat polished smooth with the behinds of generations of old villagers. We found an iron grate that would take up to five-foot logs but decided three-foot would be more manageable. With what joy we piled the sun-dried logs on the fire for a cold evening and drew our chairs up to the fire arguing as to who should be allowed to sit in the inglenook. Within ten minutes we had fled coughing, choking and weeping into the dining-room. Such smoke as you have never seen belched forth. Next morning we routed out the village chimney-sweep, now aged ninety, retired, but willing to oblige and give advice. He took one look at me and cast a reproachful eye, 'There was a nice fire wot *worked* in here before you came. My father put it in for old Mrs. Whosit, burn anything in that, you could – coal, wood, coke anything.' 'I know,' I pleaded, 'but we love this old fireplace so I ripped the other one out.' 'You done wrong,' he said gravely, 'this 'ere fireplace 'as always smoked ever since it were built and that was afore my father's time or my grandfather's.' 'If they all lived to be ninety like you,' I thought, 'that's a long long time.' If no one had stopped it smoking what hope had I?

'But what did people do to keep warm, this is a cold house.'

'Oh, they just shut their eyes and got to abide the smoke. You can get used to it if you don't want to write or read or sew.'

'Even the old people? Didn't it make them cough?'

'Ah, no, bless you, they just sat right inside there on the little seat and kippered themselves.'

I didn't quite believe him. I tried every known make of guaranteed cowl or hood, nothing worked. But fortunately we came to discover that it only smoked when the east wind was in a certain direction, and on those nights we used the electric fire. And by degrees we planted wind breaks to mitigate the wind's force.

How things grew there. I think generations of horses had manured and watered certain areas very thoroughly. We made such discoveries. I'd never known that trees had sex. But when I moaned to the old 'two-days-a-week' gardener that my lovely apple tree seemed to grow apace but never gave any Bramleys, he said 'Oh, her be female (or was it the other way round?), you must plant a nice Cox's Orange alongside and her'll do pretty.' And it was so. We had Bramleys and Cox's, more than we could eat, and cherries but the birds always got those first. And plums. Cecil bought a dreary looking little waif of a plum tree for 2s. 6d. at the Wycombe market and it gave a stupendous crop every year of the best black plums I have tasted, and no 'shop-bought Victorias' ever have the flavour of ours picked warm from the sun. And I had a 'white and silver' garden at the bottom of the lawn, close to the apple trees. Nothing in that garden but white flowers and silver-green foliage. Vita Sackville-West gave

13. above: With Mark and Jennifer at Studland, 1934

14. below: As Mona the Streetwalker in *Spring Cleaning*, 1925

15. E. Kapp's cartoon of Cathleen Nesbitt and Jack Hobbs in
The Grain of Mustard Seed, 1920

16. In *The Grain of Mustard Seed*

17. In *Hassan*, 1922

18. below: As the Grand Duchess in *The Sleeping Prince*, 1956

19. Cecil Beaton

20. The Lunts when Cathleen first knew them

21. below: Cecil Beaton's costume design for Mrs Higgins

22. As Mrs. Higgins in *My Fair Lady*

23. In Cecil Beaton's garden

me cuttings of lovely ground-covering plants with odd names, Chinese Lavender? Lambs tails? I have forgotten all their names, but they made a silver-grey background for the white flowers which came in their seasons: crocuses, tulips, peonies, Madonna lilies, roses, phlox, Japanese anemones, nicotiana, how magical they looked in the moonlight when they flourished. In the middle of the moonlight garden I placed my treasured statue, a stone Madonna by Eric Gill, my first present from Rupert Brooke. How busy we were in winter with catalogues and in summer with work. It was Cecil who did most of the work, I was apt to be clumsy with the hoe and heavy-handed with the planting.

How convenient was Penn for everywhere. My son was at the Dragon School at Oxford, easy to drive there and later when he went to Eton, Windsor was only thirty minutes away. Jennifer went, at first, to a day-school at Beaconsfield and later to a wonderful school at Gerrard's Cross recommended to me by Bronson Albery and Athene Seyler.

And best of all I could drive to the theatre, door to door in little over an hour. How I enjoyed that peaceful drive in the dark, deserted roads, home and in bed soon after midnight. And commuters' trains all day from Beaconsfield to Marylebone right up until midnight, so come winter and wet weather or fog one could leave the car at the station. I had a 'baby' Austin which on cold nights had to be cranked for about fifteen minutes by myself and the solitary porter in turns before it would start. I had taught myself to drive in London and was a bit nervous of country roads at first. One didn't have to be examined for a driving licence in those days, you just bought your car and insured it. I thought I had better have some instruction so I went to a motoring school; but they insisted I must learn about its insides first. I peered at carburettors and shafts and God knows what, couldn't remember any of the names of any of the bits and pieces or what they were for, and knew I never should, so I said, 'Oh hell! This is getting me nowhere,' and started to teach myself, round and round the Boltons, which is a sort of country village of rather grand houses with gardens, built around a church. You turn in at Old Brompton Road and emerge ultimately in Fulham Road, but in between those roaring highways it is country quiet.

When I felt secure I drove across the park to St. John's Wood to lunch with the Harwoods. Mrs. Harwood was Fryn Tennyson Jesse who wrote lovely books about the sea and was my Jennifer's other godmother. Neither she nor Mrs. Patrick Campbell took their Christian duties very seriously I fear, but they did each give her a silver christening mug! After lunch Fryn said she wanted to pay a visit to her aunt who lived in the Boltons. 'The Boltons?' I said gaily, 'I'll drive you there, I have my car outside.' Tottie and Fryn were duly impressed, neither of them ever did attempt to drive and thought it very dashing of me to do so. I drove carefully and Fryn relaxed peacefully. When we arrived at the Boltons, Fryn suddenly said 'Stop! You have just passed the house. . . . Stop darling! Just reverse back three houses.' 'I can't,' I confessed, 'I don't know how to, but I'll drive you round and round and we'll get there.' 'Oh no you won't,' cried Fryn. 'Stop right where you are, don't you know how to reverse? My God! How you *dare*,' and she jumped out indignantly. As a matter of fact I became a very good driver. My licence was endorsed only twice, once for speeding in a royal park. I was going just over 20 miles an hour which was the speed limit. Every now and then the authorities would wake up to the fact that everyone from taxi drivers to royal chauffeurs (when their Royalties were not on board) drove at 30 miles an hour all the time, so for two days summonses would be dealt out by the dozen and then it would all die down.

The other time was most shaming. I was doing a film at Denham. Getting up at 6 o'clock, when one had not been to bed till 1 o'clock every night was rather a strain so I took it easy while driving. One morning I was creeping through Beaconsfield half-asleep, turned left round the corner at Smith's bookshop as usual, thought I felt a bump in the road but did not really notice it. I thought I heard a man shouting behind me, and realised that my left-hand indicator was out, pushed the button and went on my way. So far so good. Two weeks later a policeman appeared at the cottage door and handed me a summons for dangerous driving with an injunction to appear at the Beaconsfield Magistrates' Court a week or so later. I was aghast, dangerous driving? Me! Even the date meant nothing to me. But the time? 6 a.m. . . . Something must have happened on the way to the studios. When? What?

While I was trying to decipher all of it, Cecil seized it from me and when he had read it aloud he and the children collapsed with laughter, 'Darling don't pretend you ran over a milk-cart at the crack of dawn and have forgotten all about it!' I was completely bewildered. I dimly remembered a bump, but such a little one. I couldn't have knocked over a horse as well as a cart, I couldn't have knocked over anything! However it was decided that I must have a solicitor to represent me. He took me over the accident, 'Didn't you hear a man shouting after you?' 'I thought he was warning me that I'd forgotten to turn off my indicator.' I could see that the solicitor was not very impressed with my story. However my opponent won the case for me! Mr. Milk-man, delighted to have a captive audience, made a lengthy oration with a dramatic description of how he was standing peacefully on the cart having delivered his three quarts at the Laburnums and 'this woman' came rushing round the corner 'knocked us right into the cart, the poor 'orse was frightened something 'orrible, stood right up on his hind legs, knocked about terrible he was, the poor beast, and this woman just raced on didn't even stop after the accident, though I 'ollered after 'er.' I listened incredulous and aghast, I couldn't have been asleep, if the horse had been injured I must have known. I had visions of the Royal Society for the Prevention of Cruelty to Animals pursuing me too. But Mr. Milkman did rather overstate his case. The magistrate regarded him quizzically, 'You have very good eyesight, I gather?' 'Well sir, I wear glasses sometimes.' 'Were you wearing them that morning?' 'I can't rightly remember.' 'Ah, it seems a little odd that if the lady was driving past you at such a speed you should have seen her registration number so accurately.' 'Oh yes sir, I got it correct. That's 'ow the police traced her, isn't it?'

'Now when did you take your horse to the vet?'

'Vet, sir? I didn't till next day.'

'Oh. I gather you finished your milk-round?'

'Oh yes sir,' righteously, 'never let my customers down.'

'I see, you were finishing your round?'

'Oh no sir, just beginning it, 6 o'clock it were.'

'I see. You finished your milk-round, and took the horse to the vet the next day. Did he substantiate your statement that the horse was severely injured?'

179

'Well sir, he didn't find nothing much wrong sir.'

'If he had found anything I dare say you would have had him here as a witness today?'

I think it was somewhere about there that my solicitor got up and spoke for me, recounted that I was driving very slowly, that I was accustomed to find nothing at that corner which I had been negotiating every morning for a week, that I must instinctively had been aware of something there and swayed out to avoid it and perhaps knocked against it. That if I had been aware of an accident I would never have moved on and in fact was driving slowly. By very good luck my solicitor had interviewed the cook at the house where the milkman had just delivered his bottles. Cook had come out to take them in, and heard him shouting after a car that was going quite slowly up the road and had told her that 'that woman had knocked into his cart and he was going to get her if it was the last thing he did,' but she hadn't noticed anything wrong with the cart or the horse.

So I was let off with an endorsement for reckless driving, fined £5 and subjected to some gentle irony from the magistrate as to the advisability of keeping one's eyes open when at the wheel. I drove to London very carefully that afternoon feeling very comforted that no one would ever hear about the unfortunate episode. It had been a lesson to me and a private black mark on my licence. After I had parked the car, I turned into Shaftesbury Avenue. Standing under the electric-light sign where my name was written large was a newspaper man and on his placard in large black letters was the joke of the day: 'Miss Cathleen Nesbitt drives over a milkman, his cart and his horse. She did not notice that they were there.' It was just my luck that some journalist probably in Beaconsfield to report the local flower show had drifted into the Court and heard Mr. Milkman tell his dreadful tale. It took me a long time to live it down. It was lucky that I was not acting with du Maurier at the time. He would probably have had emissaries scouring every shop in London for a milk-cart and distributing either miniature carts or horses or both all over the stage. The day Nigel Bruce's baby was born, Gerald had found a dozen little naked baby dolls and placed them strategically about on or in anything that Nigel had to touch during the evening, an ashtray, a cigar box, even a brandy glass. We all finished the evening giggling surreptitiously, Gerald himself most of all.

There is nothing more irritating to an audience than to see actors enjoying a private joke, and we must have irritated ours that evening. Mr. Chowne, the stage manager, came on stage after we had taken our curtain calls:

'That was a disgraceful performance. I must call a rehearsal tomorrow morning. I'm sorry but as a matter of fact we need one, the play has been slipping a bit lately. You too, sir, please Sir Gerald . . . at 10 o'clock tomorrow.'

Chownie was Gerald's stage manager and stage director for years. He always sat out front when Gerald was directing his own plays, and gave private notes to him afterwards. During a run he kept all the actors on their toes. I had often heard him do the rounds and sometimes finish with Gerald: 'That second-act scene ran one and a half minutes too long,' and Gerald would say obediently, 'Thank you Chownie, I'll see to it. I'm indulging too much.'

I was never a born comedienne. I lacked the inner radiance, the 'illumination' as S. N. Berman said of Lynn Fontanne. But oh! How lucky I am to have played with all the great comedians of their day during every decade of my life. In the early years Charles Hawtrey, Cyril Maude, Seymour Hicks, Gerald du Maurier, then as time went on, Alec Guinness, Ronald Squire, Rex Harrison and Roland Culver. I'm only speaking of the grand masters from whom I learned when to point a line and when to throw it away, so that when I have had the good fortune to be given a good comedy part I have never let it down, even if I have never illuminated it.

FOURTEEN

Around Europe with the Old Vic
1938–1939

Early in 1938, just as the monotony of driving up and down to
London to play in plays that did not appeal to me was beginning
to get me down, a delightful project materialised.

After my husband's illness he had had an offer to play in a
film, which he did so successfully that he decided to become an
actor.

It so happened that the Old Vic company was being sent on a
'cultural' tour of Europe: Lisbon, Milan, Rome, Florence,
Naples, Cairo, Malta, Athens. All romantic names of places I
had never seen and never thought to see. One of the repertory
plays was a drama called *Libel* by E. J. Hemmerde, K.C. What
was that well-known melodrama doing in a classical repertory?
For the simple reason that it had a court scene that lasted a
whole hour; and during the thrust and parry of counsel and
prosecuting attorney it elucidated most of the somewhat devious
intricacies of the British law of libel.

The play had been ordered as the set book of the term for all
the students of the Cairo University who wished to graduate as
lawyers, which meant practically all the students in the University; and whereas the audiences for *Hamlet* or *Henry V* would
probably consist mostly of the British population, the audience
for *Libel* consisting of all the law students in Egypt (together
with their sisters and their cousins and their aunts) could pack the
theatre for as many performances as we could give. And just at
that time, the Old Vic had not anyone of the right age to play
Gertrude in *Hamlet* and Lady Lodden in *Libel*, nor had they

anyone of the right age and presence to play the prosecuting counsel, so Cecil and I were invited to go on the tour. We had full houses every night we played *Libel* in Cairo and a great many students flocked round to try to consult Cecil on the obscurer points of law, thinking he was a real barrister which indeed he was!

We didn't play it anywhere else which meant that I had a lot of free evenings off in all the most exciting places.

Sir Miles Lampson was our ambassador in Cairo and he found time to entertain us royally. He was a man of wry humour and was most entertaining about the British efforts to keep young King Farouk 'on our side', as it were, versus the Italians.

No one of course made any reference to the shadow of war that loomed over Europe. I think we civilians all felt like Mr. Chamberlain: 'Another war – oh *no*! impossible.' Deep down we knew it was coming, but we didn't believe it.

'We'll never get King Farouk to love us,' mused Sir Miles. 'Ever since he was a baby England and discipline have been linked in his mind. He had an English nanny who was determined he should not be a "spoiled child". He was passed on to a prim English governess who practically equated pleasure with sin, an English tutor who endeavoured nobly to instil the virtues of self-control, integrity, *noblesse oblige*, all the English Public School ideals to which his temperament was singularly opposed. What with nanny always saying: *"No*, dear, you can't have that," and the governess for ever reiterating: "little boys *must* learn to obey without question," and a tutor impressing him with the necessity of *self-control* above all things for a monarch, imagine the effect when he came of age and the Italians sent a whole regiment of delightful young playboys whose theme song is: "Sire, you are a *monarch*; you can do whatever you please, whenever you please. You owe yourself some wild oats." And they are helping him to sow them in a big way. No wonder he loves the Italians.'

One of the guests was a splendid voluptuous English blonde who blew in like a fresh wind and cried in a splendid Cockney accent, 'Where's my little man, hasn't he come yet?' 'I expect he's catching up with work,' said Sir Miles, 'this is Lady Osman, her husband Sir Osman Pasha is Secretary of Finance. I saw him this morning, he's looking splendid, whatever you did to him on his holiday, it has made a new man of him.' 'Took 'im to Brighton, dear!' said Lady Osman with a fat chuckle. 'Some people say it's common, but I'm common myself, so it suits me. Good ol' Dr. Brighton; whatever you have wrong with you, Dr. Brighton will cure you.'

'Wonderful woman,' said Sir Miles at luncheon, 'can't think what I would do without her, knows more about what's going on in this town than all my intelligence officers put together.' Sir Osman Pasha had done brilliantly at Balliol and had written to his very exclusive Circassian family that he had acquired a First Class degree and a wife, whom he was bringing back with him. He had married a tobacconist's daughter, who towered above him and kept him radiantly happy. She was a great friend of the Egyptian Queen Mother who lived in a house-boat on the Nile and who was reputed to be a witch!

Lady Osman took me for an outing to Alexandria and I was startled to find that I felt so strongly that I had been there before. So much so that I said involuntarily, 'There's a palace round the next corner, in a square,' and it was so. I had been there as a child in the *County Antrim*, but had completely forgotten it. Why should something have lifted the veil of over forty years of oblivion? Was it something I had tasted like Proust's Madeleine? But I hadn't eaten anything; it was uncanny. And afterwards I had been taken to the catacombs. A kaleidoscope of memories flickers before me: Malta, one evening dining in a club when we began to notice that from every table men were quietly rising and disappearing. Alec Guinness found some elderly gentleman who explained, there had been another 'war-scare', all the Navy were being called back to their ships. We were told that it might be necessary to close the theatre. We held little meetings among ourselves when we got back to the hotel. Lewis Carson warned us we might not be able to get back away from Malta. We all groaned at the prospect. We all loved Malta, but oh! That dismal 'British Provincial Hotel'. It all blew over however, then lazy days on a little boat along the coast to Athens. Everywhere we had been so far had thrilled me. 'Rome, this is Rome!' I said to myself. And it was all I had hoped for. Milan, rather like Manchester. But one wonderful evening we all went to supper at a restaurant in the arcade, a long, long room. As soon as Alec Guinness entered the room the people at a table near the door stirred suddenly, whispered among themselves and stood up. 'Hamletto, Hamletto' they called and clapped, the whole way down the room. The whole room rose to its feet and to the rhythmic clapping, Alec, blushing furiously, walked to the other end of the room to our table against the back wall. What a touching poetic Hamlet he was, how adored by audiences he was everywhere, how pleasant it was for us to have two young honeymoon couples in the company, Alec and his Titian-haired bride Merula, Anthony Quayle and his bride who played Ophelia.

Florence, where one saw at last the pictures one had longed to see all one's life. Fascinating to be told that all Botticelli's nymphs and virgins were modelled by his little English mistress who had been brought to Florence and deserted by her soldier lover. I was taken to see an old gentleman who had a huge farm. 'What do you grow?' I asked. 'All that I need, the corn, the vine, the oil.' He showed me how the olive oil was processed, the same crop of olives successively pressed in enormous vats. 'First pressing best oil for me and my friends; second pressing oil for Italian market; third pressing oil for export!' Naples, where the rich houses were so beautiful and the little theatre such a gem, and the slums so terrifying, grey grim cliffs with caves in which ragged people lived. Everywhere one went seemed to produce something one had hoped to see and that satisfied one.

But Athens! No one had told me about Athens. 'It's the light,' they say, but also it's the sound of the names, 'Parnassus', 'Olympus', it's asking 'What is that wild flower?' 'Asphodel'. It made me feel as Rupert had felt: 'I have seen Attica . . . I can die.' I thought how aptly Stobart's great works were titled: *The Glory That Was Greece, The Grandeur That Was Rome*. Perhaps they are right, the people who tell you 'It's the light' that makes magic everywhere, that softens the glory till it is simple and without too much grandeur.

We went to visit Rhodes and were startled to find the harbour and the streets around it deserted. It was like Keats's 'Ode on a Grecian Urn':

What little town by river or seashore
Or mountain-built with peaceful citadel,
Is emptied of its folk, this pious morn?

We climbed up to the market-place and found all the inhabitants gathered there. The order had gone forth that the Leader, the Great Man, the Monster, MUSSOLINI would address his people relayed from Rome through a loudspeaker. . . . We hastened away.

I never saw any of the other islands. But a Greek friend who had toured them for many months showed us his pictures in colour. They were so beautiful. I had a sudden absurd wish that Rupert could have known he was to be buried on one.

There was a beautiful young curator who spoke French at the museum, and she gave me a wonderful moment. The men of the museum had been diving for months for a bronze horse that had been at the bottom of the sea for 2,000 years I think they said. I went down very early in the morning to see it finally brought to the surface. A beautiful creature with flaring nostrils and a proud head, and most enchanting of all there was a mechanism inside him now rusted beyond repair which had enabled him to roll his eyes. I had had no idea that such toys had been known so long ago. It was all green from the sea now but what a splendid creature he must have been when he was a shining bronze and rolled his eyes.

I don't suppose he ever realised it, but Alec Guinness contributed enormously to my happiness on that tour. He was so extraordinarily sensitive to that 'Beauty . . . by Time's fell hand defaced' and so articulate, in a gentle hesitating way about what he saw, and Merula his wife, an artist (to become a very successful one under her own name Merula Saloman) would so express with her eyes what he was expressing with his tongue that I sometimes felt that I was seeing masterpieces with three pairs of eyes!

When we said good-bye to Athens, we were all very sad and most of us had treasure laid up in the theatre prop baskets. My greatest treasure, a lovely Greek urn, I carried in my arms the whole way for fear it would be broken in transit, and how I loved to play with it. It sat in a corner alcove on a pine pedestal and I made 'flower pictures' in it by copying a book of old Dutch reproductions; I began to know when the Old Masters 'cheated', or was it just that they had a better climate? There should always be a glorious peony in the heart of every picture, and how beautifully they could surround that centre with tulips and roses and lilies! But, come the autumn of the year when my peonies were dead and gone, theirs in certain pictures were still blooming in the middle of chrysanthemums and marigolds. Perhaps it was because their peonies were blooming in their souls, mine only in my garden.

FIFTEEN

The War Begins

1939

We returned to our cottage and the peace of Penn, to April in the garden and our dear friends the Wigrams. It had been years ago, before, or just after the First World War that I had first met Robert Wigram who lived with his elder sisters in a charming old house, Yonder Lodge. He had married a girl who had died in childbirth, and remarried a delightful South African; Winnie Wigram is one of the 'life-givers' of the world with enormous capacity for making just day-to-day living seem exciting. Sometimes when sitting in the garden, I would hear the telephone ring; if there was a child at home I'd say, 'Tell whoever it is that we are all just leaving for Wycombe, unless it's Winnie of course.' If the reply was: 'It's Winnie, and she's coming to tea,' it at once became a festive afternoon, a party.

When I bought the cottage it was called The Cot. I wanted to just add an 'e', hoping that the old English spelling, as in 'dove-cote' would give it back the old English meaning of 'cot', 'a humble dwelling-place'. But the family still jeered and the name however spelt was still suggestive of a baby's crib.

I think it was Winnie Wigram who suggested Cottar's Barn. A Penn Cottage was there already, inhabited by our local celebrity, beautiful Elizabeth Taylor the novelist. Not that a *name* for a house made any difference to the village – or indeed I believe to its post office.

They knew a house by the name of the inhabitants. It was hopeless for a stranger to ask for The Cot or Yonder Lodge or

The Grange. 'Oh, you mean the Ramages' house or the Pellys' house or the Dawsons' house or the Wigrams'?' What a cosy village it was in those days. The baker would always cook the Christmas turkey in his great oven if one's own was too small. The grocer never minded one knocking on his back door at 11 o'clock at night saying 'I do apologise, but it's Sunday to-morrow and people are coming to lunch and I've run out of milk and sugar.' He was probably busy in the shop himself, decorating his window for the week. He made a wonderful 'window-dressing' each week out of all his cans and jars and groceries; he could have given points to Harrod's (and kept nearly as many varieties of everything). A sheer aesthetic labour of love, it was to him, because the traffic in the lane between him and the baker was almost non-existent. The baker lived in a lane adjacent to our cottage. We could smell the bread early in the morning, and run across for a loaf of real crusty bread of stone-ground flour. It is well known that neither fresh roasted coffee nor fresh grilled bacon ever taste as good as they smell, but fresh bread tastes even better when you have run across the grass with it fresh from the oven.

And the lady at the post office, who presided over the tele-phone switchboard on Sundays was better than an answering service. She always seemed to know where everybody was. 'No answer from the Ramage house? Well maybe they are all at the Wigrams, or the Pellys or . . . ? I'll find out,' and she could always track one down. Once indeed she practically saved my father's life! My mother was spending the weekend with us and my father had obstinately refused to come till the Sunday. Mamma sighed when he telephoned to say he would take the Sunday morning train, 'I'm sure he's up to something,' she said uneasily, 'something he does not want me to know about.' What he was up to we soon discovered. He had decided at the age of eighty-three to paint the bathroom ceiling sitting on top of a ladder on a hot July morning. He had a do-it-yourself com-pulsion to a degree rare even among sailors. Mamma always had to wait till he was out, to call a plumber, let alone an electrician or carpenter. This particular Saturday morning he had fallen from the ladder on to the tiled floor. By a stroke of good fortune the cleaning lady having left the house for her half-day off, discovered that she had left her shopping-bag and went back for it. She called out, 'It's only me, sir,' as she unlocked the door and saw the bathroom door open and father lying there with blood running from his head. Her first thought was to telephone me. And when the Penn office said there was no answer she became hysterical, poor woman, crying, 'I must get Mrs. Ramage, her father is lying bleeding.' Mrs. Winch got into action at once, rapidly calling all likely numbers. Someone said that they thought that the Ramages had taken Miss Nesbitt's mother for a picnic in the woods behind the paddock. Mrs. Winch swiftly summoned her daughter and sent her on her bicycle to the woods, rang Mr. Woodbridge the grocer to take his van and give me a lift to the station, or to my garage to take my own car out whichever I preferred. I got home, did some telephoning, drove up to London and found Papa in hospital looking contrite, 'Don't tell your mother what I was doing, I just wanted to give that ceiling a fresh coat before I left, I seem to have broken a bone in my thigh and got a cut in my head.' After a few months on crutches he was getting around at his usual sprightly pace, not even limping.

It was then 1939 and in September war broke out. '1939', I thought, 'if only it could be over by 1943.' 'My son would be eighteen in 1942, military age. Perhaps it would be over by then?' One was still raging over the rape of Czechoslovakia; was ever an honest industrious self-sufficient country so plagued with misfortune? We had sworn to protect her and treacherously betrayed her. There she is, always between Scylla and Charybdis, the Iron Heel or the Hammer and Sickle. In the last war it was Belgians we were offering homes to, this time it was our own children from the towns. I had a little Cockney who was obviously frightened of everyone and everything. She had to be tamed gently like a little wild rabbit. She absolutely refused to take a bath; she was so obviously frightened of all that water, it would have been cruel to try to force her. I had a brainwave. I put a little crimson dressing-gown of my daughter's in her room. She looked at it and loved the colour, 'Noice that is.' 'Would you like it, it's a dressing-gown.' 'Wot's that?' 'A dressing-gown is what you put over you when you get up to go to the bathroom. Then you take if off to have your bath, and then you put it on again.' 'Couldn't oi wear it as a coat?' 'Oh no! It's a dressing-gown only to go to the bath in.' For two days she

fingered it then she said shyly, 'Could oi 'ave a barf?' 'Of
course,' I said as casually as I could. 'Put on your dressing-
gown.' She put it on and walked proudly into the bathroom. I
held it for her while she dabbled a little in the bath, dried her
and wrapped her in it. 'Can oi wear it a little bit longer?' she
whispered. 'You can wear it every day as long as you have had a
bath first.' After that she began to enjoy a bath for its own sake.
The morning she dropped some of her breakfast porridge on it,
was a step towards weaning her from the dressing-gown. She
burst into tears, 'Oh, oi've messed it.' 'It's all right we can
clean it off, maybe after you have had your bath you could just
put your dress on and then put it on at night after supper.' Just
as she was beginning to be a child again, she was only six, and
had looked like a little dwarf, she was sent for by an aunt in
Wales and departed rather tearfully clutching at her dressing-
gown for comfort.

I was rather glad to see her go though, as I had no one to
leave her with and I was starting rehearsals. These rehearsals
I looked forward to with an excitement I had not felt for a long
time. Granville-Barker had been persuaded to come back to the
theatre to produce *King Lear* at the Old Vic. The theatre had
been badly damaged by fire and bombs, and in aid of the rebuilding fund John Gielgud and Lewis Casson had assembled an
all-star cast to play a short season with John as Lear. Barker
had agreed to set it up, then leave it to Lewis Casson to rehearse
for a couple of weeks after which Barker would return and
finish working on it. I think most of the cast had played at the
Old Vic before, and it was an imposing cast of classic actors:
Jack Hawkins, Robert Harris, Harcourt Williams, Stephen
Haggard, Lewis Casson as Kent and as co-producer. Cecil had
got an Army job, so I was delighted to be offered the part of
Goneril. Fay Compton was Regan and Jessica Tandy as
Cordelia. I had been a little disappointed in the Barker with
whom I had worked in his own play, *The Madras House*, fifteen
years before. He had still been fascinating to work with and
listen to. I remember how he asked if Nicholas Hannen and I
felt quite 'comfortable' playing a long scene together without
moving from our chairs. I said, 'Oh yes! it's such heaven not to
be made to get up and stroll to another chair and when one
asked *"why* do I get up?" to be told, "Well, you have been

sitting in one place rather too long." ' Barker groaned, 'The physical action is so *un*important in nearly every play; oh I don't mean when it's a question of fencing or dancing or a battle, or even in playing a broad farce like a Feydeau. Then it matters, but if an actor has an emotional or mental conflict to cope with he should never have to think "Should I move there?" or "Am I in the right place here?" He should move when his instinct prompts him, not when mine does.' 'But if his instinct doesn't prompt him to move ever?' asked Hannen. 'Then he's probably a bad actor' said Barker, 'or possibly, of course, a genius, in which case he's moving the audience' – making one of his rare jokes. But if ever we did get to a little talk about fascinating things like, 'How much should an actor feel what he is portraying, night after night?' there would come a voice from the dress circle 'Lunch time Harley!' And Harley would drop everything and disappear. We all resented that mysterious 'Helen', that American millionairess who had quenched all his passion for the theatre. But I couldn't help remembering what Norman Wilkinson, who had designed *The Winter's Tale* setting, had told me. Mrs. Huntingdon was not a millionairess and that money would not have tempted him anyway. He had fallen deeply in love with her. He had fallen in love like a schoolboy for the first time in his life, and would stand outside her hotel at night, looking up at the lighted window of her room. She would blow him a kiss from twelve storeys up and he would stand there till her light went out. I never knew which tale to believe. Whichever it was it had quenched his fire as far as the theatre was concerned.

But with *Lear* it came back, I felt. All the actors responded to his magnetic drive. Everyone wanted to work for as long as he would go on. No one was being paid more than £10 a week, all the proceeds, which must have been enormous, were devoted to the rebuilding of that part of the Old Vic that had been destroyed by bombs. There were practically no dressing-rooms left. Fay and Jessica and I had to share one room and I seem to remember that Jessica had just married and Fay was just divorcing (or was it the other way round?) and could have done with a little privacy! All of us could have done with better lighting. We had to queue for the one decent mirror with a light that we could see by.

But everyone was theatre-happy. There is no more delightful feeling for an actor than that lift of the heart that comes as one goes through the stage door feeling, 'This is my happy ship.'

And it happens seldom enough for one to be able to remember vividly the companies it happens to. Not that the average company is not happy but so often there is one little discord, a director who is arrogant, a star who is neurotic, one part badly played, even minor things like lighting too dim or too bright, or a noisy stage-hand, or one member of the cast with a chip on his shoulder – nothing anywhere to make one *un*happy but just . . . how shall I put it? One has to carry one's own 'uplift' with one. I think that outside his performance, John Gielgud had a great deal to do with the atmosphere of harmony. He is a wonderful person to be on stage with, less arrogant and egotistic than any actor of his stature that I have ever met. He and Barker had the same gift for making everyone seem important to the play. There was one actor who played a Captain, a practically non-existent part. He followed Lear on to the stage and had but one line to say after Lear's wonderful lines: 'Now she's gone for ever! – Cordelia, Cordelia! Stay a little. Ha! What is't thou say'st? Her voice was ever soft, gentle, and low, an excellent thing in woman. I killed the slave that was a hanging thee.' The Captain says, ''Tis true, my lord, he did.' The actor just said it, not ill or well, just said it. Barker called him aside and said quietly, 'That is an extremely important line. You must let the audience *feel* you have seen a miracle – you *have* – you are not accustomed to miracles – you are a rough soldier. "If it be man's work I'll do it" is about the only line you have. It has established your character and now you have seen with your own eyes a very old man, at the point of death, kill a man with his own hands, pick up a body – and a dead body is difficult to carry – and Miss Tandy is quite a tall woman. You have seen a thing that is not possible, yet you have seen it – your heart must beat faster when you say: '' 'Tis true, my lord, he did.'' It must be with awareness that almost stops Lear's rage for a second – he must *feel* you there and turn to *you*. "Did I not, fellow?" . . . Now go away and *think* about it.'

Barker had a wonderful ear for the orchestration of a scene and so, of course, had John. Between them in scene after scene they achieved effects which were absorbing and moving to watch night after night. And he made the parts of Regan and Goneril interesting to play, their wild passion for Edmund was illustrated as it were by Barker's seizing every opportunity to show the silent contest between them for his favours. Jack Hawkins made Edmund such a splendid virile lusty fellow, with such humour in his first speech on bastardy. Both Regan and Goneril lusted after him like bitches in heat. Was it the frenzy of their nerves that made them such monsters? Barker somehow brought out the odd impulses of humanity in the monsters – Edmund on his death-bed tried to make amends, not with any snivelling piety but almost with a touch of nobility. Here to the last was one whose motto, like that of one of Marston's hero devils: 'My God's my arm; my life my heaven, my grave to me all end.'

Barker knew when a great shout of laughter was valuable – when Goneril asked Edmund for a kiss he was allowed to bestow it with such passion that she was left swooning, and when he had gone from her sight and she turned to face the approach of her fussy timorous elderly husband, her sigh of, 'Oh what a difference of man to man!' made the audience laugh so much that they almost felt a wave of tolerance towards her. And, when Albany in rage having discovered her treacheries towards the King, shouted that only her woman's shape could shield her from his hands: 'Apt enough to dislocate and tear thy flesh and bones' her impudent answer: 'Marry! Your manhood? mew' was another laugh when as Barker suggested, she started a little 'mew' like a kitten and ended half-giggling with a full throated 'miaou!'; puncturing poor Albany's rage as a child punctures a balloon with a pin. I could go on and on remembering what Barker did for Goneril, putting some human flesh on to the bones of that strange profoundly egotistic insensitive creature; but it would bore anyone except another actress who has played or will play Goneril! Except perhaps that it *is* interesting to see how Shakespeare saw into the essential *childishness* of his amoral ladies (even Cleopatra) in a way that made them more credible than the pure devils of Webster and Marston and Fournier. Just as in one of Ivy Compton-Burnett's novels one sees a child of three, whose assumption that the world was created for his delight and all adult humans made to wait upon him has such enormous charm that one wants to spoil him just as his relations do, but when towards the end of the book he, as a grown man, behaves just as he did as the child of three, and one shudders at him, one realises that the modern psychiatric equation of immorality with immaturity is fundamentally sound. I think probably that everyone who like myself has worked with Barker is apt to become a bore on the subject! I do find myself *dwelling* on recollections of rehearsals. It's odd that, of all the plays that I have played in, there are only two of which my memories of standing in the wings and *watching* the principal players are so vivid and both of them were directed by Barker. I watched certain of Leontes's scenes in *The Winter's Tale* so often that I can still hear the cadences of Ainley's voice. I stood in the wings watching and listening so often to Sir John Gielgud's Lear that I can still hear the biting irony of: 'Is man no more than this, consider him well. . . . Thou are the thing itself; unaccommodated man is no more but such a poor, bare, forked animal as thou art.' And the tender moving gaiety of: 'Come let's away to prison. We two alone will sing like birds in the cage: . . . and tell old tales and laugh at gilded butterflies, and hear poor rogues talk of court . . . who's in who's out and talk upon's the mystery of things.' And the sense of grief too deep for tears one had at all those 'Never, Never's' like the tolling of a funeral bell. What wonderful warmth it brings to the heart to have such memories. When one is 'old and grey' (and *not* 'full of sleep'!) how proud one's memories.

I have seen Laurence Olivier as Macbeth and Othello. I have seen John Gielgud as Hamlet and Lear. I have seen them both together alternating in friendly rivalry between Romeo and Mercutio and I have seen them both play comedy with so exquisitely light and delicate a touch that one wants to go back again and again to see if one can find out how it is done, which suddenly makes me think of another production when I used to stand in the wings every night and watch. It was when Rex Harrison played in *My Fair Lady* and sang, 'I've grown accustomed to her face'. There indeed was a touch of genius. I find absolute perfection, a great part of genius, whether it be in tragedy or comedy. What an intriguing word is 'genius', and how careful one should be when using it. With words, the coinage is so easily debased – one smiles at little Hugh Holland's 'Lament for Shakespeare'.

These hands which once you clapt, now go and wring,
Yon Britains brave; for done all Shakespeare's dayes:
His dayes are done, that made the dainty plays.

Dainty plays? Then one is told by one who has studied words and
their origins that 'dainty' was derived from *digne*, dignity, and
implied originally worthy and excellent, and might quite
properly be used to acclaim a play of Shakespeare. So with
genius – I'm sure the real meaning of the word carries some of
the aura of a god or a devil – *genius loci*, the genie in the bottle. A
man can have enormous talent, intellect, skill, taste and still not
be a genius. I feel that Granville-Barker was a genius and so did
everyone who knew him, from John Masefield who wrote to
him, 'People talk of you as if you were a god,' to Lewis Casson
who said, 'In our time, if ever, the theatre will not look upon his
like again.'

SIXTEEN

The War Continues
1940–1945

∽∾∽∾∽∾∽∾∽∾∽∾∽∾∽∾∽∾∽∾∽∾∽∾∽∾∽∾

The war went on and on. My son, now in the 6th Form at Eton,
had to go into the Army. How thankful I was and disappointed
he was, that it was not the Air Force. He had been in the Flying
Corps at school and was 'ready to take off' but the eyesight tests
were still very strict in the Air Force, and they discovered a
slight astigmatism, so he was turned down. Much to my relief –
for the Air Force casualty list was the highest of the war – he
joined the Rifle Brigade. My daughter was already in America.
My friend, Malcolm Chase, on Great Island, Hyannis Port, had
been in London before America came into the war and had
offered to take a number of his friends' children to the States to
escape the bombing and educate them at his own expense,
knowing we were not allowed to send any money out of the
country. Jennifer went to school and to Sarah Lawrence College
there and spent her holidays at Great Island, as I had done over
twenty years before. She had one very exciting experience. I had
written to Mrs. Roosevelt and told her that I didn't want to
presume on our very slight acquaintance of so many years ago
but that I knew the White House sent out hundreds of Christmas
cards every year – and that if her secretary could address one to
Jennifer Ramage at Hyannis, the child would probably be very
thrilled. It was her first Christmas away from home. Mrs.
Roosevelt not only sent her a card but invited her to the White
House for a weekend. I think she felt, as did F.D.R., that no
opportunity of showing solidarity with the British should be
missed. Jennifer had a wonderful time, sleeping in Abraham

197

Lincoln's bed, being shown all the sights, even being given a cocktail by Mr. Justice Felix Frankfurter, which Mrs. Roosevelt, guessing it was her first, had insisted on being diluted. When she arrived back at the Chases, she was bubbling over with the desire 'to tell all about it'. Mrs. Chase stopped her politely but firmly: 'We do not talk about *that man* in this house dear.' The Republican attitude towards the Democrats in those days was as vituperative as the bitter enmity between the Whigs and the Tories was in eighteenth-century Britain and carried over into private life. It must have been quite an effort for the Chase family to reconcile their feelings about F.D.R. the *'New Dealer'*, and F.D.R. the *'pro-ally'*.

In the forties, the theatres were making desperate struggles to keep open despite the bombs. I remember in September 1940 playing in an eerie play called *Outward Bound* at the New Theatre. The scene was a ship, all of whose passengers were already dead – one of them a lovely red-haired girl, Sarah Churchill. The ship's siren had a strange unearthly sound rather like an air-raid warning and every time it moaned one could see the audience instinctively duck their heads. We got used to seeing the audience sway sideways like a field of corn in a strong wind, sheltering their faces under the seats in front. By the Saturday night of one week, I think there were about eighty people in our theatre and ninety at Wyndham's across the passage; when the plays were over we all assembled on the roof of Wyndham's Theatre to watch what seemed like the great fire of London. The great timber yards of the docks were ablaze. I was doing a five-minute poetry-reading series called 'Epilogue' every night at midnight at the BBC. That night, I was chased by a policeman half way up Regent Street calling 'Hey, Hey, Miss, you should be in the shelter. Didn't you hear the warning?' 'I know, I know, I've *got* to be at the BBC by 11.55. I'm on the air by midnight.' 'On the air' was a magic phrase in those days. The policeman put his arms under my elbows and propelled me along to Langham Place. We all went down to Studio S in the bowels of the earth, and as I passed the press-room I heard an infuriated American journalist ranting, 'Jesus Christ, I got a line to my editor in New York and whadya think the bastard said? "Another fire story? Gee! One fire's just like another!"' Just like another? When the docks are flaming and London

Bridge is burning down?' That night, all the London theatres decided to close. Mr. Beaumont of H. M. Tennent had the brilliant idea of sending most of his companies out on the road, paying a salary of £10 a week plus a percentage of the takings and a promise to do six weeks for ENSA in between every three months of the tour. I went out in Lonsdale's comedy *On Approval* with Roland Culver, one of the most brilliant comedians on the stage at that time. It was so successful that it went on for, I think, about fourteen months. Mr. Beaumont had decided it was a good play to tour, only four characters, so we could go anywhere by bus even if the railways were commandeered by the troops. The actors' first reactions were: 'Well, we may not make any money but we will escape the bombing!' On the contrary, we made a great deal of money. Some weeks were so profitable that I made more than I had ever made before. But we ran into more furious bombing in Liverpool and Huddersfield than we had ever known in London. I remember an anxious night in Liverpool. Roly Culver and his wife, Daphne, and I were staying in a little hotel within walking distance of the theatre and the din started just as we got in so we went straight downstairs to the shelter. After a time we realised that Roly was no longer with us. Men had been popping in asking if there were any soldiers or sailors on leave or any able-bodied men among those present, who would volunteer to 'give a hand at the docks'. So many men slipped away that as dawn came we were almost all women and children. Daphne was furious about Roly: 'Damn fool, the only reason he isn't in the Army is he's too old and only has one lung – why the hell did he want to volunteer.' 'I don't believe he *did*,' I said. 'I never saw him come or go.' About 7 a.m. Roly strolled in. He had found some naval pals in the audience, had gone aboard one of His Majesty's battleships, quite against every rule of the Service, been caught by the bombing and smuggled ashore in a dinghy at dawn. 'It took me two hours to get here, you can't recognise a single street, and ask anyone the way, they say "sorry pal, just as flummoxed as you are, maybe if you take the second big fire to the right, and then the first big hole to the left, you'll find yourself somewhere near the theatre".' Daphne nearly brained him in fury and relief. She was a great girl and an interesting example of how 'talent will out'. She had been engaged as general understudy and assistant stage manager and general dogsbody. By the end of the tour she was general business manager *and* stage manager and bossing the whole show. She was very firm with the actors: like Gerald du Maurier's Chownie, she would allow no nonsense. She would stand in the wings watching a scene and then waylay us as we started for our dressing-rooms. She was always extremely formal in business hours, even to her husband: 'Miss Nesbitt, Mr. Culver, I've timed that scene. You are running two minutes *over* playing-time – self-indulgent acting at its worst.' Or: 'Miss Nesbitt, Miss Churchill ("No. *No* relation" poor Diana Churchill had to answer every time a reporter looked in, eager for gossip), I don't know what private joke amused *you* so much. Please keep your private jokes to yourselves. They don't amuse the audience.' As soon as the tour was over, she became general manager and casting director in London, and sometimes directed plays for the Tennent enterprises. She seemed to have a 'talent to succeed' in everything she undertook. She and Roland separated and with a new husband she went off to start a guest house in Majorca, which became a favourite holiday resort for actors. After a time she came back to London and started a restaurant, which immediately became fashionable 'Daphne's' in Chelsea, charged enormous prices and was always full.

When the tour ended, my aim was that of every woman who had children in the forces, to keep busy, and luckily I found things to fill all my days. In the mornings I drove to London and played in lunchtime Shakespeare at the Strand with Donald Wolfit, snippets from *Macbeth*, *Much Ado* and *Taming of the Shrew*. Oddly enough we had packed houses as did the lunchtime concerts on the steps of the National Gallery.

During the afternoons I was waitress at the Amersham Hospital, mostly waiting on the nurses who were run off their feet with overwork. They were really grateful for an odd dogsbody to be on hand all the time.

'Hi, duckie!' a panting girl would call out rushing past me, her cap askew, 'I got five minutes off at 3.30. A nice cuppa, hot and sweet and a bun, could you manage?' And how rewarding to see her sink to the floor as I laid a tray on the stool beside her. 'Gawd, duckie! it's good to get me feet off the ground, thanks a million.'

In the evening I bottled, pickled and preserved the fruits of the earth.

How they rushed one, tripping on each other's heels. Cherries . . . no the birds always got the cherries! We had only two cherry trees, not worth getting in the 'bangers'.

In those days children would form groups and go to an orchard armed with old saucepans, broken frying-pans, 'any old iron', pails filled with stones, crying 'Bangers here! Bangers!' and keep up an infernal racket to scare the birds away from dawn to dusk. They charged very little and I'm sure would have done it for free. What greater bliss for a ten-year-old than to be told for once to make as much noise as you can. But strawberries, raspberries, currants, peas, plums, apples, all screaming to be bottled, beans and tomatoes to be salted down, potatoes to be 'shelved', one could never sit down, but what a noble site on the larder shelves all those kilner jars, glowing golden and crimson and green and how imposing the great brown crocks of salted green beans. And how useful the jars of blackcurrants of which I had so many and the farmer's wife so few. But she had new-laid eggs (which should, of course, have all gone to the marketing board to be rationed) and a little quiet 'exchange and mart' was set up. How pleased we were to hear that Winston Churchill had taken the trouble to write a stern letter to a magistrate in a neighbouring village, who had fined an old lady for exchanging her sweetie rations with the village children for their tea rations. 'Rationing was introduced to ensure fair shares for all. To penalise people for sharing their rations voluntarily is niggling nonsense,' thundered the great man. I fear he would not have approved of those eggs though!

By and large the whole population abided by the Law, compared to France, for instance, the black market was negligible. I remember being in Paris just after the war and going into a little pâtisserie for a cup of coffee. I saw a plate of luscious Napoleons oozing thick whipped-cream and eagerly took one, as I ate it I saw a huge notice covered with government stamps on the wall, 'Absolutely forbidden to charge more than 1.50 f. for any gâteau'. When my bill came, it said gâteau 5.50 f. I smiled and looked at the notice on the wall. 'Faut pas faire attention à ça' said madame scornfully. Obviously no one did!

And when I went to lunch with Julia James (an enchanting

ex-musical-comedy star and 'special friend' of Lloyd George),
I was delighted after the hotel breakfast of hard bread, no butter
and weak chicory, to find butter and cream and sweet French
coffee. And not only that to be told just where to buy anything I
needed, at a price!, in a little shop behind the Madeleine.

At one time during the war I rented a flat in Albany. Strange
how confused time can become in one's memory. If anyone
asked me which war had lasted longer, the First or the Second,
I would have promptly said 'Oh the First! That went on for ever
and ever. Surely the Second was over much sooner?'

To my surprise when I check up I find that the Second World
War lasted nearly a year longer than the First. Perhaps it is that
time seems endless when one is waiting and watching in a
foreign land as I was during the First World War. And partly
because in the Second one was more involved as a civilian, things
changed so rapidly. Time seemed to flash by. One barely had
time to get used to one kind of danger when a different kind
shocked one out of one's patiently acquired courage. I think the
only thing that really terrified me was the coming of the
Doodlebugs. These had such a menacing anonymity about them.
I was living in the little flat on the top floor of Albany at the
time and I can remember lying in bed listening to the 'Albany
Express' as we called it. It came straight over us heading north
every evening. One heard the buzz in the distance and as it got
louder and nearer one froze: 'Tonight perhaps it will be us.'
And one was a little ashamed at one's great relief, when it
crunched a mile away, and one knew that some poor devils in
Edgware or Maida Vale had had it.

It's strange how hackneyed old phrases come alive when one
'feels' them. I had read in thrillers about how 'fear made her
flesh creep'. It's true. If the fear is fierce enough the flesh does
'creep'. It used to be a very strange sensation. It was not as if
something was crawling up one's back or one's legs, it was the
flesh itself 'creeping'.

But there were good days in that little flat. While my son was
still in training he used to come up often at weekends from . . .
he never would say where. He belonged to a very 'secret'
division (indeed called the Phantoms).

One thing about the Doodlebugs, there was no warning, so
one didn't have to crawl all the way down the stone staircase to

the cellar. And once the 'Albany Express' had gone over one knew there wouldn't be another.

One evening Eddie Marsh and Eddie Sackville-West came to have dinner with me and one of them brought a friend, Raymond Mortimer; I remember they stayed till 1 o'clock in the morning, and I was absolutely dazzled by their conversation. I discovered they were all 'Janeites', and they all quoted Jane Austen at each other and commented on all her characters with such humour and wit that one almost felt they had written all her books between them. I found myself making a vow to re-read her works every year.

I think it was about then that I did an enjoyable radio play that Eddie Sackville-West had written. It was called *The Rescue*, and was about the return of Odysseus to Penelope. I remember a wonderful line of Penelope's when she had asked Odysseus, 'Why do you keep your eyes closed when you embrace me?' and he replies, 'I see you better like that, your image has been engraved on my eyelids for eighteen years.'

PENELOPE: *You left me a young girl, you find me a middle-aged woman.*

ODYSSEUS: *So absolute a face blunts all the weapons of time.*

PENELOPE: *You say that as if you had said it before . . . to someone else. But no matter. I do not care to know!*

Always the response of the really wise woman to passing infidelities.

I have a beautiful copy of the play with colour illustrations by Henry Moore. We played it on consecutive nights, Parts One and Two, with music by Benjamin Britten. When I remember that cast of thirty odd, and the huge orchestra, I think the BBC must have been very rich in those days. Or perhaps it has always seemed surprising when anyone in charge of entertainment is allowed to spend as much money on a good play as he would on a second-rate musical.

Then at last the war was over. My son, having acquired a scholarship to Cambridge, was demobbed fairly early. He had had, as one of his fellow officers had told me, 'A damned interesting war.' The Phantoms' chief duty, as far as I could gather, was to run around in a jeep with three or four men and carry dispatches in their heads from one headquarters to another. The idea being, I suppose, that if one was bumped off, the enemy could find no valuable written information. I say 'I suppose', because it was a highly secret organisation and I never dared ask for any information. Even when they were in training in England, they were under strict orders not to reveal their whereabouts. He used to spend occasional weekend leaves with me in Albany and when on a Sunday night he said, 'Now darling, I must catch my train,' I had no idea where the train was going to, it might have been Edinburgh or Windsor. As a matter of fact, very early on I ran into a friend of mine who was married to his company commander, and when she told me she had taken a little house at Richmond to be 'near John', I could make a good guess that the train journey wasn't a very long one. One day the telephone rang and a voice asked for him. I heard 'Yes, sir', 'No, sir'. 'Oh! Thank you very much, sir. Of course I understand.' And he turned to me and said, 'That was my Colonel – he said I might spend the night in town if I liked – I won't be needed at crack of dawn as usual.'

I thought perhaps the training was settling down to something a little less rigorous, and was delighted to have him for the rest of the evening, and said 'au revoir' as usual. Three days after, I opened my paper and read that our troops had landed and The Invasion had begun. Mark had obviously been told that Sunday that they were ready to go and had been granted an extra twelve hours' leave. I was very impressed with his acting ability. He might easily, taken by surprise, have either underacted or overacted on the receipt of such momentous news!

My daughter, who was in the WAAF, had heard that those of the girls who could read, and write, and put two and two together were going to be kept on for a long time to clear up the paper-work. (I remember that one of the minor scandals the war unearthed, was that an incredible number of young people who had suffered years of State education could neither read, write nor add!) The only ones earmarked for early release were those who had scholarships to one of the universities. Jennifer promptly got to work and managed to achieve one to Lady Margaret Hall, Oxford. It's an achievement I have always been awed by.

How anyone who had had the peripatetic education that she had had, starting as a child at the French lycée, moving to an

English boarding school, then to an American boarding school, then to an American university, then to becoming, I think, an assistant in the photographic laboratory of an Air Force camp, could satisfy an English establishment examiner, has always mystified me. Mark already had a scholarship to King's College, Cambridge – so they were both with their 'Army Grant' splendidly independent. Both of my children, when I confessed that I was trying to write a 'book about myself' were most encouraging, but added firmly, 'leave me out please'. I promised I would, but they keep breaking in! After all they are both people I would like enormously, even if I weren't related to them, and have given me more satisfaction than almost anything else in my life.

SEVENTEEN

Life Begins at Sixty
1949

∽∽∽∽∽∽∽∽∽∽∽∽∽∽∽∽∽∽∽∽∽∽∽∽∽∽∽∽∽∽∽∽∽∽

For the third time in my life a visit to America was to lift me out of a 'slough of despond'. It's odd that, on that first voyage around the world, the one country that I hadn't visited, North America, was the one that fired my imagination by just reading about it. When I joined the Irish Players in 1911 it wasn't only the prospect of work that delighted me, it was the prospect of going to America. When I went again in 1915 to play a dreary part I had already turned down in England I had the odd feeling of being rescued from myself, of beginning life all over again.

Now at sixty I was going through a period of dispirited nostalgia. It seemed to me that the best of life was over for me; for reasons that it is pointless to go into now, my marriage had broken up. My career didn't seem to be going very well either, after being stuck in a bad part, in a bad play (which ran for a year, financially comforting but rather destructive to the morale), I seemed to have done very little work for several years. I was beginning to wonder if my long years of good fortune had exhausted my ration when Henry Sherek sent me *The Cocktail Party*. I didn't know then that it was destined for New York. He was planning to produce it at the Edinburgh International Festival. I read the first act with delight; 'a good part at last,' was my first thought, the usual actor's egotism! 'And in an Eliot play, a verse play, every dream come true,' I rejoiced. But I am ashamed to say I became more and more bewildered as the play went on, question after question, 'Who is Julia? What is she? What is a Guardian? Why do three ordinary people, or are they "ordinary people", suddenly turn into priests and perform an occult ceremony?' In fact I found myself behaving like the angry lady who saw Harold Pinter's *The Birthday Party*. She wrote, the story goes, to Pinter, 'Can you tell me the meaning of your play? There are three things I do not understand. 1. Who are the two men? 2. Where did Stanley come from? 3. Were they all supposed to be normal! You will appreciate that without the answers to these questions I cannot understand your play.' Mr. Pinter replied politely, 'I would be obliged if you could explain the meaning of your letter. There are three points I do not understand. 1. Who are you? 2. Where do you come from? 3. Are you supposed to be normal? You will appreciate that without answers to these questions I cannot understand your letter.'

I remember I rang up Alec Guinness and asked, 'Do *you* understand this play? Do you think *anybody* will?' Alec's grave beautiful voice calmed me without reproach, 'I would not, until I know the play a good deal better, presume to say I understand it. All I can say is that it has a great meaning for me.' I think if it hadn't been for Alec I would have been afraid of it, but he was so inspiring to play with, and played the play so magnificently on two levels, the wry ironic mischievous humour of Harcourt-Reilly and the priest-like authority of the Unidentified Guest. I never really found meaning in the last act of *The Cocktail Party*, or what meaning I did find seemed monstrous to me; and I have never really enjoyed Shelley as a poet, the way I enjoy Donne or Keats. But when Alec spoke his quotation from Shelley in the third act, I was for a moment persuaded that it was extremely arrogant of me to presume to 'criticise' either Shelley or Eliot!

How kind he was to those of us who got tied up in our efforts to keep the rhythm and the fun going effortlessly. I remember one day when everything I did seemed a little leaden, Alec took pity on me and said, 'I think we are all taking this too seriously, come on, we'll go and have a really good lunch somewhere and forget about it and come back "all-alive" and rehearse with gaiety.' I forget where he took me but the food was wonderful, we drank champagne, Alec's dry humour made me giggle helplessly. We got back to the playhouse a few minutes late, we who were always the essence of punctuality, and, as we thought, floated on to the stage, and began to give delightfully gay high-comedy performances. After about an hour Martin Browne, the director, came on stage and said with his usual gentle politesse, 'I think you two are just a bit tired. It all seems a little flat. Perhaps you'd like to leave a bit early today?' He was not being ironic, I don't think he had the faintest idea that we were both ever so slightly inebriated, no not even that, pixilated, to use the lovely movie euphemism. But it was a great lesson, no amount of inner gaiety in the actor's mind is of any help towards making the audience gay, unless that actor is directing that gaiety with cold and cunning concentration!

The opening on 22 August 1949 at the Royal Lyceum, Edinburgh, was a revelation; the audience took it as a comedy, and we all floated on their laughter. I felt that the tide had turned for me (Alec's performance alone would ensure eager offers of theatres in London) and that I was going to have happy moments to work on the sketch of a character I had achieved. But not a single London manager would take a chance on it. As with *My Fair Lady* they waited till New York had set the seal of approval on it. But Gilbert Miller who had his own theatre there bought it for New York, and in November 1949 we set off by plane.

'This is my first time to cross the Ocean by aeroplane,' I said to my children who came to see me off. 'Life begins at sixty, darling!' said my son. I had a sudden feeling of zest for living again. 'Do you know I do believe you're right,' I replied seriously and both the children laughed at me. But none of us imagined that I was not only going to stay in *The Cocktail Party* for a year, but that it was the beginning of a twenty-year sojourn in America. Delightful years of almost continual work, many delightful parts, and above all wonderful new friends – not only Americans, Anita Loos, Helen Hayes, Margaret Sullavan, Anne Seymour, George Cukor, the Joseph Cottens, the Moss Harts, the David Selznicks, Frank McCarthy, Rupert Allen, just writing down their names makes me feel joyful, calls up so many pictures of good times and kindnesses and warmth, and that amazing unrepayable American hospitality. What seems strange to me now, but what I took for granted at the time, was the number of English friends I made. I suppose it was partly the spontaneous camaraderie that always seems to spring up between Britons abroad and partly the very quiet retired country life I had been leading since the war in England, just driving back to Penn every night and rarely seeing anyone but the people I was acting with.

I had met, but only had an acquaintance with, Gladys Cooper, for instance, or Margaret Leighton, Rex Harrison, Audrey Hepburn, Lynn Fontanne, Alfred Lunt, Richard Burton. I didn't know any of them well till those American years. Perhaps the most exciting thing that happened to me was meeting Enid Bagnold. It was odd that I should never have met her before; we had known many of the same people during our girlhood in London, but I had never seen her until she arrived to stay with the Lunts while I was there. All her books had for years been on my 'precious' shelf, next door to Jane Austen's. Not that they are the least alike as writers but I think they both have 'masculine minds'. I can hear an acid murmur from the 'Women's Lib' corner, 'Do you consider the masculine mind, as you call it, superior to the feminine mind?' to which I can but reply, 'Yes, I do.'

We opened *The Cocktail Party* in New York, all a little anxious, all of us having decided that New York was a wonderful city and one in which we most eagerly wanted to stay. The opening night seemed a little flat to us all, compared to Edinburgh. John Van Druten came round to me and said: 'Sorry love, it just doesn't quite come off. I'm afraid it's going to be just a short sharp "succès d'estime".' To cheer me up he suggested I dine with him on the next day and we could dine late and read all the press notices.

'But tomorrow is Sunday. We'll have to wait till Monday before we get any reviews?'

It was then that I learned that one of the delightful facts of life in America, for an actor, is that one can always buy tomorrow's papers tonight and always get the press reviews within an hour or so of the curtain falling. Hence all those hectic first night parties, at which no one can settle down till the manager's 'scout', who's been telephoning all the newspaper offices comes round with the verbatim reports. One can then enjoy the party and sleep in peace, knowing the worst or the best. Now I believe there is only one paper left, one soars or falls by the *Times*. Then there were a good half dozen, even some of the evening papers for Monday had gone to press by

Sunday night. After dinner Johnny rushed out to buy all the morning papers. As we read them through we were astonished, 'For heaven's sake! You're a hit! Do you realise these notices mean at least six months, probably longer.' Johnny was flabbergasted, he didn't really like the play. I was enchanted, I already loved New York.

We were a very happy company, Alec Guinness, Irene Worth, Robert Flemyng, I not only loved them as people, I admired and respected them as artists, and we had such fun together. Even at large parties we tended to drift together, Irene and I used to walk home together, very often. 'Exercise is good for the figure', we reminded each other, 'and we must remember to keep fit for the sake of our elegant clothes' (not that Irene ever had a weight problem, slender willowy reed that she was). But on a certain corner of Fifth Avenue there was a great plate-glass window, 'Childs', with three white-hatted chefs tossing pancakes in the window. 'Hot buttered pancakes soaked in maple syrup!' Who could resist them? Not I or Irene. 'Just this once,' we would say to each other almost every night.

No one had expected such a long run; Alec, Irene, Robert all had after three, or six or eight months, film or theatre commitments to take them back to England. I stayed for the whole run. I was enjoying myself highly.

One of the replacements for Alec was Hugh Williams; Tam, as he was known to all his friends, was a creature of infinite charm and wit. He was at the moment a bankrupt, but he never allowed it to curtail his style of living. His lovely wife, Margaret, tried hard to economise. They had a little flat in Washington Square which she managed to make attractive by all sorts of devices, buying cheap Indian bedspreads and secondhand enormous damask tablecloths, no longer used anywhere, which dyed brilliant colours, so that there were colourful curtains hanging everywhere. But Tam was occasionally given to furious rages. 'These bloody commissioners or whatever they call themselves, not content with attaining most of my salary, they write saying, "How dare I, as an undischarged bankrupt, put both sons down for Eton?" How dare *they* tell me where I may educate my children!' No one could ever stay angry with Tam. His first wife who left him before he had met Margaret, 'because she couldn't stand the racket "financially",' came out to New York to do a play. Tam always appeared at parties with Gwen Whitby (his first wife) and Maggie (his second) one on each arm, making sure that both his wives had a good time. He and Maggie made a fortune afterwards as successful playwrights. Just before their first success he and Wilfred Hyde-White were both playing in a farce at The Criterion. Someone told me that they were both at the moment undischarged bankrupts, but were nobly struggling to see that their creditors were paid in full. I went round to see Tam after a matinée one day, half expecting to see him eating fish and chips and drinking tea. Not so. He and Willie Hyde-White were both sitting comfortably in Tam's room with a couple of dozen oysters and champagne. I think they would have considered it indecent to be starring at The Criterion and not living it up.

Perhaps that is why I am so fascinated by the mystery of people who 'believe', like Alec Guinness or Tam Williams. Tam used to be quite worried about me. 'You know you really are a very Christian woman if you only knew it,' he would say. 'I can't see how you can live that way if you don't believe in a future life.' Your true believer would think it a sign of immaturity (perhaps it is?), but I still feel as I did as a schoolgirl, 'A gentle scepticism is the height of human happiness and wisdom. You should not believe in anything, not even your own disbelief.'

The frequent changes of cast led eventually to my coming back to New York after the run of *The Cocktail Party* finished. I got into the habit of helping Gilbert Miller with the 'new girls' who replaced Irene Worth as Celia. He tried several, none of them very good, and I tried hard to coach them. I hadn't realised myself what quality Irene brought to the part, a curious dedication that she brings to everything. It is something that cannot be taught. Finally we had Faith Brooke, who brought a quality of her own. She was a real worker and good to work with.

I left New York rather sadly and with very little hope of returning, but within a few months Gilbert Miller decided to do Anita Loos's adaptation of Colette's *Gigi*. Colette herself had picked Audrey Hepburn to play Gigi, and Gilbert who had an old-fashioned actor-manager's desire for an established star to play a leading role, was nervous about her lack of experience.

I believe she had only once appeared on the stage in a minute role in a review, in which she brought down the house every night. Gilbert asked if I would come to the St. James Theatre one morning and see if I could 'hear her from the pit', as he put it. I never let him pay me for these adventures in teaching. I thought it such good experience in case I found myself having to teach in my old age. I couldn't as a matter of fact quite hear her but I realised as soon as she stepped on the stage that she radiated star quality to such an extent that it really didn't matter. I think it was more that I had fallen in love with her at first sight and wanted to see more of her, than any belief that I could *teach* her anything that made me suggest she might like to come down to the country where I was living and just let her voice go in my three-acre field where she could shout and test any range of voice. I can still see her jumping off the train and racing along the platform calling 'Hi! Cathie here I am' and a whole crowd of people who had been waiting for that same train standing staring as though they had seen a being from another world, the guard standing rapt too, till he suddenly remembered to blow his whistle.

We worked together a little, just on projection and she went off to Paris to be fitted for her dresses. I got amusing accounts of how Gilbert was sending actress after actress to Paris to audition for the part of Tante Alicia and how Raymond Rouleau who was to go to New York to direct the play turned them all down, till finally one morning Gilbert telephoned me. 'Look I've sent every one I can think of to that damned Frenchman, and he won't have any of them, Audrey thinks you might do.' It was spoken rather grudgingly and I was not surprised. If I had even thought of myself in the part I'd have been begging for it! But I didn't think I had the right sort of allure for the ageing 'most successful cocotte of her day', and a king's ex-mistress to boot.

However, off I went to Paris and to the Hotel La Reine Elizabeth and faced Rouleau with trepidation. I don't think he even asked me to read the part, he was so delighted to have someone who could talk French and listen to his criticisms of the ladies who had read the part to him, that he telephoned Gilbert at once, 'Yes'.

I stayed on and was fitted for a ravishing wardrobe by Nina

de Nobile, a famous French designer. I can say it without vanity because as I think I have already mentioned I don't admire my own face at all, but in America I did acquire the reputation of being a beauty. I think I owe a lot to people like Nina de Nobile, Lucinda Ballard and above all to Sir Cecil Beaton; de Nobile for *Gigi* clothes; Lucinda for *Romulus*, and Cecil for four plays, ending up with *My Fair Lady*. Those dresses were so ravishing that I could almost hear the little gasp from the audience on my first entrance. I really did look superbly decorative.

I remember with such pleasure the melting colours of the yards and yards of rainbow-hued chiffon that floated around Tante Alicia when she first appeared. And chiffon again in *Romulus*. Lucinda Ballard, the wife of Howard Dietz, the composer and lyricist, is an American designer whose designs for the Metropolitan's production of *Giselle* and Helen Hayes's *Wisteria Tree* are still a high-water-mark in any history of stage design. And as for Cecil, one gets a wonderful sense of authority and poise from just seeing oneself in one of his creations. He was responsible for one of the happy moments that startle one with the pleasure of the unexpected. I was playing a very amusing role, not the star part, in Henry James's *Portrait of a Lady*. I had had my entrance round of applause. How warmly a New York audience greets its old friends on an opening night. Delicious of course to the recipient, but how maddening for the author whose first act is half spoiled by those 'rounds' every few minutes till all the cast has appeared.

As I was saying I had had my entrance greeting and, having a very amusing little scene to play, had made my exit to gratifying applause. My next entrance merely required me to stroll across the stage. I was greeted on entrance *and* exit with applause! I say *I* was greeted, but it was Cecil who was greeted and with real enthusiasm, as well he might be. He had designed a riding habit from top hat to boots all of such an elegance, and such a glorious true emerald green that the effect was dazzling. Long after the rather dull play was forgotten and even the names of those who had played in it gone with the wind, people remembered that green riding habit and that hat. What a fortune Cecil could have made if he had abjured all his talents and just set up as 'The Greatest Man Milliner in the World'.

If I could wear the grey ostrich-feather hat I had in *My Fair*

Lady every day, even in my bath, I believe I'd go out feeling beautiful, which as Lynn Fontanne once said is half way to *being* beautiful. I remember telling her the story of Simone, the great French actress, who had in her hall a full-length mirror lit with the greatest care, with soft rose and mauve lights veiled with tulle. In her dressing-room was a table with a huge magnifying glass and glaring brilliant lights. Before going out to a great occasion she would spend an hour at her make-up rectifying every blemish, enhancing every perfection. When she had done her best she would dress without looking in a mirror again and then stand for a moment in front of the 'kind' mirror in the hall. She would smile at herself softly and murmur, 'Oh! Dieu! que je suis belle.' And everywhere she went people would turn and murmur, 'Dieu! qu'elle est belle!'

'Sensible woman', said Lynn approvingly, 'anyone who can't look beautiful when she has to look beautiful shouldn't be on the stage at all.'

It was Raymond Rouleau who told me that story of Simone so I haven't wandered as far from *Gigi* as it might look. Poor Raymond, he found himself really 'dépaysé' at first. Not knowing a word of English, he had to have Audrey or myself to translate his instructions to the rest of the cast. He couldn't understand the power of the unions; that we should have to stop at 6 o'clock whether we had finished or not enraged him. 'Mais c'est imbécile. Demain matin on aura tout a refaire, tout.' On the other hand he was much struck by the discipline of American actors. 'You say, "take one hour for lunch and come back at two o'clock please" and they come back. In Paris we should still be looking for half the artistes in the near-by bistros at 3 o'clock.'

He began to learn a little English, sometimes becoming a little confusing in his directions. There was a scene I had to play with a young man during which Tante Alicia had to sweetly and languidly turn him inside out. 'Is coming good', said Rouleau, 'mais un peu plus de snak chère Cathleen.' 'Snak?' I thought, 'does he mean snap? Perhaps I'm taking it too slowly; well, I'll try it a little more swiftly.' He looked perturbed at the result and we were halfway through the morning when I discovered that 'snak' was 'snake'. He wanted me to uncoil slowly and gracefully to strike, as it were. 'Ah! serpent?' I asked, at last,

'C'est ça, c'est ça, snak!' I thought it was a word he was un-
likely to use much so I didn't hurt his feelings by correcting his
pronunciation. The play itself didn't get very good notices but
Audrey, quite literally, became a star overnight. She had already
signed a contract to do the film *Roman Holiday* for Paramount,
and they were so delighted with her notices they offered Miller
a large sum of money to publicise the play on condition that
Audrey was starred above the title. The original billing was to
star Colette to which we all agreed and the cast below the title
reading 'Cathleen Nesbitt, Constance Collier, etc., and introducing Audrey Hepburn.' But by the time I arrived in New
York, Rouleau had quarrelled with Constance who walked out.
Then Florence Reed was brought in who insisted on having
precedence over me which I thought reasonable as she was a
big star in her own country. Then she and Rouleau had a
formidable fight and Miss Reed walked out. So I was back to
square one, with top billing and the star dressing-room. Miller
rang me up in the middle of the week to tell me about Paramount's offer and explained that he would like to co-star me
with her, but Paramount insisted on sole billing for Audrey, and
of course I agreed. As he said, 'I'm afraid we'll have to come off
if we don't take advantage of this offer.' It was rather a blow to
me to come to the theatre next night to see Audrey's name in
huge letters, Colette's *Gigi* in equally huge letters, and in very
very small type way down underneath came Cathleen Nesbitt,
Miss A., Mr. B., Miss C., Miss D. I'm surprised now as I look
back at how much that upset me. It seems such a small matter,
but to my equal surprise something similar happened to me just
a few years ago while I was still in America. And it annoyed me
just as much! I thought at my age I really would have grown out
of caring so much about such trivial things. I am reminded, too,
of an evening years ago in Blackpool. I was trying out a play
there for 'Binkie' Beaumont and as I had gone to London on the
Sunday I met him on the train on Monday and he gave me a lift
to my hotel in Blackpool. 'Oh dear, oh dear!' he murmured
peering out of the window, 'I hope Miss A. doesn't take this
route to the theatre when she arrives next week.' When asked
why, he said, 'I've had such billing trouble with next week's
play between Miss A. and Miss B. I finally compromised by
promising to print an equal number of posters, one group

putting Miss A. first, one putting Miss B. So far I've seen nothing but Miss B.'s taking precedence! Oh, you actors! One could give an actor a starvation salary, murder his grandmother, give him a rabbit hutch as a dressing-room and get away with it, but when it comes to billing, he is out for one's blood, and will shed his own in defence of his "rights".'

Audrey's beauty, warmth and simplicity lit up that theatre every night, back-stage as well as front. I looked forward every day for the moment when she would poke her head round my door and say, 'Cathie dear, here we are again!' and kiss the top of my head before racing back to her own room like a young gazelle, with her slender limbs and large glowing eyes. We had a delicious scene together when Tante Alicia taught Gigi the importance of knowing a good 'stone' when she saw one, and acquiring as many as possible as early in life as possible. I used to feel sorry for the audience that they couldn't see as closely as I could the look of awe and wonder and delight with which she looked up at me when I held up a ring and asked, 'What is that?' and she replied under her breath, 'An emerald!' No amount of adulation could spoil her, her manners were always exquisite, but behind her gentleness was a very strong character. She fought Paramount for weeks over her refusal to sign a seven-year contract with them. They tried everything, bribes, promises, even a little quiet blackmail, 'We have just tested a girl who will be equally good for *Roman Holiday* and if you refuse the contract we offer you, we must regretfully . . .'

'Do you think they really have got someone?' she would ask me, 'but I am right, aren't I? I *can't* be tied up with them entirely at their mercy for seven years?'

I had seen her test and knew there wasn't anyone in the world except Audrey for what they wanted, and reassured her. Once I remember she was so much wiser than me, she had had an offer to go to Stratford-on-Avon for a Shakespeare season, 'Oh, how wonderful! How splendid for you,' I said, but she shook her head. 'If I could just go and have a season learning, doing the Celias and the Nerissas and the small parts, but you know what it would be, they'd make me play the Violas and the Juliets and give me a blaze of publicity and I'm not ready, not nearly ready, I'd flop.' I can see her now, her worried, eager little face, looking in her black slacks the 'little scrubbed boy' that

216

Shakespeare must have dreamed of for all his 'girl-boys'. But she was right, she was a wise child.

I always thought she showed remarkable courage breaking off her engagement to James Hanson, as soon as she realised that he was going to interfere with her career, after he had promised he wouldn't. It was only ten days before the wedding, with the wedding dress waiting and the whole of Huddersfield agog with excitement. How relieved her mother was. 'Imagine Audrey living in a huddle of horses in Huddersfield,' she moaned when it was first rumoured that Audrey was going to marry into a hunting family!

How I wish Warner Brothers hadn't been so adamant about someone else singing the songs in *My Fair Lady*. I went to her house one day to hear the tape of 'Wouldn't it be loverly?' and thought it very 'loverly and moving'. I have not seen very much of her since she gave me a surprise party on my seventieth birthday. We meet occasionally in Hollywood or New York. I am happy for her that she has stopped working but keep hoping that when her children are a little older there will be another Audrey Hepburn picture to look forward to.

Two friendships with people nearer my own age resulted from the production of *Gigi*. During the somewhat stormy rehearsals of *Gigi*, Anita Loos's imperturbable good humour was a godsend, and she was always full of practical advice about where to live and where to eat and where to buy clothes, realising that although Audrey and I had thought our salaries were adequate by British standards, they shrank enormously when confronted by the cost of living in New York.

Anita must be nearly seventy now but she still seems to look exactly as she did when I first saw her over twenty years ago. She looked like a little brilliant tropical bird, always dressed by Balenciaga. She told me that by a streak of good fortune for her Balenciaga's favourite model was an exquisite tiny Burmese girl, and the things he designed for her were always right for Anita. 'Dressed by Balenciaga' wasn't so wildly extravagant for Anita either, as when the annual sale disposed of the model-worn items, there was no competition for the prettiest coats and dresses – Anita was the only woman in Paris who could get into them.

Through her I knew Helen Hayes. How I wish I had seen her in her famous part of Queen Victoria! I think there are places in

America where people believe that she *is* Queen Victoria! Especially in Cuernavaca in Mexico where her house is in a little street which is called Calle Victoria. People often asked her whether she bought the house because of the address. But I know she bought it because of the view across a valley with Popocatepetl in the distance. I had read a poem, as a child, which had the name of the great mountain in it. I never learned to spell it, I don't know just how to pronounce it, and I didn't learn at Cuernavaca; the natives called him 'old Popo', and regarded him as a mixture of Weather Bureau and National Monument and Ancient Idol – the Magical Pocopatepetl!

Helen has a genius for discovering a house with a view. I shall never forget waking up on Sunday morning on my first weekend at her house in Nyack. We had motored down from our theatres on Saturday night, and all I'd been aware of was a round hall from which doors led right and left, in every direction, and stairs leading upstairs and downstairs and to my lady's chamber. Often as I have stayed there, I never quite knew whether the door I opened led to my bedroom, or the kitchen or the library or the drawing-room, or another bedroom. And I never minded going the wrong way round because there were such fascinating bits of 'things Victorian' everywhere. On one wall a group of pictures of her young ladies-in-waiting in prim early Victorian dresses, with oval faces and rosebud mouths: I used to search among them for my great-great-aunt Alice, but they all looked alike and some of them had no names attached. Or one could open a door and find oneself gazing at a Renoir, the Renoir that Helen had bought on her way to spend $20,000 on a sable coat! She had suddenly decided she owed it to her public to dress like the star she was, instead of going about in an old camelhair; so she would have a sable coat, and look like a queen. Les messieurs Revillon Frères were ready waiting with superb skins to fit the toile, but on her way she passed the Durand-Ruel Galleries, where hung in solitary splendour Renoir's *Girl in the Lace Hat*. Helen stopped and gazed. 'Why that's exactly how my Mary will look when she grows up! That picture really belongs to Charlie (Charles MacArthur, her husband) and me, it's a *portrait* of our daughter!' She went in and bought the picture, and cancelled the coat.

But Helen has told that story, better than I could, in the

delightful book* about the city of New York on which she and
Anita Loos collaborated for a year, and have recently published.
It's a book which gives me much pleasure, being full of ammuni-
tion for me in my warfare with those American friends who say
that New York is not a city for any civilised person to live in
any more. Perhaps it's not very 'civilised', though even that I
dispute, but I do think it is the most exciting city in the world.
I suppose Paris is the most civilised, New York the most
exciting and London the most livable-in, or do I mean lovable?

I used to dream that if a fairy godmother were to leave me a
fortune, I would have a house in Paris for the spring, in London
for the summer, in New York for the autumn – and in every
house would be clothes and make-up and kitchen-ware, so that
I would never have to pack. But, lacking fairy godmothers,
ordinary mortals have to pay for their pleasures, and the nightmare of packing is a small price to pay for the good fortune of
having had a chance to live in all those cities, and at the chosen
time of year. What would I do in winter? Hibernate I think, with
an occasional week in Palm Beach or in Mexico.

I seem to have digressed slightly since I left myself waking up to a view in Nyack even more beautiful than the
view from the Calle Victoria in Cuernavaca! I had arrived at
midnight and fallen happily into bed in the cosy 'country' bedroom; someone came in, almost immediately I felt, so sound
was my sleep, with coffee and the French toast which Helen
makes so superbly. 'Would you like the curtains drawn?' 'Yes,
please,' I answered, sleepily. A blaze of light awakened me
thoroughly. I stood entranced at the window. Just below me was
the terrace, gay with white iron chairs and green cushions.
Below it, a grassy bank with stone steps in it led to the rose
garden, another grassy bank sloped down to the pool, another
went right down to sea-level, and beyond it the great river
Hudson shimmered in the sun.

The whole vista was framed by descending avenues of the
most beautiful tree in the world, the dogwood tree, with its
snow-white and glowing pink stars. I had never seen them in full
bloom before. I could understand the story I had heard of how
Laurence Olivier had so fallen in love with the dogwood trees

* Helen Hayes and Anita Loos, *Twice Over Lightly*, Harcourt Brace Jovanovitch,
1972.

that he had refused to believe that you couldn't grow them in England. He bought a dozen at just the right age to transplant, had them most carefully packed, even travelled on the freighter with them to make sure they were watered and nurtured on the way over, had them carefully planted by whoever was the Capability Brown of the day, and they all died. I was sad to hear that story, I had been making plans to take some young trees back to my own garden.

What pleasure I have had from trees in America; the maples in Vermont state, so ablaze in the autumn one felt one could warm one's hands at them; the palm trees in Florida, and the grapefruit trees with the grapefruit hanging in magnificent clusters like blown-up grapes, and best of all, the lemon trees growing under one's window in California. When I first went out to Hollywood to do a film I found a little garden flat in a real garden with orange and lemon trees, flowers and fruit blooming together. I used to think the lilac tree had the sweetest scent, till the philadelphus came with summer and was still sweeter. Then orange blossom seemed better still, the best I decided. But I now think the lemon is the most fragrant of all.

I had no sooner returned to London after *Gigi* and done a play at the Edinburgh International Festival than I was back in New York again to do Sam Taylor's comedy *Sabrina Fair*. I found the play delightful but my part dull. I nearly turned it down till I heard that two of my favourite film stars were going to be in it. Margaret Sullavan and Joseph Cotten. People told me that Maggie was 'difficult' in the theatre. I discovered that it was for the same reason as Marie Tempest was said to be difficult: she was an absolute perfectionist. At rehearsals she would almost drive everyone mad, most of all herself, in her quest for truth. She had mannerisms of speech that made people say that she was affected. But she was the most honest actress I have ever played with. Immensely disciplined on the stage, she was not so in life. I have always been fascinated by people who vent their emotions unrestrainedly. Maggie could suddenly flare up like a thunderstorm; if the lightning blasted you, you suffered for a moment, but forgave her long before she came begging forgiveness like a child. In fact sometimes when she said something to her director or a fellow actor that I thought unforgivable, I would find myself within a few hours trying to make her forgive herself! She and her husband Kenneth Wagg lived in Connecticut and I spent many weekends with them. During the week Maggie would stay in their New York flat if the weather was bad, but every Saturday we would rush out of the theatre into the waiting taxi, and subside panting into the train. At Greenwich either Kenneth would be waiting with his car, or would have left Maggie's car at the station. She was such stimulating company that we would talk all the way; once we were so busy talking that we passed Greenwich without noticing and with horror heard a sleepy porter call Hartford. We had to hire a car to drive back to Greenwich. I can't remember what we were talking about. I hope it was important. 'It's been a most expensive conversation,' said Maggie.

She was, I think, very much like Colette must have been in her 'concentration of love' on animals and birds and plants. I remember one night, we were alone in the house, I had a dream of an avalanche; I awoke thinking, 'I still hear that crash, what a vivid dream!' Then I heard Maggie's voice 'Cathleen . . . come . . . the tree is dying!' At the bottom of their garden there was a little river and over the river hung the tremendous branches of an elm; it had been shored up with steel and seemed more solid than the house. I raced downstairs, stumbling over the Abyssinian cat, for once startled out of its languorous grace. The tree was falling into the river. One last wrench, one could almost hear it groan and it lay still. 'We bought the house because I fell in love with that tree,' said Maggie softly. 'Listen to the silence, all the birds have fled, even the ducks. Let's get our dressing-gowns, we can't go back to bed.' 'Let's hold a wake,' I suggested, and we sat with a bottle of wine and drank to that immemorial elm, and talked of ourselves to each other till dawn. I think that was the moment I was the closest to Maggie in all our friendship. I remembered the sadness I felt in the destruction of three of the five beautiful elms in our paddock at Penn. There comes a moment in the life of an elm when it becomes a danger to the public and has to be cut down. When it has become centuries old its death is unpredictably sudden.

Maggie died so tragically young and so suddenly that I felt I had lost a beloved sister.

When I think of her, which is often, I remember the haunting lines of Walter de la Mare.

Life Begins at Sixty

Look thy last on all things lovely,
Every hour. Let no night
Seal thy sense in deathly slumber
  Till to delight
Thou have paid thy utmost blessing;
Since that all things thou wouldst praise
Beauty took from those who loved them
  In other days.

There was so little I could give to her, I like to think that loving someone is itself a gift, that loved ones do take beauty from those who loved them.

During the next year I settled down in New York. I became a 'resident alien' and furnished a little flat on Central Park West. I played in many successful plays and had many delightful parts in *The Sleeping Prince, Anastasia, Portrait of a Lady, My Fair Lady*, and toured with Judith Anderson in *The Chalk Garden*. In fact I was never out of work for twelve years, largely I think because I had very little competition – there were hardly any actresses of my age and experience – whereas in London there were at least half a dozen.

I went out to 'The Coast' as the Easterners called Los Angeles, every now and then to do a TV role or a 'bit' in a film. In fact I was quite in demand for TV for a time, as I could do 'dialects' very well: Irish, Scots, Welsh, Deep South, even a kind of Brooklynese!

I shall always be grateful to two authors, Paddy Chayevsky who wrote *The Mother* and Sydney Carrol who wrote *The Playwright and the Star*, for the best parts I have ever played in any medium – or should I say the most successful. Those were the days of live television; one did it right there in the studio at Radio City, in one evening, live to a live audience. And afterwards the applause rained in from one's audiences everywhere; a splendid excitement of 'telephone call for you from L.A., Miss,' 'phone call from Chicago,' 'phone call from Washington,' and the next morning bundles of telegrams and the next week letters, letters. I was so overwhelmed by them (never having had real fan mail on that scale) that Cecil Beaton lent me his secretary who had a wonderful method for classifying.

1. This group: I think you must answer yourself in your own hand.

2. This group: You dictate replies to me and sign them when I've typed them.
3. This group: I will write a charming letter from you and you will sign them.

Somehow when taping and filming came in, the thrill for me was gone – one had an endless tedious few days with cameras and mikes, and then one looked at it coldly weeks later with a cold appraising eye, muttering to oneself, 'Oh my God! why did I do that?' and 'Heavens! how phony I sound.'

But of course it wasn't *au fond* the medium that changed things, so often the writers weren't very good – a Chayevsky or a Carrol doesn't grow on every bush – and star writing makes for star performances in any medium. One of the TV stints in Hollywood was to make a pilot for a projected series. I came back to New York and forgot all about it till a couple of months later I was notified that the series had been sponsored and they were ready to go into production early in the following month.

EIGHTEEN

Three Years in Lotus-Land
1962–1965

⌒⌒⌒⌒⌒⌒⌒⌒⌒⌒⌒⌒⌒⌒⌒⌒⌒⌒⌒⌒⌒⌒⌒⌒⌒⌒

When they heard that the pilot for the TV series that I had
made in Hollywood had been sold, and that I was to be at the
studio's disposal for between three and five years, my New
York friends were horrified: 'Live in Hollywood? Oh, my dear,
how awful for you – it might go on for years.' Nobody believed
me when I said I *liked* Hollywood.

I found a garden flat again, with orange and lemon trees and I
was very contented during my three-year 'servitude'. How I
loved the sun, which was always shining – the heat, sometimes
90° for several days running – the weekends by the sea – so
many friends had houses at Malibu or The Palisades, they all
seemed to have spare rooms and 'working girls' were always
offered a day by the ocean to refresh them from the week at the
'Factory', as Gladys Cooper called the studio where she too was
making a series.

She had a house in Pacific Palisades where I'd once spent
several weeks when we were doing a picture together: *Separate
Tables* it was, and what fun we had. Harold Hecht the producer
gave a lunch party in a small studio to introduce the cast to each
other, the day before we started. We were all old stagers who
had known each other in London, except for Burt Lancaster and
David Niven. We all ended up crowded round David Niven, the
world's best raconteur; he made us laugh so much we none of
us wanted to go home, which inspired Hecht with a wonderful
idea. When we reported for work the following day he announced that he had set aside that same small studio as a private

lunch-room for us and that lunch would be sent in every day from
The Brown Derby.

'You all seemed as if you'd been living together for years,
and that's just the atmosphere we want for this picture, we must
keep it.'

Gladys offered to pick me up at my hotel and drive me to the
studio, but after a week she said, 'This is silly – I have lots of
empty rooms, why don't you come and stay.' So I spent I can't
remember how many blissful weeks. We both had contracts for
a minimum of six or eight weeks, after which we were on a
'daily rate' – more advantageous financially. Gladys chuckled
with glee every time anything went wrong, or someone fluffed,
or a scene had to be re-shot: 'Two more extra days and I'll have
enough to pay for heating my pool.' How delighted we were
over the affair of the egg-cup. The property department was very
proud of the authenticity of everything on stage, but occasionally
Gladys or I had to hint that, for instance, in a British guest-
house they don't serve pots of tea at the dinner table every
night. 'I thought the British had tea with everything,' muttered
the prop man. At the breakfast scene Gladys had to order boiled
eggs for her daughter's breakfast. She found American egg-
cups on the tray. 'But we don't break our eggs into a large cup,
we have a small cup that fits the egg and we eat the egg out of
its shell.' 'Props' looked puzzled: 'I guess I never seen anyone
eatin' an egg outa a *shell*,' he said. 'Well we *must* have British
egg-cups. It's a *British* guest-house.' said Gladys. There were
no British egg-cups in the property room, and apparently none
in the nearest village. After several hours' delay the scout
reported he couldn't find any in Hollywood either. Gladys murmured to me 'I know *just* where you can get them but let them
look for themselves – it will take them all day – another day for
the pool!' However, the production manager decided that rather
than wait all day, the order could be changed to scrambled eggs –
which are eaten on a plate on both sides of the Ocean.

The only dull days were the days when David Niven wasn't
called – not only did he tell extremely funny stories, mostly
against himself, but he told them so well. And he never was one
to hog the scene. He could draw tales from eighty-year-old May
Hallat about her childhood, or from Felix Aylmer about his
terrifying attempts to find an exit from the freeways.

I can remember one day they wanted to take close-ups of his reacting to the glances of the other guests at the boarding-house. To save time he sat at his own table and we were grouped at strategic distances around him.

He looked at us gravely and murmured, 'Gladys Cooper, Deborah Kerr, Cathleen Nesbitt, Felix Aylmer, Wendy Hiller. Oh my God! what a jury of experts – might as well plead guilty, here and now.'

Once David invited me to his house for lunch on a Gala Day, where I met his wife; Hjordis is one of the most beautiful women I have ever seen, and how I love to look at beautiful women. The food was wonderful. I had never taken to that great American delicacy cheese-cake, but when I refused it, David said, 'Oh! but you *must* taste it – it's the "specialité de la maison". I bet you'll come back for another helping.' I did and a large one at that. Indeed that and George Cukor's *crême brulée* are side by side in my private list of 'great dishes I have eaten'. It's odd now I come to think of it that they are mostly rich *sweet* desserts. Cecil Beaton's Monte Cristo *soufflé* is another that comes to mind. Perhaps I subconsciously think of them as 'forbidden fruit'. For so many years of my youthful dieting, I had never eaten fattening dishes without a sense of sin.

The first thing I was told on arrival was that one could *not* live in Hollywood without a car. So I fished out my old British licence, which I had not used for fifteen years and asked if I might have a visitor's permit.

I was told I must first take a road test. Not being used to a left-hand drive and American rules of the road I thought I'd better take a few refresher driving lessons. Within a week I had lost my nerve entirely. The size of the car I was learning in terrified me to begin with. It had power-assisted steering and I wasn't happy without gears. I couldn't even park the great monster 'six inches from the kerb, and absolutely level with it'. A row of sticks indicated the kerb – they had all gone down like ninepins by the time I had parked, all askew at that. I gave up the whole idea, I decided I might be a menace on the road. I was glad of my decision when I heard that Gladys Cooper, who had driven in Los Angeles for fifteen years, was told she must take a test before her licence was renewed on her return from an English trip. She failed the test three times. It took her studio some wire-pulling at the highest level before she was given a licence.

Gladys's friends all declared that she *was* a menace on the roads; and indeed being driven by her was always a little hair-raising. But in fifty years of driving she had never had an accident which was a good answer to all criticism. I started depending on taxis, which were not always to be depended on to turn up at 6 a.m.

Once again an 'ever-loving son' came to Mum's rescue. Bill Windom passed my way *en route* to the studio, and picked me up and took me home nearly every day. Even on days when he was released earlier than I was he would almost always hang about to give me a lift.

Inger Stevens and William Windom and I were co-stars in the series, myself as a Senator's widow, Bill as her son, a Member of Congress and Inger, as the beautiful Swedish au pair girl. Bill was certainly a loving son, beyond the call of duty, and eased life for me considerably.

He and Barbara, his wife, had a house practically right on the ocean and I had some lovely lazy weekends there gossiping with Barbara while Bill sailed his boat all day long.

Barbara was the granddaughter of Louis B. Meyer and made me laugh one day when she showed me a little house in Beverley Hills, with a great brass plaque: Louis B. Meyer Foundation. They always say to the rich about their money, 'You can't take it with you, you know.' Nobody said that to Louis B. Meyer; he could and he *did* – he keeps it all in that little house.

It seems that he had quarrelled violently with Barbara's mother, and had tied up all of the fortune that should have been left to her in so many trusts of various kinds that the first descendants to touch any of it were to be Barbara's children, and probably not even them, till they had achieved a ripe old age.

At first the change in one's daily routine took a little adjusting to. For years I had been accustomed to theatre hours – never getting to bed till after midnight, spending ten hours in one's dressing-room on Wednesdays and Saturdays. Now it was an 'easy' day on Monday, 'plotting' and reading the script; four days of being at the studio by 6.30 a.m. for make-up and free by 6 o'clock in the evening. For me there was often Friday free too, and for everyone, that blessed Saturday and Sunday. I had to learn to go to bed early to try to get in the eight hours I have always needed. At first that 6 a.m. alarm-call was paralysing!

And there was the continuous effort to escape the ministration of the make-up artist and the hairdresser, both of whom belong to extremely powerful unions, and their will is law. How often have I seen actor and director on edge (wanting to strike while the iron is hot and do a retake of a scene that was nearly perfect) because someone from 'make-up' or 'hairdressing' would rush on to the set to powder a nose, or tuck in a stray piece of hair. That is one tyranny the new wave of naturalistic films has done away with!

I was surprised that *The Farmer's Daughter* lasted as long as it did. Such suspense as there was was supplied by the question: 'Will he? Won't he? Isn't he going to marry the girl?' 'He', being a young widower, a Congressman, with two small sons, living with his mother, Agatha, a Senator's widow. Mother Agatha's great desire was to see him happily married to their charming Swedish au pair girl. When the series began I had rather hoped that, mother and son being descendants of several generations of political families, there would be a political angle to some of the stories, and I should get some sidelight on the intricacies of American politics and the way Presidents were elected and the way the Constitution worked. But the producers probably quite rightly had decided that, to their particular public anything of a political nature would be a bore, so to this day I am sadly uninformed as to how the American Constitution works. One only really hears about it when it is *not* working and then 'The Man in the White House' is always blamed.

I got accustomed to the friendly proprietary manners of our public, so often was I assailed in a supermarket by some female shopper: 'Say! Hi! Aren't you "Agatha"? Yeah I thought you were. Why isn't this *something*! Say, meet my friends will ya? Edna! Mary-Belle! Marilyn! come here – meet Agatha. When are those two going to get married? My, that was a good plan of yours teachin' Katie how to make him jealous. What next have you got up your sleeve to give him a push?' I don't think they ever knew my real name. I was just Agatha who came into their living-room every Friday large as life – in close-ups rather larger! – and who enchanted their children by riding up and down stairs on a 'personal elevator', a chair attached to the banister which rode up and down at the push of a button.

'Why does she have to use that damned chair?' I asked once, 'she doesn't seem to be crippled, she cooks and gardens like mad so she doesn't have a weak heart. Why can't I *walk* upstairs?' It was frustrating to use, it made so much noise that one's lines couldn't be heard, so that they had to be dubbed afterwards, and it moved so slowly that one's lines suddenly sounded silly if one waited till one got to the bottom to utter them.

I finally inspired our press agent with curiosity, so he did some research and came up triumphantly with the answer. 'Agatha *has* to have an elevator because there was one in the film. Ethel Barrymore played her and she had a fall early on, and they wanted to get on with the shooting, so the minute she could walk they gave her a cane, and instead of waiting till she could manage stairs they put in the little elevator.' 'If I fell down off that platform at the head of the stairs and broke a leg what would they do?' I asked. 'Put it in a cast and put *you* in a wheel-chair,' he answered brightly, 'and then some day in the future, if they ever did a re-make of the picture, or of the series, Agatha would have to have an elevator *and* a wheelchair.' 'Quod erat demonstrandum.' I confess I sometimes got a little tired of Agatha. She was so endlessly good and sweet and kind and charming. There were times when I longed to be a witch in the next-door studio where Elizabeth Montgomery was doing *Bewitched*. But we had our compensations. We had a very busy and competent press agent who arranged delightful trips to Disney Land, everything laid on *de luxe* including beds at the hotel, and no waiting in a queue for any of the attractions, so that Agatha and her son could give the grandchildren a day out at Disney Land. Once Bill and his wife and I were flown down to New Orleans for the opening of a new hotel. We were given the 'celebrity suite' at the Hotel Monteleone, and spent a few energetic days sight-seeing, or rather *they* did. It rained all the time, so I sat in my room and read a delightful history of New Orleans from its very beginning, and ended up knowing the town better than either of them. The press man's best stunt was persuading the great Washington hostess Perle Mesta to give a wedding party for the young couple in Washington. After all, what could be more appropriate? The family was supposed to live in Washington. So the wedding having been solemnised in the studio we all packed our best clothes and were flown to the capital. An exhausting evening it was too, as we had to stand to receive an endless procession of guests. Bill's wife came along too; one could forgive some of the guests for not being sure which *was* his wife, the beautiful blonde who helped him receive the guests or the beautiful brunette who hung on his arm when at last the reception line broke up!

Once one had settled down, life was really lived in a Lotus-Land. Sundays by the ocean, walking along the sands, stopping for a pre-luncheon drink here or a pre-dinner cocktail there and parties galore, at weekends. Sometimes a magnificent formal dinner at George Cukor's. When one asked, 'Should one dress?' George would always say, 'It would please *me* to see you in a long dress.' His house with its formal elegance and wonderful pictures was a background for elegant clothes. Even after the war, in England men automatically wore a black tie to a dinner party, but in California black tie had to be heavily underlined on the invitation before the average man would think of 'dressing'. Sometimes in summer there would be informal parties in the garden. George, always solicitous of his guests' comfort had a collection of wonderful pure cashmere dressing-gowns to wrap around the girls in their summer dresses, all of whom always forgot the sudden bitter chill that descends when the sun goes down. George's parties were always exciting. The food was wonderful and the guests were such a mingling of all worlds, not only the great movie stars I had always hoped to see in the flesh, but artists and musicians, writers and journalists, such as André Previn, Christopher Isherwood, Alistair Cooke, Hugh Trevor-Roper. And George always quiet, courteous, a catalyst of any warring elements. And warring elements are always a possibility in a room full of personalities, which means almost automatically a room full of egoists!

Rupert Allen and Frank McCarthy would give parties, too, in their house far up in the hills. Everyone helped themselves from a long refectory table laden with tempting food; one couldn't help overloading one's plate! The parties were generally given for some visiting V.I.P. I remember once Rudolf Nureyev was the guest of honour. I had only seen him at a distance on the stage looking like a young god – close to, he seemed like a god

of woods and jungles, a young Pan. Very *alive*, but wary and
aloof; probably bored with the enthusiastic females who rushed
at him telling him they had also seen Nijinsky (how tired he
must have been of hearing that). He retreated to a corner with
Natalie Wood. They talked Russian together with growing
excitement and abandon. I didn't understand what they were
saying, but I could almost sense the moment when, as one or
two 'piss elegant' guests looked at them disapprovingly, 'the
children decided to be naughty'. I felt sure they were saying:
'So . . . they think we are just behaving like a couple of peasants?
We'll show them!'

They started eating their chicken legs in their fingers (the
only sensible way to eat chicken legs), crunching the bones and
chucking the debris on the carpet. Some of the guests were
shocked, others said delightedly, 'I guess if Tolstoy had given
parties in his youth, all the guests were having fun just like that.'

Some five years later I met Nureyev at Douglas and Mary-
Lee Fairbanks's country-house outside San Francisco. He had
come over with Margot Fonteyn and her husband Señor Arias to
spend a day by the pool. Nureyev turned out to be one of the
people whom success had not spoiled. His manners were impeccable, his kindness and gentleness with Señor Arias were un-
affected. It was curiously moving to watch his pleasure when
Margot 'translated' a witticism of her husband and made us all
realise that though Arias's speech was affected by the wounds
received in Panama his mind was still keen. She seemed to grasp
instinctively what he was trying to say, and when we all laughed
at his *bon mot* his blue eyes twinkled merrily and we all felt he
was one 'of the party'. And when Nureyev moved his chair into
the sunlight, or when Margot 'fed him' his lunch, it was done so
simply and unostentatiously that one was hardly aware of it. I
have seen wives being 'kind' to a disabled husband so very
obviously aware of their own kindness and patience that it was
almost embarrassing; with Dame Margot there was such a
sense of it being the most normal and natural thing to do that
it became charming and moving. When the little group had gone
Mary-Lee and Douglas and I all felt, 'There goes a very great
woman.'

And now I have once more run ahead of myself. Several years
ahead in fact. Back to *The Farmer's Daughter*. We had three years

of it, until finally the Congressman married the au pair girl to the great satisfaction of our ever-loving public.

And by that time my vague dream about California that this was the land where I would like to end my days had faded. Happy as I had been I realised that though Hollywood was a splendid place to *work* in, it wouldn't be good to live in when not working. I was within a few years of my eightieth birthday, and my roots were in England; not only my roots but my branches. I had always longed for grandchildren and my daughter for twenty years had longed for a child – then when she was over forty she gave birth to a boy and two years later to a girl. There can be nothing more rejuvenating than suddenly to find oneself the grandmother of two small babies!

To watch the development of Crispin and Carey-Kate would be a delicious excuse for retirement.

But of course old actresses don't retire! Like old soldiers they 'only fade away' and even then only when *very* old. I didn't feel old at all – in fact the next few years were so busy that I never had time to think about age. I was so busy commuting every-where – exactly *where* and *when* I did my jobs is something I can never recall precisely – which Christmas was it that I spent with Helen Hayes in Cuernavaca and saw the Museum of Mexico City? It was the most beautiful museum architecturally that I had ever seen. And what gaiety! In the pre-Columbian room for instance one would come upon shelf after shelf of the merriest pornography imaginable. You look at the tiny clay figures, wondering vaguely what on earth they are doing and suddenly you dissolve in laughter as you realise what they *are* doing! They seem to wink at you: 'Isn't sex fun?' and continue on their mad gambolling.

Was it the next summer I went to visit Noël Coward again, and was taken to dine with a friend of his in whose living-room hung the only abstract picture I have ever *felt*; it was just *blue*, washes of blue, but the blueness seemed to come right out of the canvas as an ideal of blue, a Platonic essence. It was over fifty years since I had been so aware of the blueness of blue in a valley of hyacinths in the Chiltern Hills. I knew then what people meant when they said that a painter was painting what he *felt* rather than what he *saw*; it had never made sense to me before.

It was about then that I went to Guildford to play Amy in

T. S. Eliot's *Family Reunion*, a part I had longed to play for many years.

And the following year I was back in Los Angeles.

I went to stay with my friend Barbara Poe while playing there in a revival of *My Fair Lady* with Douglas Fairbanks Junior. 'We are none of us going to give you another farewell party,' she said, 'you'll be back.' Perhaps I shall yet! It would be good to see all my friends again. 'All my friends'; I'd like to pay tribute to them in a chapter to themselves.

NINETEEN

All My Friends

ᡐᡐᡐᡐᡐᡐᡐᡐᡐᡐᡐᡐᡐᡐᡐᡐᡐᡐᡐᡐᡐᡐᡐᡐᡐᡐᡐᡐᡐᡐᡐ

'I do sometimes let others say for me things that owing either to the feebleness of my language or the feebleness of my judgement, I cannot say so well myself,' said Montaigne. I suppose the reason we admire him so is that he attributes to himself at times every human weakness he has seen in humanity at large. One can always find in him an excuse for one's besetting weaknesses. I quote him to apologise for mine, a passion for quoting. I am always haunted by someone who has 'said it better'.

'There is nothing in the world like friendship and there is no man in the world who has such friends as I, so many, so multiform . . . so trustworthy, so courteous . . . so apt to make jokes and to understand them. Also their faces are beautiful and I love them. I repeat a long list of their names before I sleep. Friendship is always exciting, and yet always safe . . . it is cleaner than love and older; for children and old people have friends but they do not love. It gives more and takes less, it is fine in the enjoying, and without pain when absent and leaves only good memories.' Thus Rupert Brooke in a letter to Jacques Raverat.

It is a very wise statement from one so young. Now that I am old I realise how wise it is. How pleasant it is to repeat a long list of their names before I go to sleep.

So many of my beloved English friends, who happened to be in America when I was there, are now near me here. My beloved Leueen McGrath has a great gift for friendship; she has more friends, and does more for them, than anyone I know. I have known her for eighteen years, and she has the gift of seeming younger every year. She comes into one's room, as her husband

George Kauffman used to say, 'like spring bearing spring flowers,' and always if a friend is in need she will enlist herself promptly as chauffeur, nurse, or gay companion.

I once used to think a female lunch party was to be avoided. Now I should like to have a lunch party every week with Zena Dare, Dorothy Dickson, Deborah Kerr, Margaret Leighton, Mary Mills, Leueen McGrath: enough, no party should have more than six people at once. They are all talented. 'Also their faces are beautiful and I love them.' I like to think they are all here and near and I can see them when I will.

And the two I have known for – is it possible – fifty years? We have grown up together in the theatre, and with so many other fans I count myself lucky to have seen *Joan of Arc* and *Milliment* – those illustrious Dames, Sybil and Edith.

And those other friends who have given me such blissful weekends. Stanley Hall and Noël McGregor, whose atelier, Wig Creations, really did re-create the art of theatrical wig-making and have coiffed all the great stars on both sides of the Atlantic.

They live with their friend Charles Cassel in the deep country with an aviary alive with exotic splendidly plumaged birds and white peacocks, and a stable full of prize-winning ponies, and last of all a flock of sheep. Stanley knows them all by name. You think all sheep look alike? So did I once. But now I can go with Stanley to the gate and hear him call 'Rameses' and know that an elder statesman with a long serious face will advance with dignity; and when he calls 'Charlotte', a slim-legged creature will step up and make eyes at him, cooing 'm-a-a-a-a'.

And Rodney Millington and Maurice Evans who don't have 'zoos' – but what libraries, what theatre records to browse in. And Johnnie Mills whom I know as only actors who have been on tour together know each other, and whose acting I admire as only actors can admire other actors. The Millses, to the sorrow of all their friends, have had to sell their famous house, The Wick, in Richmond, to a pop star. Pop stars are the new 'millionaires' these days. I wouldn't wish to be contemptuous of pop stars; I applaud anyone who can give pleasure. But oh! how my heart goes out to those old-timers, from Sybil Thorndike to Ethel Merman who can advance on a stage without that hideous trailing snake of a microphone, and speak to you and me instead of into its toad-like head.

I have sat with Bobby Flemyng on the verandah of his high-up flat in Brighton looking at the sparkling sea and reminiscing about the time in New York when we shared Margalo Gilmore's flat. Hospitable Margalo who always allowed her friends to stay in her luxurious apartment at a 'pepper-corn' rent while she was away.

I have sat also in 'Bumble' Dawson's garden of rare plants, and fondled her 'rare' cats and eaten her rarer-than-rare food and wondered how the busiest theatrical dress-designer in London can find *time* for all her friends. Time! Time! There seems so little of it as one grows old and so much to *do* with it.

In my 'wishful dreams', I'm torn between wanting to see one friend or two each week, or have a grand and splendid house, The Wick at Richmond, for instance, and have a luncheon party every month for *all* my friends.

In all my years of travel I had never been to Switzerland, and had no conception of how I would love it. But I did first see one of its great lakes under the best of circumstances. I went to visit Noël Coward at Montreux.

To stay at Les Avants to begin with is an experience. Shall I ever forget the view from the balcony in front of my bedroom, or the bathroom decorated in blue and white frills and ribbons like a boudoir for Marie Antoinette and yet of a *practicality*. The first bathroom I had seen with a thermometer attached to the 'mixer' tap over the bath, so you didn't have to try too hot or too cold water till you got the right temperature. But all this was just extra fun and stage setting for the company I could have happily enjoyed in a fisherman's hut.

Cole Leslie, 'dear Coley' to everyone. I've just realised that whenever I hear a group of people talking about Coley, I'm sure to hear someone say rather diffidently, 'It's an odd word, but don't you think Coley is rather a . . . saint?' and there's always an enthusiastic 'Yes' from everyone. And Graham? always warm and kind and thoughtful.

And Noël himself. But I can't write about him. *Everyone* has written about Noël, and said everything that there is to be said about him, and what is interesting is that if it is anything particularly penetrating or even a little wryly critical he always said it first himself. It has been my misfortune (though I have acted *with* him) never to have played in a play of his. But yes! I have.

We discovered it in that wonderful compendium of all his staggering output (*The Theatrical Compendium of Noël Coward* by Mander and Mitchenson). Tucked away among the addenda is the programme of a 'special sketch entitled *Pretty Prattle* by Noël Coward. The manuscript of this is now lost. It does not appear to have been submitted to the Lord Chamberlain.'

Pretty Prattle 26 April 1927

Lady Gwendolen Verney	Miss Lillian Braithwaite
Zushie Winkett	Miss Cathleen Nesbitt
Marian Pheda	Miss Hilda Moore
The Hon. Millicent Blood-worthy	Miss Heather Thatcher
Roger Brompton	Mr. George Grossmith

And members and guests of the night club – a very distinguished company from John Gielgud to Eric Portman.

'There!' I cried with delight, 'I have played in a play of yours – who *was* Zushie Winkett – *what* was she?'

'You ought to know, you *played* her,' said Noël.

'You ought to know, you *wrote* her,' I complained. But we had both completely forgotten. 'It *was* nearly fifty years ago,' we admitted, 'and at a "charity matinée" at that' – and what visions of confusion that called up!

But at least I could announce at the glorious party for 'All my Friends', 'I once played in a play of Noël's. Interesting part – Zushie Winkett in *Pretty Prattle*'. When I think of my Californian friends, I want to quote Rupert Brooke again.

'California is nice . . . the Californians are such a nice *friendly* bunch . . . there is a sort of goldenness about 'Frisco and the neighbourhood, and about the people. Everyone is so cheerful and cordial and simple and *kind*.'

Kindness, that is what I remember most clearly about almost all my Californian friends.

Barbara Poe for instance. I had met her, I think, at a showing of her pictures – she is a delightful and original artist – and once or twice at parties had been struck by her appearance, for she looks rather like Nefertiti.

I didn't really know her well, but when she heard that I was in hospital she was the first person to come and see me. I had had a fall and broken a pelvic bone, and had to be rushed to a hospital where the only bed was in a room with two other patients.

When I told Barbara that I didn't mind their company but that their taste in TV programmes was driving me mad – 'I'm not really worried, as I have two weeks off from my TV series anyway, but the doctor won't let me go home, I have to be on crutches for at least another week or ten days – and I must not attempt to negotiate stairs.'

'You must come and stay with me *at once*,' said Barbara; 'my house is all on one floor-level with the garden and the pool – you can live in a wheel-chair quite happily for weeks if need be – don't argue I'm coming for you in the car tomorrow morning.'

She came and when we arrived at the house there was a wheel-chair waiting for me in the garage. I could so easily run about from room to room in it that I became lazy about using the 'walker-machine' that the hospital had supplied me with. I was made welcome for several weeks, and indeed ever since I have regarded Barbara's house in Mandeville Canyon as my home from home, and stay there every time I go to Los Angeles. Her friends became my friends, Mildred Knopf, for instance, whose cookery books are among my favourite bedside-books. To be a beautiful woman *and* a superb cook, what a pleasant combination. Vincent Price and his Mary, Boris Karloff and his Evie; will our grandchildren, glued to TV re-runs of their pictures, be pleased or disappointed to learn that these bloodthirsty monsters were in reality the gentlest, kindest and most domesticated of men? Disappointed probably – children are mostly such blood-thirsty little monsters themselves! And Frank McCarthy and his wise and witty friend Rupert Allen. How thrilled I was when I heard that Frank had at last fulfilled a life-long ambition to become a producer; and then to hear that the picture he had quietly been 'working on' for years had been shown. It was *Patton – Lust for Glory* and a big success. Such a quiet, gentle, modest man. I had known him for years before I happened to penetrate into his own private cubby hole, and discovered that every niche of the walls was covered with citations and orders and decorations from every country in Europe, even from Russia and Turkey! He laughed it off saying, 'Well I was with Ike all the time (he was Eisenhower's top aide during the war) and of course I was in the way when they were being dished out.' But I knew that some of them were little letters that are only given for bravery under fire.

In Coldwater Canyon – what romantic names they have (Julie Andrews lived in Hidden Valley Road) – lived Bill Frye and Jim Wharton, inveterate party-givers and 'most sought after' party-goers. And Greer Garson with whom I had done a couple of television programmes, before we discovered that the aunt who lived with her had been at school with me in Belfast. And pretty Dolores who really 'belonged' to Angela Lansbury, but who was my 'dresser' and friend while Angela was filming. She saw me through the run of *My Fair Lady* and often took me home to dinner at her little house.

Angela is the only star I have ever seen who could dance as well as the best dancer in the chorus – and if you have ever seen the average musical-comedy star just 'getting away with it' in front of the chorus line you will appreciate what fantastic work that must have meant. Her husband told me she had determined to dance as well as sing, as Auntie Mame, and *dance* she did!

And Juliet and Hayley Mills. I stayed with them once in Gladys Cooper's house which she had rented to them, and found the complete absence of sibling rivalry between them quite moving and delightful. It's really very rare to find such absolute complete friendship between sisters in the same business. Even when Juliet's career seemed to be having a slight hiatus, and Hayley's to be soaring there was no sense of rivalry. A living compliment to John and Mary Mills's upbringing!

There was Glynis Johns who like myself never quite knew to which side of the Atlantic we belonged, but whom I always associated with the Pacific Ocean.

And Anne Seymour whom I loved first because she was a friend of Maggie Sullavan's, and who then became my dear friend.

And in golden San Francisco, there was Ina Claire. I once went on my own to have a little holiday. I had been told I must not ever go east without having seen the fabulous city.

I was wandering among the flower shops – one sees more flowers in the shops and in the streets there than in any other city – and I ran into Ina Claire. She insisted I go and stay with her in a country house she had just bought. 'It's a *beautiful* house,' she said, 'they were going to just destroy it, imagine! I offered them as much as it would cost them to demolish it, and they let me have it.' It was, as Noël Coward aptly remarked, a cross between Versailles and Le Petit Trianon.

When I was shown my room I admired the wrought-iron tops of the radiators. 'They are exactly the same as the ones in my bedroom at The Langham in New York.'

'Both houses must have been built during the nineteenth century and it was such a good period,' said Bill, her husband.

'It's such a pity they don't work now,' I said, 'at least mine don't.'

'Everything works in this house,' said Ina proudly. I thought I heard a faint snort from the Chinese butler who had come to announce dinner. At bedtime Ina and Bill took me up to my room. We opened the door and gasped. The radiator was leaking – leaking was an understatement – it was flooding the entire room. As we all got down with buckets and pails to mop up I found it hard not to exclaim, 'That's just how mine behaved in New York.' Finally Bill had to put his foot down; the Chinese butler announced firmly that they must choose between him and the house. He was a superb cook, a perfect valet, and, usually, a man of smiling good humour, and had been with him for years before Bill married Ina. They went back to a luxury flat in San Francisco.

The next time I went to San Francisco I stayed at David Pleydell-Bouverie's ranch. Reflecting that it was one of the most comfortable houses I have ever visited I began to wonder, 'Can it be that here too, in what should be our own domain, the men can beat us?' They are, I fear, the best cooks, the best milliners, the best couturiers, the best hairdressers. Are they also the best hosts? Reflecting on David's house, and Noël Coward's house in Switzerland and Cecil Beaton's house in Wiltshire and Stanley Hall's house in Kent I almost think: 'Perhaps they excel us in that too?' But then I think of the Lunts, and the Fairbankses and the Howard Dietzes, and say 'Nonsense! No one anywhere could excel *them* as hosts.'

Is it perhaps that one is instinctively a little surprised and apt to give more marks therefore, to the bachelor gentlemen for managing so successfully without a woman about the place?

Twice while in California I saw the terror of a great fire. Once after a tour of *The Chalk Garden* with Judith Anderson I went to stay with her at her house in Santa-Barbara and we saw the great fire raging over the mountains. Judith lived in a large house on top of a hill – we didn't *think* the fire would really come our way but we spent the time racing between it and the radio which was given over entirely to news of the fire and questions: 'Could anyone give accommodation to twenty race-horses? Fire rapidly approaching so-and-so's stables. Could anyone help to evacuate so-and-so's kennels. Home offered to eighteen dogs – station-wagon urgently needed.' I would go out to watch the glow suddenly flame up skywards as the embers sparked on a fresh coppice of dry wood, and would hear Judith moan, 'Oh! Oh! They have just announced it's struck so-and-so's house in Montecito; he's away but all those priceless *pictures*.' Judith, who doesn't easily make friends but loves very passionately those she does love, was in 'pain' that night.

Then there was a tremendous fire one New Year's Eve in Los Angeles. A number of us were drinking in the New Year with Clifton Webb and going on to a party at the Vincent Prices. Clifton came back from a phone call white-faced, 'The Prices place has been cordoned off, they are under notice to be ready to evacuate within fifteen minutes if necessary. The only guest there at the moment is Eddie Robinson. They *may* come down to us.' By one of those miracles that happened that night the fire suddenly turned east and though some of the garden was roasted, the house was intact. When I asked Mary Price afterwards, 'What did you *do* when they said it might be on you in fifteen minutes,' she laughed. 'We rushed about like a colony of ants.' 'The *pictures*!' cried Eddie; and started pulling them down from the walls. 'My Columbians!' cried Vincent, who has a famous collection of pre-Columbian art; 'My *silver*,' thought Mary who had all her most precious silver out for the party, and started filling baskets with it for the servants to take down and dump in the pool. 'We thought we were too busy to be frightened, but I knew *I* was when I found myself stopping in the pantry, looking at the dozens of petit poussins all laid out to be roasted for supper. "What a waste," I said to myself, and found myself starting to put them in the fridge. I *must* have gone slightly dotty.'

For the next few days wherever one went one found oneself quoting Pepys on the Great Fire of London. Plus ça change!

When I got back to New York I started to say good-bye to my New York friends – not immediately, I did a couple of television programmes and a play before I actually left, and I always had a feeling that I would be back. Indeed it wasn't for several years that I finally gave up my little flat in Central Park West.

'Don't say good-bye, you'll be back,' my friend and agent Milton Goldman would say, and indeed I did come back on several occasions, sometimes for only a week, *en route* to somewhere else, time to look up all my friends. Milton Goldman and Arnold Weissberger, who come to London every year and give such star-studded parties that they are as well known to the local columnists as they are in New York, are always ready to spoil me. Milton has that rare quality in an agent of being as good to the clients who are temporarily down on their luck as to those at the top of the tree. I remember at one of their parties Maureen Stapleton, who had not yet become a big star, and I who would never become one, were both out of work, and feeling the eternal actor's nightmare, 'Shall I ever work again?' But Milton treated us as honoured guests, rushed us round to make sure we met everybody, leaving his big stars to look after themselves. Buoyed up by Arnold and Milton and champagne we left the party on 'cloud nine' as they say over there. My lawyer Aaron Frosch is another old real friend who 'looked after' Alec Guinness and myself as our income tax accountant when we first arrived in *The Cocktail Party*. To such good effect that Alec said to me when we saw the amount of our indebtedness to the internal revenue, 'Aaron is either a crook or a very clever man indeed, and as he is obviously *not* a crook he must be *brilliant.*' Brilliant indeed, and kind 'beyond the call of duty'. Now, with all the legal and financial affairs of people like the Burtons and the Harrisons on his hands he still finds time to cope with *my* financial ignorance, listening to my queries and advising me on everything as though I were one of the millionaires his office copes with. And Radie Harris, who is famous as being a Hollywood columnist as eagerly read as Hedda Hopper was, without ever having said a malicious word about anyone, or published a scoop at the expense of a friend.

I had in the fifties many contemporary friends whom I had known from my early years in New York. But one finds in one's old age fewer and fewer contemporaries left. Margalo Gilmore and Bea Macdonald and Ouida Rambone seem to be the only ones left. Ouida Rambone found for me the little flat in Central Park West where I lived so contentedly for so many years. They had a huge apartment on the top floor – when I 'wished for company' – I could repair me there, and browse in Basil's splendid library. And in their apartment I met all the musical stars who lived in or passed through New York, including the young man I had first heard play in Bridget Guinness's drawing-room fifty years ago – *still* a young man, Arthur Rubinstein. How I would like to have a little room like Frank McCarthy's little hide-away with all his decorations and citations colourful on the wall, only my room would be papered with photographs of *all* my friends. And when I get, *if* I get, to a really ripe old age, tied to a wheel-chair, and a little deaf – I could spend endless happy hours remembering, and reciting my little Litany, 'Blessed am I to have had so many and so various and so pleasant and comely friends.'

I have left the best to the last. The ones I met late in my life and whom I deeply love and am most beholden to, the Lunts and Enid Bagnold. Actually I had 'made acquaintance with' the Lunts before they met each other.

I first saw the Lunts' house at Genesee Depot *over* fifty years ago. It was Alfred's boyhood home, and when I was acting in summer stock in Milwaukee, the nearest town, Alfred came over to act with us – and once took me to spend a day at his house.

How intriguing it was, one enormous room with staircases leading up to a gallery which had doors leading to bedrooms. I was so fascinated by the spaciousness and spareness of everything that I can't even remember how many of his family I met! Then I lost sight of Alfred for many years.

Lynn I *had* met very briefly in London before the war, but it was just as I was leaving America to go back to England that Lynn arrived in New York with Laurette Taylor.

When I finally saw them together in London they had both become famous stars. I went to see all their plays and finally summoned up courage to go back stage to tell them how I admired them.

How warm and welcoming they were then and when I went to live in America.

And what a 'fairy tale' house they have made of the old farm-house at Genesee Depot, adding to it through the years, a house where one could easily get lost, except that all ways lead to the centre – a charming little room known as the flirtation room. I never discovered why. Perhaps because it looked such an impossible room to conduct a flirtation in! So many *doors*, one to a staircase winding its spiral way downstairs to the garden room, another leading up to the bedrooms, and doors every-where opening on to the dining-room, a step or two down to the drawing-room, a step up to the library and on the level again as the boudoir, now known as the television room; the room where they sit murmuring, 'What *good* actors they all are.' They have always been so generous in their appreciation and admiration of other actors.

And how generous their hospitality, especially to tired actors needing a rest. With a visitors' book (only they don't *keep* a visitors' book) resplendent with all the great names of more than one generation, there is always a bed for some weary strolling player.

I remember an actor in New York, who had once played a supporting role in a long run with them, telling me that some time after, he had had a lean period, and had been ill. 'I was shuffling along Madison Avenue, feeling kind of sorry for myself, and suddenly there was Miss Lynnie tapping me on the arm and saying "You don't look too well" and I said I didn't *feel* too well, and it ended up with her saying "we are just going back to Genesee, come and stay there for a week." I just couldn't believe it, it seemed like a beautiful dream. And all the time I was there, I was treated like I *was* somebody . . . they were like that with all of us in the company – big featured players – bit parts, stage managers, just all one family. You know I got back to New York and I was walking on air and singing, "Everything's going my way".'

I knew just what he meant. They are wonderful hosts; they both are so busy with so many interests that one is never con-scious of being a 'visitor', one is absorbed into the life of the household. They have so many talents and such unexpected ones. Alfred is an artist whose drawings and 'designs for decoration' are genuinely creative. He is also a *cordon bleu* cook, and a skilled gardener. Lynn arranges flowers better than any professional 'Spry', going through the garden plucking the exact balance of colour and form that she needs. And she is a brilliant dressmaker. I shall never forget a black silk suit she made for herself, the skirt bias cut (nothing more difficult to handle!), the jacket beautifully braided, the zipper, always so tricky, lying flat and invisible. 'When are we going to see it Lynnie?' asked Alfred.

'I'll model it for you after dinner.'

Later in the evening she appeared on the steps leading down to the drawing-room, wearing exactly the right shoes, the right hat, the right gloves and handbag. She glided round the room, the skirt swaying gracefully, a top model from Paris, wearing the latest Balmain. And she has one quite unique accomplishment. She can tame a chipmunk. I think very few people have ever *seen* a chipmunk, they are such timid creatures they scramble to cover at the flicker of a leaf.

Lynn can sit on the ground, in an old pair of blue jeans, infinitely still for hours and end up with a chipmunk quite literally eating out of her hand.

During the years I was in Hollywood doing the TV series, I used to go to New York or back home to London frequently during our vacations, and the Lunts very often allowed me to break the journey with a few days or even weeks with them. So I have seen Genesee in the spring when Lynn filled the house with peonies till their delicate fragrance floated in every room. And in high summer when one spent most of the day in the pool, coming out for a light lunch brought up by Jules the master cook.

'Which is really the master cook,' I asked Lynn, 'Jules or Alfred?'

'Ah well that's a difficult question. I can only tell you they are equally professional. Once in Paris they took a course together at the *Cordon Bleu* School. I *think* Alfred came out one mark ahead!'

There was one never-to-be-forgotten Christmas Day when we suddenly decided to 'dress to the nines' for our *dîner à trois*. Lynn ineffably elegant in a 'Valentina', me preening myself in borrowed plumes in one of Lynn's 'Lanvin Castillos', Alfred suddenly looking very Scandinavian in a white linen Russian tunic that Lynn had bought for him 'because the embroidery on it was so fantastic'.

We were all so 'entertained', or was it the champagne? that we were ready to assure each other that it was the best Christmas party we had ever been to.

And the next morning, as though my cup were not already full, when I gave back the beautiful coral-coloured dress Lynn had lent me, she refused firmly to take it. 'Alfred and I have decided that it suits you so well that you *must* have it.' It has been my best dress ever since!

If I were to start thanking the Lunts for all the gifts tangible and intangible that I have received from them I should sound like an Oscar-winning starlet, but I must record that it was at Genesee that I first met Enid Bagnold. It seemed strange that we had never met, though we were practically contemporaries and had known many of the same people in London during the twenties.

Did she stay a week, a month? I can't remember, only that we all fell in love with her. I didn't think she would have time to even notice me. There was so much to discuss about the play; so much lively conversation between her and Alfred, with Lynn suddenly capping a story with a quiet comment so wonderfully timed that we all laughed.

To my amazement and delight we *did* become friends. How exciting it is when you are seventy-five to find a completely new friend to love and admire. I won't try to describe her; she has told so much about herself in her wonderful autobiography.* Her wonderful *youthfulness* is one of the most astonishing things about her. If ever two people have made me reconciled to old age, she and Lynn have done so. Once past seventy one does, a little, begin to count the years: seventy-four, seventy-five, seventy-six, seventy-seven, -eight, -nine, -*eighty!* Eighty-one, eighty-two, eighty-three, Good Heavens – it can't be *eighty-four!* But when I think that Enid is only a year younger than I am, and Lynn (I have never known her age – but she must be about the same), I think, 'What a meaningless thing chronological age is. Who would ever dream of calling these youthful creatures old ladies? Or come to that, Lady Diana Cooper, who sits radiant in a box at the theatre and rivets every eye? Or Zena Dare who

---

* Enid Bagnold, *Autobiography*, Heinemann, 1969.

at eighty-seven walks into a room with such a straight back and sparkling eyes and rises from a chair with such easy grace?'

Thinking of them it's easy to stop thinking even of oneself as an 'old lady'. And of course when I read of someone who has undergone some accident or misfortune and the press adds that she is 'eighty years old', I at once think, 'Poor old thing how awful at *her* age!' with no sense at all of being, after all, her contemporary!

It's a great help of course to belong to a profession that has no set retiring age and in which 'there is always something new around the corner'.

TWENTY

All My Sons

∽∽∽∽∽∽∽∽∽∽∽∽∽∽∽∽∽∽∽∽∽∽∽∽∽∽∽∽∽∽∽

Billed in the order of my meeting them! Alec Guinness, Emlyn
Williams, John Mills, Joseph Cotten, Marlon Brando, Hugh
O'Brien, Rex Harrison, William Windom, Eric Portman,
Richard Burton, Douglas Fairbanks Junior, Nicol Williamson.

One of the pleasure of the life that begins at sixty is that you
begin to play mother roles. It's a special pleasure in America!
I had 'played Mother' in England to Alec Guinness in *Hamlet*,
to Emlyn Williams in *The Case of the Frightened Lady*, and to
John Mills in *The Uninvited Guest* but none of them was a very
'motherly' mother. Gertrude in the first play, Lady Lebanon in
the second, Lady Lannon in the third, were all mothers from
whom their sons might wish to be spared! Perhaps it was owing
to my having played Julia in *The Cocktail Party* on my American
début – a lady of warmth, wit, wisdom, and character – that all
the mothers I played there, were endowed by their authors with
just those qualities.

They were all good-humoured women with a tendency to
treat their successful middle-aged sons as little boys who needed
to be chided or comforted, as the case might be. And the sons
responded with that mixture of affection, respect and occasional
irascibility that such mothers command. When you 'act' such
a relationship daily for long periods you are both apt to find
that some mutual affection and respect spills over into real
life.

It was certainly so in my case. Who could *not* regard with
affection and respect such sons as Joseph Cotten, Cary Grant,
Rex Harrison, Richard Burton, Marlon Brando, William

248

Windom, Hugh O'Brien and last the Benjamin (who is always the best beloved), Douglas Fairbanks Junior.

Alec and Emlyn and Johnny were all friends outside the theatre. I might never even had met any of the others most of whom became friends afterwards, if it had not been for the theatre.

As a matter of fact most of those gentlemen have two qualities in common that probably contribute to their being so beloved by their public. Firstly, they genuinely *like* women (unlike so many Don Juans and Casanovas who merely like to chase them) and secondly they have the natural good manners that spring from an affectionate disposition.

But I can't help suspecting that I would not have received the attention and affection that I did if I had merely been playing one of their sisters or their cousins or their aunts. With Joe Cotten for instance, the courtesy and consideration he showed during the very first rehearsals when we had only just met; and the generosity with which he insisted on my having the 'second star room' to dress in (which was his by every right of billing and status) quite overwhelmed me. He always has an instinctive Southern chivalry and good manners, but I suspect that I wouldn't have profited to quite such a degree if he hadn't begun to think of me as his mother. 'Don't argue, I can't have my mother running up and down stairs all evening,' he would say about the dressing-room. Joe has that same quality of inherent 'loving kindness' in a man that Audrey Hepburn has as a woman.

And Richard Burton . . . I had known him off and on in New York; I had gone to see *Camelot* several times just to revel in his performance and when I took part in a poetry reading with him I was really awed by him. Hearing him recite *In Parenthesis* by David Jones the Welsh poet was a shattering experience. I was ignorant of the author and found 'understanding' difficult, but one didn't need to know what the poem *meant* in order to feel the tremendous shattering emotion. I had always thought of myself as a reasonably well-read person but compared to Richard I'm an ignoramus!

I played the role of his mother, years afterwards, in a film which was badly written and directed, but which was illuminated by Richard's performance as a sad, jealous, vain little homosexual barber, always with a chip on his shoulder.

But somehow under the petulant often ridiculous exterior Richard managed to convey an inner glow of something like 'saintliness', if there is such a word? As his mother I had to lie in bed all day, a helpless, crippled, wrinkled toothless old woman, a kind of decaying vegetable. Sometimes after a last look in the make-up room mirror at the monster the make-up artist had achieved I felt, 'If *I* ever came to look like that I'd spend my time praying for death.' But every time Richard came to play his scenes with her, he would listen to her whining and dress her and feed her with such tender patient sympathy, so oblivious of her looks and her temper, that as 'old mum', I felt myself relaxing and retreating from the emptiness of life into the long years ago when she had been young and comely and exulting in the baby on her knees. Even if none of her dreams for him or his dreams for himself had come true no life could be said to be quite empty where there had been some giving and taking of love.

How Richard would have laughed if I had sat up in bed and uttered such words: 'Dear me who would have thought the old girl had so much Pollyana in her!' Strange how *right* that 'saintly' aspect that Richard gave to the part.

As I look back over my life there are only three people I have regarded as worthy of canonisation, and they are all homosexuals. I had always realised that a few of the greatest artists, wittiest writers and most successful dramatists have been homosexuals, but I had forgotten the 'saintly' ones. Saints are so rare anyway.

What a delightful three months I spent in Paris doing *The Staircase*. Here I was living in my beloved Paris at the film company's expense in a charming flat adjacent to my favourite Paris park, Le Parc Monceau, sometimes only 'working' two days a week. So much time to browse around by myself – lunching in the sun on a 'bâteau-mouche' seeing all my favourite views of Paris; loitering in the fantastic new Métro station of the Louvre – where one can be reminded of all the pictures and statues, not only in the Louvre but in little forgotten chapels and museums that one wanted to look at again. Of course one agreed with one's friends that Paris was becoming sadly Americanised and Anglicised, especially if one had fought one's way through the Prix Unique or Le Drug Store to buy a needle or some aspirin, but then one could always walk out and look at the clear evening sky behind the Arc de Triomphe and find one's way home across Le Parc Monceau, admiring the newly gilded tops of its handsome iron gates – and find oneself on home ground behind the boulevard de Courcelles, with the network of little ancient streets where la pâtisserie and la charcuterie and l'épicerie and even la mercerie and la pharmacie were, all little separate 'special' shops, cheek by jowl down one street. One could buy one's evening paper and laugh at the latest joke in the 'Franglais' column – 'Monsieur s'habille. Il met son smoking, il va dans son living, prendre un whisky – soda. Il attend sa femme qui fait son walking dans le bois. Il espère qu'elle aît pris son pullover.' And then one could relax and listen to the gentleman who reads the news and revel in the sheer beauty of the French language when spoken by some one who *enjoys* speaking it – and to me it sounded as if all the newscasters took pleasure in the purity and elegance of their diction.

And there was the theatre – with delightful comedies like *Cher Antoine* and *Quarante Carats* – which somehow like certain wines, don't really 'travel'. Something of the flavour gets lost in the Anglo-Saxon dialogue and acting. There were 'showings' at the grand couturiers, but now that Balenciaga and Molyneux have given up only Balmain makes me wish I were rich enough to buy! But Ginette Spanier who to me *is* Balmain, and one of the great Parisian personalities would let me come and take a good seat. The Balmain 'showings' are always successful, and Ginette is always as nervous as a Siamese kitten for a week before – just as any great star of the theatre is before her opening, however experienced she may be.

Rex Harrison was also in *The Staircase*, and I often went down to the studio on a day when I wasn't really needed to watch him and Richard rehearse together.

Observing Rex rehearse had always had the same fascination for me as observing Gerald du Maurier. To see the enormous concentration, the time and energy spent in achieving, in a few lines or even a few moments without a line, an effect of absolute spontaneity, was absorbing to watch. I remember once being allowed by John Van Druten to watch a rehearsal of a play of his. Rex had a moment when he had to listen for a brief time to someone on the telephone, cut off the conversation abruptly, walk half way to the door, stopping when the phone rang, looking at it, shrugging his shoulders and walking out of the door. He 'played' with it for nearly an hour, found the exact force with which to put the phone down, the exact position of his feet when it rang again so that he could turn automatically, half step towards it, and abruptly swing round and make for the door. Too swift a turn, the wrong foot forward, could have given an ungainly lurch. He put the movements together with the meticulous precision of a watchmaker, did it over once or twice, and then left it. When one saw it in sequence it looked so casual that one merely wondered how he had managed to convey to the audience what the unseen other person had said, and was going to say, and what he was thinking about. I remembered Granville-Barker's rule: 'You can make an audience unaware that you have carried on a long conversation with a person they can't even see, if you *concentrate* deeply enough – and you can't concentrate if you are wondering, "Should I move here or sit there?" That must have become so automatic as to have become spontaneous.' But as I have often seen, the preparation for that spontaneity has to be as tough as a dancer's limbering-up.

I played Rex's mother in *My Fair Lady* and often thought how Barker would have enjoyed his sheer professionalism, and his loyalty to Shaw's own words – I remember him prowling about the stage during the rehearsals of *My Fair Lady* with his little Penguin copy of *Pygmalion* in his pocket, occasionally button-holing Moss Hart or Alan Lerner when he found a line that he considered 'non-Shavian'. There was a delightful moment at the final run-through, when Moss solemnly announced to the company that before they dismissed he would like to make a 'presentation' to Rex. Then Alan Lerner came on staggering under a magnificent Penguin nearly five feet high from Schwartz, the famous toyshop. When Moss said, 'Maybe you would like to give us your old Penguin? it's gotten to be a bit dog-eared – we'll give you this in return,' Rex with a cheerful grin surrendered his little book.

Fritz Lowe always said of Rex that if he had had the right larynx he would have been the great singer of his day, his pitch and phrasing are absolutely perfect.

How I enjoyed *My Fair Lady*. It was one of the happiest companies I have ever known. Bill Liff the stage manager was

largely responsible for that. Being a man of great natural
authority and of great sweetness of nature, he could run a 'happy
ship' with perfect discipline and no 'bullying'. And Moss Hart
was a very great director and one of the most lovable men I have
ever known. His death was a cruel loss to his friends and to the
American stage. At first I rather hesitated about going into *My
Fair Lady* – it was much the smallest part I had ever played –
but I wanted to be in a musical. I wanted to watch Rex rehearse,
and when I heard I was to be dressed by Cecil Beaton, I really
wouldn't have minded having no lines at all. No! that's not
true – one can't be in a huge electrifying success without longing
to be more of an integral part of it, longing for one 'good scene'.
But it had its moments, and I always enjoyed the little chuckle
of appreciation that ran through the audience when Professor
Higgins having been well and truly routed by his Eliza, stands
alone for a moment and then cries desperately, '*Mother! Mother!*'

At one time he had a little yacht moored at an East River
pier, and on Saturday nights I sometimes went down with him
and Kay Kendall and Jack Merivale to their house at Westbury
on the Sound. Kay and Jack would go fishing at dawn and bring
back live-caught fish which we all refused to eat for breakfast.
The Monday afternoon drive back to the theatre was always a
little hair-raising; Rex so hated to leave his country retreat that
he was apt to cling to it till the last minute, but always managed
to get there just in time. Sometimes we would find Bill Liff the
stage manager standing at the stage door anxiously scanning the
horizon. 'You'll find your understudy putting on your clothes,'
'Biff' would say grimly. 'He can take 'em off then,' Rex would
say. 'Sorry old man, can't think what happened, started late. . . .'
'And I bet you drove like a lunatic,' 'Biff' would groan. 'I drove
with the *utmost* care, I had my mother aboard.' I refrained from
confessing to 'Biff' that 'mother' had almost had a heart-attack
on the way!

Other 'mother' roles have taken me to Hollywood. I always
looked forward to those trips. I confess that when I was asked
'Would you like to do a "bit" in a picture or a television film to
be shot in Los Angeles?' I always said 'Yes' often before even
reading the script. To be quite honest I've rarely been able to
read a film script; their format is so confusing – I just rifled
through the pages to find my part, which often seemed to be

practically non-existent, and then said to myself: 'Hollywood! – that lovely sunshine – those delightful hospitable people – all of whom seem to have a house on the Pacific shore which one can reach in less than an hour; the gardens with orange and lemon trees heavy with fruit and starry with blossom.'

The first time I 'went west' was to play Napoleon's mother, with Marlon Brando as Napoleon. I was tremendously interested to meet him; one had heard such rumours of his unpredictable behaviour, his talent, and his occasional misuse of it, his lack of good manners. I was pleasantly surprised to find him courteous, good humoured and professional to his finger-tips. As his mother I had to sit at his right hand at a dinner party for thirty guests, which went on for at least ten days, during which an interminable series of 'close-ups' of all the famous guests were taken, necessitating moving of walls and doors and windows practically with every shot. We had plenty of time to discuss our opinions of the script. I had read all the books about Lucrezia that I could find before coming out and been fascinated by her colourful character and the part she had played in her son's life. I didn't think she could be made uninteresting. I had counted without the script writer. What little of her there was was practically non-existent. Poor Brando suffered much more. 'I had always wanted to play Napoleon,' he confessed. 'After this appalling travesty I shall never have the chance again.' He did his very best to infuse life into the tin soldier they had constructed, but he was occasionally defeated. His unerring instinct for *truth* rejected one speech entirely. It was a long speech made towards the end of the dinner party. Long speeches never troubled him and he never fluffed or needed extra 'takes', but this speech defeated him. He dried up several times, then lost grip and fluffed again, and finally he got up and said, 'I must leave it till tomorrow, it's getting too late. I'm tired.' He apologised to me for keeping us all hanging around for so long, and I ventured to wonder whether it was not the fault of the speech itself. 'It sounds so unutterably corny and muddled and meaningless; it ought to be rewritten.' 'Don't think I haven't told them so,' he said, 'but they get back at me saying, "there is not one word in that speech that Napoleon did not utter himself." And our research department is supposed to be infallible.' When I got home that night I sat up very late glued to all the books I had found about Napoleon (when hoping I'd really have to play a real woman as his mother) and did indeed discover among the more familiar passages most of the sentences given to him to say – but the whole speech was an amalgam of purple patches from occasions when he had indeed spoken those very words. But a paragraph from the oration to his troops delivered in Egypt before the Pyramids was stuck on to an excerpt from an official letter to Caulaincourt, which in its turn was joined to some entries from his private diary, the whole enriched with odd 'telling phrases' from here, there and everywhere like cherries stuck on a cake. When I showed him the result of my research next day, he laughed so much that everyone thought I must be quietly showing him a dirty picture!

However he decided it was too late to really do anything constructive about the picture and delivered the speech as it was at a good thumping pace. I never met him again and I should imagine he has forgotten the incident as thoroughly as I have forgotten the film. All I can remember is the truly magnificent appearance made by him and Merle Oberon, he in a brilliant uniform glittering with stars and crosses and medals and Merle Oberon in regal velvet and diamonds; the lids of her magnificent eyes were heavily painted with silver – I wondered whether the research department had been caught 'embroidering' again or whether Empire ladies really did paint their eyelids with silver?

Recently I have been 'mother' to yet another star, Nicol Williamson, who had such an outstanding triumph as Uncle Vanya in Mike Nichols's all-star production of the play.

'Give a dog a bad name,' as the saying goes. I imagine every great actor has at one time or another been 'hanged' in the public eye for the wildness of his youth. Yet surely everyone who has a touch of genius also has a strong rebellious streak. I had heard so much about Nicol as a 'wild man' that it came as a surprise to find him so well-mannered, so professional in his control over the apparently uncontrollable anguish and hysteria that his part demanded. After exploding so much pent-up energy that it brought the cheering audiences to their feet at the close of *Uncle Vanya*, Nicol would hare off to the Little Theatre where he was giving a one-man show and proceed to sing rock and country songs with a steel band, interspersed with an occasional turn at the piano and readings of poetry and prose from Eliot to Beckett. Next day he would be full of energy and ready to take one to the hospital where his wife had just given birth to a son; how touching to see the gentleness in his face when he peered through the glass of the baby-room and spotted his first-born among the thirty-odd infants. The 'wild one' seems to have tamed his talent without in any way impairing it.

Epilogue

When I came to my eightieth birthday, I did not really expect to work very much more, but in the last five years I have paid 'working visits' to all my favourite cities, and found some exciting new ones. I was in Paris during that year, then I went to Los Angeles and San Francisco and played mother to Douglas Fairbanks in a revival of *My Fair Lady* and later had the privilege of seeing him play in *The Pleasure of his Company*, giving a performance that reminded me of Gerald du Maurier so irresistibly that I saw it twice. And he and Mary-Lee took me for a holiday in the sun in Palm Beach.

I have basked in the sun, for which my old bones crave, there, and in Marseilles, doing a 'bit' in a film; and in the splendid warmth of a New York summer, I went to play in Mike Nichols' production of *Uncle Vanya*. This time I had only an infinitesimal part, but I remember Granville-Barker's maxim: 'There is no such thing as a part too small to be played well.' Working with Mike was like working with Barker again. I found myself in the company of stars who respected each other and their director: George Scott, Julie Christie, Nicol Williamson, Lillian Gish, Elizabeth Wilson, Conrad Bain, Bernard Hughes. And once more I saw an audience stand up to cheer, swept away by the old theatre magic.

It was then that my friend Richard de Combray, who is writing a book about Venice, gave me a copy of the best book about that magical city ever written, *Venice*, by James Morris.* I

---

* *Venice*, by James Morris, Faber and Faber, 1960.

had never been, in all my peregrinations, to the one city I longed to see, so when I got home my son took me there! And it is now enthroned in my memory with Athens, two cities whose magic surpasses rather than fulfils expectation.

And now that I am, as Bertrand Russell once said, 'Eighty-five years young', there is time to enjoy the second childhood that old age brings. By second childhood I mean the renewal of the sense of wonder, of curiosity, of a desire to know the answer to everything, and a child's acceptance of the fact that there is so much in life to which there is no answer.

I grieve for the loss of old friends. I am sad that I shall never again see Elizabeth Pollock and Bunny Bruce and Tam Williams and Jack Hawkins and Gladys Cooper and Max Adrian, and so many others, but it is no longer the *passion* of loss that one feels in youth or even in middle age. And that great man of the theatre Noël Coward has left us a lovely little last poem which I quote as an envoi:

When I have fears, as Keats had fears
Of the moment I cease to be,
I console myself with the vanished years,
Remembered laughter, remembered tears,
The peace of the changing sea.
And remembered friends who are dead and gone.
How happy they are I cannot know —
But happy am I that have loved them so. *

Index

Adrian, Max, 258
Agate, James, 104
Ainley, Henry, 59, 61, 62, 64–5, 66, 67–70, 71, 72, 78, 157, 158
Ainley, Susanne, 70
Albery, Bronson, 177
Alda, Frances, 108
Alington, Lord, 48
Alington, Napier, 48–9
Alington, Lady Susan, 48
Allen, Rupert, 208, 230, 238
Allgood, Sally, 52, 56, 77, 86
Anders, Glen, 140
Anderson, Judith, 222, 241
Andrews, Julie, 145, 239
Arias, Roberto E., 231
Asquith, Arthur, 97
Asquith, Cyril, 96, 144
Asquith, Herbert, 91–2, 124, 160
Asquith, Margot, 99
Astor, Alice, 131
Atwill, Lionel, 112–13
Avon, Lord, 147
Aylmer, Felix, 225, 226

Bacall, Lauren, 116
Bagnold, Enid, 133, 209, 243, 246
Bain, Conrad, 257
Balenciaga, 217
Ballard, Lucinda, 213
Balzac, Honoré de, 38
Bankhead, Tallulah, 116, 140, 142–3
Barrie, J. M., 83, 84–5, 90, 111, 114, 151, 160
Barrymore, Ethel, 229

Barrymore, John, 103–6, 107, 111, 149
Barrymore, Lionel, 149
Baylis, Lilian, 171
Beaton, Cecil, 12, 147, 213, 222, 226, 240, 253
Beaumont, Binkie, 199, 215–16
Belasco, David, 60, 114–15
Belgeddes, Norman, 113
Bennett, Ethel, 27
Beresford, Lord Charles, 132
Bernhardt, Sarah, 21–2, 26
Boucicault, Dion, 83–5, 90
Brancker, Sir Sefton, 28
Brando, Marlon, 248, 254–5
Britten, Benjamin, 203
Brook, Peter, 62
Brooke, Faith, 211
Brooke, Mrs. W. P., 90–100, 107, 111, 133, 151, 160
Brooke, Rupert, 71–100, 101, 111, 123, 137, 177, 185, 186, 234, 237
Browne, Denis, 90, 93, 97
Browne, Martin, 208
Bruce, Bunny, 258
Bruce, Nigel, 156, 167, 180
Burton, Richard, 65, 209, 248, 249–50
Byers, Mrs., 23, 25

Campbell, Mrs. Patrick, 133, 148–9, 163–4, 178
Campbell, Violet 'Bunny', 143–4, 156
Cannan, Gilbert, 71, 72
Capel, Joan, 143–4, 156
Carrol, Sydney, 222
Carten, Audrey, 167

Index

Carten, Waveny, 167
Cassel, Charles, 235
Casson, Lewis, 191, 196
Cavalieri, Lina, 108
Cecil, Lord David, 147
Chambers, Haddon, 111–12, 121–4
Chase, Malcolm, 114, 197
Chatterton, Ruth, 57
Chayevsky, Paddy, 222
Chesterton, G. K., 83, 106, 114
Chowne, Mr., 181
Christie, Julie, 257
Church, Richard, 88
Churchill, Diana, 200
Churchill, Sarah, 198
Churchill, Winston, 93, 201
Claire, Ina, 239–40
Clancy, Mrs., 20–1
Colette, 211, 221
Collier, Constance, 108–9, 215
Compton, Fay, 191, 192
Connaught, Duke of, 130
Cooke, Alistair, 230
Cooper, Lady Diana (Diana Manners), 86, 130, 133, 246
Cooper, Gladys, 144, 209, 224, 225, 226–7, 239, 258
Cornford, Frances, 91
Cotten, Joseph, 208, 220, 248, 249
Coudray, Mlle, 36–7
Coward, Noël, 20, 144–5, 232, 236–7, 240, 258
Cox, Ka, 97
Cukor, George, 208, 226, 230
Culver, Daphne, 199–200
Culver, Roland, 181, 199–200
Curzon, Lady Irene, 130, 131
Curzon, Mary, 131

Dare, Zena, 235, 246–7
Darlington, W. A., 171
Dawson, Bumble, 236
Dean, Basil, 60, 157, 158, 161
De Combray, Richard, 257
De Glehn, Wilfred, 138
De la Mare, Walter, 71, 221–2
Delius, Frederick, 157, 158
De Wolfe, Elsie, 125
Dickson, Dorothy, 235
Dietz, Howard, 213, 240
Dolin, Anton, 158
Donne, John, 94–5, 112
Dowson, Ernest, 38, 77

Drouet, Juliette, 79
Du Maurier, Gerald, 144, 167–8, 180–181, 251, 257
Dumble, Miss, 164
Dunsany, Lord, 127
Duputel, Demoiselles, 32–7

Eliot, T. S., 206–7, 233
Evans, Edith, 104–5, 135, 235
Evans, Maurice, 235

Fagan, J. B., 125
Fairbanks, Douglas, Jnr., 123, 231, 233, 240, 248, 257
Fairbanks, Mary-Lee, 127, 231, 257
Filippi, Fanny, 46
Filippi, Rosina, 45–7, 48, 61, 133
Flecker, James Elroy, 93, 157
Fleming, Meta, 24
Flemyng, Robert, 210, 236
Foley, Frank, 48
Fontanne, Lynn, 133, 140, 214, 243–6
Fonteyn, Margot, 133, 231
Forbes, Helen, 24
Frankfurter, Felix, 198
Freyberg, Bernard, 97
Frohman, Charles, 121
Frosch, Aaron, 242
Fry, Roger, 91–2
Frye, Bill, 239

Galsworthy, John, 90, 103, 152, 171
Garson, Greer, 239
Gary, Madame, 39–41
Gary, Mimi, 39
Gary, Pierre, 39
George V, King, 161
Gérard, Mlle, 37
Gielgud, John, 105, 171, 172, 193, 195
Gill, Basil, 157
Gilmore, Margalo, 236, 243
Gish, Lillian, 257
Goff, Moyra, 143
Goldman, Milton, 242
Gosse, Edmund, 86
Grant, Cary, 248
Granville-Barker, Harley, 59–67, 69, 71, 74, 83, 163, 191–2, 193–6, 252, 257
Green, Hughie, 132, 156
Gregory, Lady, 52–4, 56, 58
Grey, Lord, 159
Grock, 59

Index

Guinness, Alec, 181, 184–5, 186, 207, 208, 210, 211, 242, 248, 249
Guinness, Benjy, 132
Guinness, Bridget, 106, 107–8, 127–33, 136, 143, 148, 160, 243
Guinness, Loël, 108, 129
Guinness, Meraud, 108, 129, 131
Guinness, Merula, 185
Guinness, Tanis, 106, 108, 129, 131

Haggard, Stephen, 191
Hall, Stanley, 235, 240
Hallam, Basil, 90
Hallat, May, 225
Hannen, Nicholas, 153, 191–2
Hanson, James, 217
Hardy, Thomas, 72
Harris, Radie, 242
Harris, Robert, 191
Harrison, Rex, 181, 195, 209, 248, 251–2, 253
Hart, Moss, 208, 252–3
Hartnell, Norman, 167–8
Harwood, H. M., 139, 145
Hassall, Christopher, 71
Hauser, Frank, 146
Hawkins, Jack, 191, 194, 258
Hawtrey, Charles, 89, 90, 181
Hayes, Helen, 208, 213, 217–19, 232
Hayman, Alf, 121–3
Hecht, Harold, 224
Heggie, Peter, 105–6, 107, 113–14
Helburn, Teresa, 107
Helena-Victoria, Princess, 156
Hemmerde, E. J., 182
Hepburn, Audrey, 116, 209, 211–12, 214–17
Hicks, Seymour, 181
Hiller, Wendy, 226
Hobbs, Jack, 139–40
Hoey, Elizabeth, 18
Hoey, Jane, 18
Hoey, Katherine, 18
Hooker, Henry, 115–16
Hope-Crews, Laura, 121–2
Horner, Katharine, 86
Hughes, Bernard, 257
Huntingdon, Mrs., 192
Hyde-White, Wilfred, 211

Illingworth, Miss, 115
Isherwood, Christopher, 230

James, Henry, 86, 213
James, Julia, 201–2
Janis, Elsie, 90
Jesse, Fryn Tennyson, 178
Johns, Glynis, 239
Johnson, Maud, 160
Jones, David, 65, 249
Jungman, Baby, 129
Jungman, Zita, 129

Kapp, E., 140
Karloff, Boris, 238
Karloff, Evie, 238
Karsavina, 140
Kauffman, George, 235
Kendall, Kay, 253
Kerr, Deborah, 226, 235
Kerrigan, Jimmy, 53–6, **110–11**
Klay, 102
Knopf, Mildred, 238

Lafargue, Jules, 38
Lally, Gwen, 58
Lampson, Sir Miles, 183–4
Lancaster, Burt, 224
Lane, Sir Hugh, 52
Langner, Lawrence, 107
Langtry, Lillie, 109
Lansbury, Angela, 239
Latham, Ned, 140, 141, 144, 148–9
Laure, Madame, 39, 41–2
Lawrence, Sir Geoffrey, 157
Lawrence, Gertrude, 116, 144
Lawrence, Margaret, 57
Lee, Robert E., 17
Leigh, Vivien, 116
Leighton, Margaret, 209, 235
Lerner, Alan, 252
Leslie, Cole, 236
Leslie, Shane, 162, 171
Lewis, Rosa, 126–7, 128
Liff, Bill, 252–3
Lillie, Bea, 156
Loines, Russell, 139
Lonsdale, Freddie, 161–2
Loos, Anita, 11–12, 208, 211, 217, 219
Lorne, Marion, 172
Lowe, Fritz, 252
Lunt, Alfred, 113, 209, 240, 243–6

MacArthur, Charles, 218
McCarthy, Frank, 208, 230, 238, 243
McCarthy, Lillah, 61, 63, 112

Index

McCarthy, Rachel, 47
Macdonald, Bea, 243
McGrath, Leueen, 234–5
McGregor, Noël, 235
McKinnel, Norman, 149–50, 153
MacWhirter, Miss, 23–5
Mainwaring, Generis, 131, 136
Mainwaring, Sir Harry, 131, 136
Mainwaring, Zara, 156
Mallarmé, Stéphane, 38
Malleson, Miles, 135
Mamoulian, Rouben, 113
Maney, Richard, 54–5
Manners, Diana (Lady Diana Cooper), 86, 130, 133, 246
Manners, Hartley, 131
Marie-Louise, Princess, 156
Marsh, Eddie, 71, 72, 86, 90, 93, 97, 98, 99, 107, 137, 203
Marshall, Herbert, 143
Mary, Queen, consort of George V, 161
Masefield, John, 112, 196
Maude, Cyril, 121–3, 181
Maugham, Somerset, 140–1
Maugis, Madame, 35
Maugis, Jean-Paul, 35–6, 37–8
Merivale, Jack, 253
Merman, Ethel, 235
Mesta, Perle, 229
Meyer, Louis B., 227
Miller, Gilbert, 208, 211–12, 215
Millington, Rodney, 235
Mills, Hayley, 239
Mills, John, 235, 239, 248, 249
Mills, Juliet, 239
Mills, Mary, 235, 239
Moeler, Philip, 107
Montaigne, 234
Montgomery, Elizabeth, 229
Moore, George (Americantycoon), 111
Moore, George (novelist), 151–5
Moore, Henry, 203
Morgan, Charles, 145
Morgan, Sydney, 52
Morris, James, 257
Morris, Margaret, 60
Mortimer, Raymond, 203
Moscowitch, 125, 134

Nares, Owen, 46
Nesbitt, Anna, 16, 18, 29, 45, 58, 120–121, 136, 139
Nesbitt, Courtney, 43

Nesbitt, Hugo, 15–16, 17, 29, 57–8, 106, 139
Nesbitt, Mary Catherine (Cathleen's mother), 15–18, 19–20, 23, 26–30, 31, 35, 43, 44, 45, 47, 57, 120–1, 136, 139–40, 147, 148, 156, 172–4, 189
Nesbitt, Terence, 29, 58, 106–7
Nesbitt, Thomas (Cathleen's father), 15–18, 20–2, 26, 29–30, 43, 44, 139, 189–90
Nesbitt, Tom, 15–16, 17, 18, 29, 57, 126
Nichols, Mike, 255–6, 257
Nielson-Terry, Dennis, 61, 65, 67
Niven, David, 224, 225–6
Niven, Hjordis, 226
Nobile, Nina de, 211–12
Nureyev, Rudolf, 230–1

Oberon, Merle, 255
O'Brien, Hugh, 248, 249
O'Donovan, Fred, 77
Olivier, Laurence, 104, 170, 172, 195, 219–20
O'Neill, Maire, 51, 53, 86
Osman, Lady, 183–4

Parry, Sir Hubert, 35
Perkins, Frances, 102
Peto, Ruby, 86
Pinter, Harold, 207
Playfair, Nigel, 61, 62, 66, 135, 151–3
Pleydell-Bouverie, David, 240
Poe, Barbara, 233, 237–8
Polignac, Marquis de, 140
Pollock, Sir Adrian, 144
Pollock, Elizabeth, 143, 156, 258
Pollock, Lady, 144
Portman, Eric, 248
Previn, André, 230
Price, Mary, 238, 241
Price, Vincent, 238, 241

Quartermaine, Leo, 61
Quayle, Anthony, 185
Ramage, Cecil, 146–9, 156–7, 158–60, 164–5, 166, 176–7, 179, 182–3, 191, 206
Ramage, Jennifer, 163, 164, 177, 178, 197, 204
Ramage, Mark, 142–3, 160, 164–5, 177, 197, 203–5, 257
Rambone, Ouida, 243
Raverat, Gwen, 12

Index

Raverat, Jacques, 234
Reed, Florence, 215
Ribblesdale, Lord, 131
Rimbaud, Arthur, 38
Robinson, Eddie, 241
Rodgers, Mary, 127
Rolland, Romain, 38
Roosevelt, Eleanor, 197–8
Roosevelt, Franklin, 115, 116, 198
Ross, Ruby, 125–7, 128, 175
Rossetti, Christina, 38
Rouleau, Raymond, 212, 214–15
Rowe, Enid, 60
Rubinstein, Arthur, 108, 243
Rutherston, Albert, 62, 64, 76
Ryland, George, 147

Sackville-West, Edward, 203
Sackville-West, Vita, 176–7
Saint-Simon, Louis de Rouvroy, 41
Saloman, Merula, 185, 186
Sassoon, Siegfried, 92
Schubert Brothers, 52, 55
Scott, George, 257
Selznick, David, 208
Seyler, Athene, 177
Seymour, Anne, 208, 239
Shank, Edward, 146
Shanks, Leslie, 171
Shaw, Bernard, 135, 252
Sheldon, Edward, 113
Shelley, Percy Bysshe, 207
Sherek, Henry, 206
Siddons, Mrs., 157
Simone, 214
Sinclair, Arthur, 54
Smythe, Ethel, 27
Soldadenkov, Boris, 116–17
Spanier, Ginette, 251
Squire, Ronald, 181
Stevens, Inger, 227
Strange, Michael, 104
Sturt, Lois, 48
Sullavan, Margaret, 208, 220–2, 239
Swinburne, Algernon Charles, 38
Synge, John Millington, 90, 91

Tandy, Jessica, 191, 192, 193
Taylor, Elizabeth, 188
Taylor, Laurette, 131–2, 243
Taylor, Sam, 220
Tempest, Marie, 58
Terris, Ellaline, 84

Terry, Ellen, 111, 140, 146
Teyte, Maggie, 108
Thesiger, Ernest, 150
Thomas, Blanche, 104
Thomas, Leonard, 104
Thorndike, Sybil, 133, 172, 235
Tree, Sir Herbert, 102, 108–10, 111–12
Tree, Iris, 110, 111
Trevor-Roper, Hugh, 230
Twain, Mark, 17
Tynan, Kenneth, 146

Van Druten, John, 209, 251
Vedrenne, Mr., 47
Voltaire, 41

Waddell, Helen, 24–5
Wagg, Kenneth, 221
Wallace, Edgar, 169, 172, 174
Webb, Clifton, 241
Weissberger, Arnold, 242
Wellcome, Syrie, 140–1
West, Rebecca, 171
Westly, Helen, 107
Wharton, Jim, 239
Whitby, Arthur, 61, 62
Whitby, Gwen, 211
Wigram, Robert, 188
Wigram, Winnie, 188
Wilkinson, Norman, 62, 192
Williams, Emlyn, 172, 248, 249
Williams, Harcourt, 191
Williams, Hugh, 210–11, 258
Williams, Margaret, 210–11
Williamson, Nicol., 248, 255, 257
Wilson, Elizabeth, 257
Wilson, Paul, 102
Wilson, Sandy, 146
Wimborne, Lord, 128
Winch, Mrs., 189–90
Windom, Barbara, 227, 229, 230
Windom, William, 227, 229, 230, 248
Wolff, Mr., 43
Wolfit, Donald, 200
Wood, Chalmers, 126
Wood, Natalie, 231
Woodbridge, Mr., 190
Woollcott, Alec, 17, 117
Worth, Irene, 210, 211

Yeats, W. B., 52–3, 56

Zola, Émile, 38